P9-CCM-802

HELSINKI CATCH

MARKKU REIMAA

HELSINKI CATCH

European security accords 1975

TRANSLATION MARK WALLER

Edita | Helsinki

© The author and Edita Publishing Ltd.

Design: Edita Publishing Ltd. / Marjut Heikkinen
Cover photograph: Lehtikuva

ISBN 979-951-37-5359-7

Edita Prima Ltd.
Helsinki 2008

Contents

Introduction

The CSCE, the spirit of Helsinki and the CSCE final document or the Helsinki accords, the last-named formally known as the Final Act, signed in the Finnish capital on 1 August 1975, reflected the cooperation, the atmosphere and the fresh efforts to build a safer Europe that characterised the period of détente. It marked an end to the sharp antithesis of East and West in the post-war period. The blocs and the neutral and non-aligned countries outside them adopted new ways to discuss tricky and novel issues. Out of this situation an expansive forum took shape for dialogue and cooperation among 35 European countries, the United States and Canada. Only Albania, China's sole European ally, remained outside the forum.

In reality no one who joined the process initiated by Finland in May 1969 could tell what it would lead to or that this cooperative network of 35 participating states would operate despite the conflict in the Middle East and the 1973 oil crisis, the 1974 partition of Cyprus, the military coups in Greece and Portugal, the deployment of SS 20 missiles by the Soviet Union in 1976 and its occupation of Afghanistan in December 1979, the revolution sparked by Solidarity in Poland and the subsequent declaration of martial law in December 1981, the deployment of US medium-range missiles in Europe at the end of 1983 and early 1984; or then the death of President Pompidou in the summer of 1974, the resignations the same year of president Nixon and Chancellor Brandt, and the deaths of General Secretaries Brezhnev, Andropov and Chernenko in Moscow all within a short period in the early 1980s.

These crises and events tested the viability of relations among the main CSCE participants and the overall credibility of the CSCE. The CSCE offered a channel for dialogue at a time of international unrest. An effort was made to curb crises from coming to a head. There was no resort to force in Europe following the occupation of Prague, and not even when the Soviet Union collapsed some twenty years later.

The Helsinki Summit has often been compared to the 1815 Congress of Vienna. Both forums concerned the post-war construction of a new European system. In Vienna a new balance of power was sought, brokered to counter France's policy of expansion. The aim was to safeguard the internal development of the leading nation states – Austria-Hungary, Russia and Britain. The principle of non-interference in internal affairs played an important role in this.

Multilateral diplomatic skills and experience did not directly depend on the greatness of states. It is often the case that the more power and strength there is the fewer nuances are in play. The tendency of power hubs was to set out clear alternatives and challenges on a black and white axis. The lesser powers were often left with only difficult options: to join in or get left out. The principle proposition of Finland's non-alignment policy was that in European politics the palette was more varied. This mindset was hard to put over credibly in banner headlines and to large audiences.

At the start-up phase of the CSCE some viewpoints were presented according to which once the Federal Republic of Germany's (FRG) treaties with the Soviet Union, Poland and the German Democratic Republic in 1970 plus the 1972 four-power joint agreement on easing communications in Berlin were ratified, the main aims of détente would be met. The CSCE process, if it were to get going, would constitute just a momentary and harmless one-off sideshow. On the other hand, the treaties resulting from the FRG's new Ostpolitik would contribute to ensuring that the German question would not emerge at any point as a definite issue on the CSCE agenda. Both Germanies wanted to avoid this, and so did many others.

Over thirty years after the signing of the 1975 Helsinki Final Act and the Summit meeting of CSCE heads of state, the CSCE process remains conspicuous in permanent institutions and the OSCE. The architecture of the Cold War has now been torn down. The ideological, political and military tension between the eastern and western blocs has dissipated. This situation begs the question why the Cold War did not come to an end practically speaking in 1975.

This book examines Finland's involvement in the CSCE process from 1968 until the end of the Vienna follow-up conference in January 1989. This period preserves the original character of the 35-state forum for security and coopera- tion. Throughout, the Soviet-led Warsaw Treaty Organization, the West as a whole, the EEC countries and the US-led North Atlantic Treaty Organization acted as unofficial reference groups. In addition there were four neutral and five non-aligned countries that formed the nine-country Neutral and Non-aligned Group, N + N.

The nature of alignments and the level of coordinated cooperation varied greatly. The neutral and non-aligned group of countries was a new CSCE crea- tion. This offered room for manoeuvre with respect to different solutions, par- ticularly when compromises were made by the consensus requirement. Thanks to the CSCE Finland was able to consolidate its position as one of Europe's four neutral countries. The achievement of such a position was by no means axiomatic, either within this group or outside it.

The World War II legacy

Soviet Foreign Minister Vyacheslav Molotov proposed the organisation of a European security conference at the conference of the foreign ministers of the four victorious powers on 10 February 1954. The proposal was geared to "securing the collective security" of Europe, taking charge of the post-war division of Germany, possible German neutrality and exclusion from military alliances and the prevention of its rearmament. This arrangement would have naturally meant an end to US commitments and guarantees on the European continent.

The idea, attributed to Molotov, was originally Stalin's. The Soviet Union had lost 400,000 troops in the occupation of Berlin in May 1945. Victory Day and the overthrow of Nazi Germany were achievements of historic magnitude to Soviet leaders, as they continue to be in Russia today. International recognition of these achievements remained a central Soviet aim in the CSCE.

The message of the 20th Congress of the Soviet Communist Party in the spring of 1956 was also of internal importance to the socialist system: it was a sign of the renunciation of the terror of Stalin's rule. The events in Poland and Hungary in 1956 nevertheless demonstrated that national aspirations were still exaggerated. They were suppressed.

Unrest in East Berlin in spring 1953 and the Hungarian uprising in autumn 1956 were expressions of crisis in the socialist system. In Poland, Vladislav Gomulka was returned to power after spending several years in prison. A climate of greater freedom was anticipated. On 14 December 1964 Foreign Minister Adam Rapack addressed the UN General Assembly. In his view the time was ripe for convening a European security conference, in which both the USA and the Soviet Union would participate.

At the end of Khrushchev's rule relations worsened between the Soviet Union and China. Writing in 1969, Andrei Amalrik predicted that Soviet and Chinese military confrontation might bring down the Soviet Union by 1984. The Chinese accused the Soviet Union of 'revisionism' and of trying to replicate the western lifestyle. It was on these grounds that China's only faithful ally in Europe, Albania, refused to take part in the CSCE process.

The end of colonialism in the Third World led to a powerful independence process that created new states. The competition to gain the favour of the new states intensified. The Soviet Union looked as if it would gain a significant foothold in the areas left by the former Western colonial powers by virtue of its economic might and propagandist peace policy. The Soviet Union's ambitious goal was to overtake the US in economic competition and to ensure parity in military build-up.

Hungary's Foreign Minister Janos Peter defined the "borders of the international socialist community" in his speech to the UN on the occupation of Czechoslovakia in autumn 1968: "It extends from Cuba to Vietnam, and includes China and Albania."

The policy of peaceful coexistence brought with it a new challenge for the West. Already in 1958 Milovan Djilas had written in his book 'The New Class' that this policy in no way aimed at the melding of two systems. The goal was to preserve the communist system and to wait until the capitalist system lost the contest or caved in.

The removal of Khruschev in October 1964 and the changeover to the period of the seemingly more pragmatic troika of Brezhnev, Kosygin and Podgorny, the detonation by China of its atomic bomb and mounting US difficulties in Vietnam essentially dominated the events of the 1960s. The transition to the Brezhnev era signified the questioning of ingrained beliefs and a reassessment of the interests and aims of countries' foreign policies.

At the end of the 1960s the military alliances sought by communication exchange to find a common denominator for closer dialogue. In December 1967 NATO issued the Harmel report, named after Belgian foreign minister Pierre Harmel. This showed a more pragmatic thinking to the possible East-West arrangement in Europe. Along with the strengthening of the Western alliance's defence capability was the readiness to open up dialogue with the Eastern military alliance. The Warsaw Pact countries responded to these signals.

President Urho Kekkonen paid particular attention to FRG Foreign Minister Willy Brandt's March 1968 speech in Nürnberg. Brandt said that the Federal Republic needed a new settlement with Poland, because no one knew when the German people might achieve unification under a peace treaty. Such a settlement would in any case recognise and respect the Oder-Neisse Line until the arrangement of a peace treaty. For Poland, the clear and irrevocable recognition of its western border was central to its post-war initiatives.

Prague spring and autumn 1968

The acceptance by the Czechoslovakian communist party in its manifesto in January 1968 of the Prague Spring was an indication that citizens considered the past in a more critical and open way, the better running of daily affairs and the economy, and a freer climate of opinion and information. The Stalinist leadership style of Antonin Novotny that had continued since 1953 changed to the reforming socialism with a human face of Alexander Dubček.

Priority was given to the renewal of the political system and the broadening of economic reform, plus new regulations on freedom of opinion and expression. The 1966 censorship decree was abrogated. Persons persecuted under the oppressive machine of the Stalinist era would be rehabilitated. The activities of the state prosecutor, the law courts, parliamentary committees, party organs and national committees would be made accountable. Already in February 1968, Poland's communist party leader Wladyslaw Gomulka had in discussions with Dubček warned that such measures could lead to "uncontrollable political consequences".

Intense negotiations started among the party leaders of the five members of the Warsaw Treaty – the Soviet Union, GDR, Poland, Bulgaria and Hungary – on the adoption of Prague's new manifesto. They sought to test Dubček's loyalty to common values and courses of action. In addition, the five countries raised their level of military readiness, held military exercises close to the Czechoslovak border and increased other forms of political pressure through the media and party channels.

Following the 3 August meeting of Warsaw Pact countries in Bratislava, Prague considered that it had won a certain amount or acceptance for its reforms. In Finland too this way forward might have been fairly satisfactory. Foreign Minister Ahti Karjalainen told the parliamentary committee on foreign affairs on 19 August: "The Czechs could develop their own way that recognised its national circumstances without blemishing the path of socialism. It certainly deviates from the courses of other socialist countries. Taking into account the assurances of the Czech leadership, it is not however seen to be at the stage of endangering the existence of socialism or of causing a foreign or military policy threat within the group of socialist countries."

Mr Karjalainen's statement to the foreign affairs committee two days before the dramatic events unfolded suggest that the occupation of Czechoslovakia on 21 August 1968 came as a complete surprise to Finnish politicians.

The situation developed in precisely the opposite direction than predicted. Warsaw Pact troops entered Prague on the night preceding the 21 August and demolished both the Prague Spring and any possibilities for its political leadership to continue their work.

On the first day of the occupation the Finnish government's foreign affairs committee gathered in Helsinki at 12:30 under the chairmanship of the President for a lengthy session, after which it issued a very brief statement in response to the situation.

The statement regretted that certain "differences that have emerged among East European countries" could not be solved through negotiation. The government said that it was following the situation vigilantly and that "it was adopting its stand as called for by Finland's established policy of neutrality." The government emphasised its position, according to which "nowadays, under existing circumstances, including in Europe, all matters of dispute between states should be resolved peacefully by negotiation and avoiding increase in international tensions."

The situation also came as a shock to Finnish communists. In a historic statement party leader Aarne Saarinen said that the Communist Party of Finland, which was celebrating its 50th anniversary, was not, under the circumstances, in a "festive mood." The party conference was cancelled. The political committee of the CPF convened on the afternoon of the first day of the occupation and agreed unanimously that the measures carried out by the five Warsaw pact states "harmed the entire international workers' movement."

Protestors gathered outside the Soviet Embassy in Helsinki to demonstrate a more candid opinion on what people in Finland thought of what was happening. Finland's political leaders were in agreement that 'protest activities' should be limited so as to be as few as possible. The preservation and care of bilateral relations with the Soviet Union remained a priority.

Romania's disassociation with the occupation was impressively revealing. It indicated that the key decisions on the occupation were not necessarily taken inside the Warsaw Treaty Organization.

A shock for Kekkonen

President Kekkonen was shocked. He "felt distressed" because Kovalev, the Soviet Ambassador to Helsinki, had visited him on the morning of 21 August at 8:00 to announce that troops from certain socialist countries had, at the request of the Czech authorities, arrived in the country. This did not correspond with what he had been informed by Ambassador Zdeněk Urban from Czechoslovak sources. Kekkonen was arriving at the view that the Soviet Union had made a massive political mistake. "I felt depressed," Kekkonen wrote. "The consequences would be conspicuous in international politics for years to come."

Kekkonen's diary for 1968 contains many fretful references to the development of the Czechoslovakian situation. From May there were various degrees of information about the concentration of Soviet troops on the Czechoslovakian border. The inner solidarity of the Warsaw pact was tested in particular by the Romanian authorities. The pronouncements of the Romanian Prime Minister and Foreign Minister during their visit to Finland were fairly openly critical of the Soviet leadership, in particular concerning Prime Minister Brezhnev's policy compared to the Khrushchev period.

Kekkonen found that the occupation of Czechoslovakia also had strong repercussions in his own relations with the Soviet Union. "The events had wrenched the achievements and basis from this work." "My bow is broken." "I can't go on." Amidst preparations to travel to attend the wedding of the Norwegian Crown Prince he predicted that he would be singled out for blame. "As if Kekkonen had been the one to invade Czechoslovakia!"

The situation assessment following talks held with Prime Minister Alexei Kosygin at Hiittinen, 7–8 October 1968 altered considerably. In conversation with the British Ambassador Scott Fox on 18 October, Kekkonen said that "Finland's position would strengthen if the West's and the Soviet Union's relations grow colder."

Faith dwindles in the power of ideology

The occupation of Prague on 21 August 1968 was an epoch-making event in many respects in Europe. The British historian Eric Hobsbawm has characterised the occupation and the frustration of the socialism with a human face experiment as a grave blow to the entire credibility of socialist ideology.

At the Cierna nad Tisou conference on 29 July 1968 General Secretary Brezhnev outlined to Czechoslovakia what was later to be known as the Brezhnev Doctrine, namely that socialism's achievements and the destiny of Czechoslovakia as a socialist country were not purely an internal Czechoslovakian affair. "They were the common affair of the whole international socialist community and of the whole communist movement."

Meeting in Bratislava on 3 August, the six representatives of the Warsaw Pact had sought to respond to the challenges set by Czechoslovakia's 'socialism with a human face'. At the same time they reaffirmed the principles of conduct of fraternal parties on matters of socialist development. The gains of socialism and communism had to be defended at all costs.

The aggressive policy of the imperialists had upheld 'a complex and dangerous international situation.' The socialist countries' parties continued the struggle to preserve world peace and security. West German neo-fascists, militarists and revanchist circles were a threat to world peace and the security of the socialist countries. "The socialist countries have to fight all efforts that aim to reassess the outcome of the Second World War and alter Europe's existing borders." "They were prepared to do anything to ensure that a conference of European nations would convene to defend the peace of the European continent."

The surging currents of the Prague Spring ran dry almost immediately. Soviet tanks surrounded Prague in the early hours of 21 August 1968. The mood throughout Europe was intense. The Czech leadership was taken to Moscow. In light of this it was apparent that Alexander Dubček could not be 'liquidated' or replaced right away. Brezhnev (...) said that force had to be resorted to because the Czech leadership were unable to keep the situation under control. Dubček responded that from what had happened it appeared that "neither the Czech communist movement, nor the communist movement of the Warsaw Pact countries, nor the world communist movement was any longer under the control of Moscow's rulers."

Moscow was aware that the events in Czechoslovakia worried President Kekkonen. This was why it was decided to send Prime Minister Kosygin to Finland to meet Kekkonen on 7 October and clarify Soviet policy in Europe. When Kekkonen expressed astonishment that following the aforementioned conference there was a quick shift of opinion in Moscow in favour of dispatching troops, Kosygin denied that there was. At no stage had there been any satisfaction in Moscow with the results of the negotiations. Kosygin refuted the impression Kekkonen had gathered that the Soviet leadership had not been unanimous in its chosen course.

When in January 1969 Kekkonen made a flying visit to Paris, his and President de Gaulle's assessment of the Prague situation were very much along the same lines. Kekkonen considered that the occupation was the military bloc's internal dispute, and likewise de Gaulle commented "the Soviet Union did not at that moment have aggressive designs on the West".

Party leader Dubček returned to Prague. The purging of individuals in the party leadership was started and the situation came to be termed "normalised". Dubček eventually had to throw in the towel and make way for Gustáv Husák in February 1969.

Non-interference with borders of spheres of interest

At the level of high politics the situation between the superpowers was once again almost back to normal. The US appeared to quietly accept the Soviet Union's actions within the area of its sphere of interest. The Brezhnev doctrine received fresh affirmation from a prestigious quarter. As master of the socialist camp the Soviet Union could even use force to keep its allies and system on a tight leash.

Finns received very up-to-date information on this directly from the US as well as in Helsinki and Washington. The Soviet Ambassador to Washington Anatoly Dobrynin had visited President Johnson already the evening before the Prague occupation to inform him that the Czechoslovakian government had requested Moscow's help and military intervention to prevent imminent counter-revolution. Dobrynin tried to convince Johnson that intervention was not a threat to peace in Europe. "On the contrary, it was intended to secure European security." In the same vein, Moscow's assumption was that it would not affect US-Soviet bilateral relations.

At a press conference held 22 August State Department representatives said that because of the events in Prague there was growing resistance in Congress to continuing with the policy of rapprochement towards the Soviet Union. The same might be the case with the ratification of the nuclear non-proliferation treaty, which could run into difficulties.

The Czechoslovak Ambassador to Helsinki, Urban, tried to keep Finnish officials abreast of events during the days following the occupation. The Czechoslovak Foreign Minister Jiri Hajek travelled to New York. It was expected that the events in Czechoslovakia would be discussed by both the UN General Assembly and the Security Council. The political leaders of the Prague Spring had been taken to Moscow, where, according to Urban, negotiations were being conducted in a "correct spirit".

Foreign Minister Karjalainen issued a statement on 27 August in which he said that in all probability the Soviet and Czechoslovak delegates would reach a negotiated solution. Karjalainen said that he did not feel that he was not acquainted with all the factors that had finally led to the unfortunate series of events, to military intervention. He also did not know the details of the compromise reached. "In today's world resort to arms does not achieve a permanent solution to disputes between states."

The CSCE process and particularly its discussions concerning inter-state relations constituted a key challenge to the Brezhnev doctrine. The principle of non-interference in internal affairs was interpreted differently in the East and the West. The argument centred closely on whether it concerned non-interference in the internal affairs of another state or the principle of non-interference in the internal affairs of another ideological camp.

The Prague events and the occupation of Czechoslovakia can serve as a benchmark for how the situation in Europe could not have got any worse. Thereafter it could only change for the better.

The Conference on Security and Cooperation in Europe became a useful device, while Finland and Helsinki were the midwives that made it functional.

Out of the cul-de-sac

Warsaw pact activity intensifies

In the wake of the occupation of Prague the alliances and governments endeavoured to ward off any worsening of the situation. After Prague, the government in Bonn was determined to continue along the path of its new *Ostpolitik*.

Despite the occupation, the Warsaw Treaty Organization sought, under Soviet guidance, to present an image to the outside world that a consistent policy of peaceful coexistence with the Western world would continue and even expand.

Meeting in Budapest on 17 March 1969, the Warsaw Treaty's political advisory committee issued for the second time the declaration issued in 1967 in Bucharest. This was an appeal to the European states to hold a pan-European conference. In addition, Hungary's Ambassador to Helsinki had already sent the appeal to the Finnish Ministry for Foreign Affairs, and the Soviet Ambassador, Alexei Kovalev, presented it to President Kekkonen on 4 April. Kovalev appealed to Finland to take a positive view of holding the conference and to be involved in its preparation.

On 8 April, Ambassador Kovalev showed President Kekkonen the basis of the Budapest declaration, the appeal mandated by his government for the organisation of an all-Europe conference. The aim would be "to resolve outstanding issues necessary for promoting European security and peaceful cooperation". The appeal included an admission that there were problems. There were, in addition, states that were not happy with the status quo. It was imperative to arrange the conference.

The Budapest declaration stated that no preconditions would be set, success would require thorough preparations and a preparatory conference would convene to draw up the programme and agenda. All European countries would be invited, including the FRG and the GDR. The Europeans would work out to what extent the US could participate in the arrangements. Kovalev stressed that the Warsaw Treaty countries took a "flexible" attitude to US participation. Flexibility is always a complicated matter. It often entails positive expectations, but sometimes with extra conditions. It can be used as bait.

It was hoped that Finland would now appoint a representative for the preparatory conference. In this respect the Finnish initiative and the inclusion of the US and Canada among those invited did not happen by chance. It was remarkable that the Warsaw Pact countries had said that they were flexible on the question of US participation. This was interpreted in Helsinki as meaning there was no objection in principle to inviting the US.

On 29 April 1969 Ambassador Max Jakobson went to the President Kekkonen's residence at Tamminiemi, just outside Helsinki, to discuss the basis of a memorandum for developing Finland's CSCE initiative. Finland was not satisfied with simply responding to the Soviet and Warsaw Treaty appeal, but wanted to make its own independent suggestions. It also offered to host the prospective conference. This willingness was based on the grounds that Finland had good relations with all countries involved with European security. Its attitude to the main European security problem – the German question – was unbiased.

The discussion formed the basis of an express memo drawn up by Risto Hyvärinen, a head of department at the Foreign Ministry. At the beginning of May Kekkonen was to visit Sweden. The government foreign affairs committee discussed the matter on 2 May and approved it. On 5 May the memorandum was sent to all European governments and to the USA and Canada. When the grounds for the initiative were presented to the heads of foreign missions in dispatches, the main point was that the Finnish initiative could prevent the contention of other such proposals, "which could become matters of dispute between the superpowers".

Finland's initiative

The Finnish government's CSCE initiative was announced on 5 may 1969. Although it began, erroneously, with the words "The government of the Soviet Union", the content of the initiative indicated that the initiator was the Finnish government. No one was sure whether the initiative would lead to definite action. At that point the initiative clearly had a more immediate aim than a solution to the overall European security situation. In its initiative for a CSCE Finland indicated that it was itself concerned about the matter. It shared its worries about European security and in light of them was ready to consider measures that it could help promote.

The initiative enabled Finland to effectively repel demands for the unilateral recognition of the GDR. On the other hand there was a presumption that the real conference host was the Soviet government. In the rush the opening words of the initiative had remained unchanged but at that stage it was a plus that the Soviet Union looked right away to be onboard.

The invitation to convene a CSCE particularly encouraged and spurred on the smaller member states of the Warsaw Treaty Organization. They were keen to get out of the dead-end caused by the occupation of Prague, the break in relations with the West and the restrictions directed at the Soviet Union's fraternal countries. With the CSCE they would once again have open relations with Western Europe. In place of bilateral links, the multilateral CSCE forum would in the prevailing circumstances offer a better, more effective and less dramatic channel for relations. These countries needed relationships with the West for their own economic development. Closer economic cooperation, particularly between Prague and Bonn had been a source of envy within the socialist camp. Outside information on the superpowers' outlooks suggested that the West too had expectations of breaking the ice of the Czechoslovakian events and of opening up relations with the East.

The Soviet Union's activity in the CSCE would indicate a significant change from the Czechoslovakian occupation. Before the occupation, Austria had been an active location for Soviet diplomatic contact. In their bilateral meetings Soviet representatives had noted the possibility that Austria could take the initiative for convening the European conference. During his visit to Moscow on 16 March 1967 Chancellor Josef Klaus said that Austria was of course interested in the solution of Europe's security problems but "that to take up the political initiative would be beyond Austria's resources."

Soviet activity on the CSCE in its connection with Vienna was linked to Austria's attempts to have closer economic relations with the European Economic Community. When these failed in the face of opposition from France and Italy, Soviet activity towards Vienna receded.

The idea of a European security conference was prominent in the discussions held between foreign ministers Karjalainen and Gromyko in Moscow on 17 July 1969. Many countries had responded positively to the Soviet Union's latest proposals, but this was not enough as far as Gromyko was concerned. State representatives should get together, and negotiations had to be prepared. This would not happen without someone to take the initiative. "Perhaps Finland could do something about this."

In Finland, the German question weighed heavily on the shoulders of the government. This was a focus of a committee that was active advocating the recognition of the GDR. Risto Hyvärinen, now retired after a distinguished career as a diplomat, remarked in 2006 that the Finnish government had been in a situation where "If it had done nothing, pressure to unilaterally recognise the GDR could have got out of control and then could have forced the government to do something at odds with its original wishes."

Ambassador Max Jakobson sent some fresh observations to Kekkonen on 13 May 1969 concerning the Finnish initiative. It appeared to be achieving its aim in every respect. At the same time, because it had received a positive response in Moscow, it seemed to bolster Helsinki's policy on Germany and so reinforce the Finnish position of neutrality. "We now just have to work out the means for discussions with other governments on pursuing the initiative," Jakobson wrote.

Kekkonen replied to Jakobson's letter on 27 May. He referred to his recent discussion with Kosygin. This had shown that it might be a long time before the conference took place. The observation also reflected Kekkonen's fear that the consequences of the occupation of Czechoslovakia had put the brakes on bringing about the conference.

The idea for the conference and the matters to be dealt with during it were the subject of high level discussions in Moscow. Deputy Foreign Minister Vladimir Semyonov wanted to visit Kekkonen in October 1969 to present the results of these discussions. The meeting took place at just a few hours' notice. Semyonov said that the Central Committee of the CPSU had taken up Kekkonen's initiative for realizing a security conference and had noted the considerations the President had presented. Semyonov confirmed that the Soviet

Union and its allies did not oppose the participation of the USA and Canada. Due to the Potsdam conference the USA had a responsibility for the European situation, particularly the status of Berlin.

Another point of departure concerned the prospective participation both Germanies – the FRG and the GDR – with the same entitlement as other European countries. This did not however mean de jure recognition of the two states by all participants. Semyonov stressed that the Soviet Union was now putting two overall subjects on the conference agenda:

- a prohibition on the use of force in Europe, and
- the development of peaceful cooperation among European countries in the areas of economy, science and technology, as ways of promoting political cooperation.

It was with this in mind that the signatories of the Budapest appeal intended to meet in Prague from 30-31 October and to accept the convening of a security conference on the basis of the Finnish initiative. They would come to recommend Helsinki in early1970.

Semyonov's presentation contained the particularly eye-catching Soviet aim to get a treaty concerning the non-use of force ready within a short time and specifically in connection with the CSCE. Semyonov said that the Soviet Union and the FRG had been holding vigorous bilateral talks on the matter. "But if the security conference does not reach such an agreement, only then will the Soviet and FRG bilateral agreement become relevant."

On 13 November Semyonov paid another visit to the President to detail the results of the Prague meeting of 30-31 October. The discussion indicated that the more precise the proposals made for the security conference the greater the probability that they would form a principle or formal obstacle even to the convening of the conference. The Finnish government memorandum had stressed that there should be no preconditions set for the conference. Kekkonen thought that the demand for the *de jure* recognition of current borders would be too ambitious and become a direct obstacle to bringing about the conference. Semyonov replied that if the matter was not presented now it could be difficult to raise it during the conference. Kekkonen wanted to stress that his main objective remained to realize the conference and not yet to talk about its actual issues and challenges.

At the end of the discussion Semyonov posed the question of whether Finland could put forward the documents adopted at the Prague meeting in its own name. The request was arrogant and undiplomatic. Kekkonen turned it down flat. But he did not dispute whether the conference would not deal with such proposals. Throughout the early months of 1970 he was sceptical about whether it was realistic to summon the gathering. Semyonov responded merely be saying that the matter was urgent because the forces opposed to the conference had been aroused.

Poland's Deputy Foreign Minister Jozef Winiewicz visited Finland following the Prague meeting of the Warsaw Treaty countries and met with Kekkonen on 22 November 1969. Winiewicz energetically congratulated Finland on its work, as various countries, including Austria, were keen to get things moving. Kekkonen said that perhaps the favourable response was to seek our impartial attitude to the issue of the Germanies. This aroused Kekkonen's curiosity about the Warsaw Treaty countries' anxiety. He asked why the Warsaw Pact was presenting such an early deadline for the convening of the conference. Winiewicz replied that the aim was to hurry things up. He asked Finland, among other things, to prepare a summary of the subjects to be dealt with by the conference. Kekkonen refused. Because of its position Finland would not be responsible for various proposals concerning the subjects to be dealt with.

Winiewicz responded with rapid terseness. He said that according to his information the Czechs' problems following the occupation of Prague were not yet over. The success of Gustáv Husák, who had taken over the leadership of the party in March 1969, after the occupation, was uncertain. In any case, "the socialist countries felt themselves more secure" – meaning amidst the preparations for the security conference and closer multilateral dialogue. "This is partly due to their common willingness to negotiate." This was obviously also linked to their previously expressed "flexibility" concerning the possibility of US and Canadian participation. In December 2007 Professor Dobrosielski underscored the idea that from the CSCE perspective the Prague events had hastened rather than slowed its development.

In his 1996 book KSZE – Fossil oder Hoffnung the veteran GDR Ambassador to the CSCE Peter Steglich dealt with the same notion. Steglich writes that the Warsaw Pact's sense of urgency about convening the conference was because "it wanted to get out of the difficult situation caused by the crushing of the Prague Spring as quickly as possible." Steglich affirmed this view during a discussion held in Berlin in June 2007.

The occupation of Czechoslovakia was therefore a most effective instrument for speeding up the CSCE and addressing the Warsaw Pact's flexibility. There was nothing certain about the Soviet Union's future intentions in relation to the socialist countries. Romanian representatives from various quarters expressed deep worries about their own situation, as did those from Yugoslavia. It is a paradox of the development of détente that less than eight months after the Prague occupation of August 1968 the Finnish government received highly positive feedback on its initiative for organising a conference on European security.

The Polish government's main aim was to diminish Europe's dividing lines and not to reinforce them, as the Soviet Union repeatedly suggested. Fairly qualified attention was given to the individual actions of the different member states of the socialist camp prior to the start of the CSCE negotiations. Historical and political matters appeared to have the same roles within the socialist came as elsewhere in Europe. The emphasis on distinctive national characteristics was normal, though their visibility and active room for manoeuvre were often extremely limited. Just as in the West one was often guilty of simplifying the decision-making process of the Soviet leadership as monolithic and single-tracked, by the same criteria the policies of other socialist countries were all too often measured as merely derivative of Soviet policy.

At the end of 1969, Warsaw Treaty representatives affirmed that their attitude to US and Canadian involvement was "flexible". In terms of the hosting, convening and scheduling of the conference, the issue of the participation of both Germanies nevertheless amounted to an acid test.

Responses from the field and the media

Finland's CSCE initiative was a typical example of the energetic foreign policy of the Kekkonen era. Preparatory work was carried out by foreign ministry experts, who at the time were the champions of the policy of neutrality. President Kekkonen's active foreign policy did not necessarily require the preparatory input of the government or the Parliamentary foreign affairs committee. Though there were many factors involved in the initiative, even risks, there was a readiness to go along with them without substantial debate on their possible consequences.

On 13 May Foreign Minister Karjalainen reported to the parliamentary foreign affairs committee on the initial responses to the initiative. He said that the reactions had been positive, apart from Albania's. Certain key countries had not yet responded. The issue could be looked at again later. The first responses had nevertheless confirmed his view that the idea of the conference was timely. In June the French foreign ministry notified the Finnish embassy in Paris that France was in principle in favour of the idea. There was no hurry "as the security conference could be held in 1971 at the earliest." "The German question was not yet ripe for discussion."

The initial responses of the German Federal Republic, on 12 September, and the Netherlands, on 8 August, welcomed the Finnish initiative "in a constructive spirit". The British did likewise and would examine with its allies how the idea could best be advanced. Several responses from members of the Western alliance referred to the NATO conference to be held in December 1969. More specific views would be expected from that.

When the Swiss government deliberated on the matter at its 10 July session, it set clear conditions on Switzerland's participation: the conference must be carefully prepared and in such a way that it suited the framework of Switzerland's neutrality policy. It must not take the form of a debating forum on superpower disputes arising from the Second World War.

The American response, which came in January 1970, expressed satisfaction that Washington and Ottawa had been included among the recipients of the Finnish memorandum. At the same time, the authorities in Washington emphasised the importance of careful preparations. The conference would not be useful unless real progress could be registered "in areas key to European security."

The Albanian government announced its views to Ambassador Jussi Mäkinen in Vienna on 24 February 1970. Albania considered that a European security conference was necessary but the Soviet Union's support for it was purely "demagogic".

In its May memorandum the Finnish government had pledged to consider new measures. The main parts of successful progress on the initial stage of the CSCE process comprised holding on to the role of conference host and the preparation of practicalities.

Belgium's Foreign Minister Pierre Harmel visited Moscow from 23-27 July 1969. Both sides wanted to inform the Finns of the course of the discussions. According to the Belgians, discussions with the Russians had from the start reflected a common vision. At first there should be focus on issues on which there could be prior agreement and the achievement of mutual understanding. According to the Belgians, the discussions had not touched on more detailed proposals.

The chargé d'affaires at the Soviet embassy in Helsinki Farafonov gave Finnish officials an account of the discussions on 20 August. According to Farafonov, the Belgian Foreign Minister had dealt in some detail with NATO's prospective agenda. This would envisage putting on the agenda, among other things, issues related to military security, such as balanced disarmament agreements, the prohibition of the use of force, the drawing up of an international code of good conduct – or principles concerning interstate relations – prior notifications of military exercises and the prohibition of military exercises close to state borders. In addition, the agenda could include matters concerning techno-scientific cooperation.

The Finnish government publicly commented on the Warsaw Pact's Prague meeting of 31 October 1969 that emphasized the imperative of achieving a consensus. Finland also announced that it was continuing with its own bilateral contacts with those governments that had been sent the original memorandum. When the Foreign Ministry head of department Risto Hyvärinen offered an assessment of the situation at the beginning of December he said that Finland sought to perform a duty that a neutral country could do to alleviate tensions in Europe. A basic assumption was that results could be expected only by creating a broad international consensus: "In each stage Finland's line of action was to influence the creation of this consensus." By the beginning of December, judging by the written responses, the Finnish initiative had in principle received affirmative feedback. None of the replies were negative.

The CSCE agenda – the challenge of careful preparations

On the one hand the need for "careful preparations" was the key message of the Finnish government's 5 May 1969 memorandum; on the other it was the specification of all those countries responsible for European security.

The Finnish government did not want to go into any further detail about how carefully the prospective meeting was to be prepared. Careful preparations were something of a guarantee to the main Western nations that matters they considered important would be the bases for serious discussion. Careful preparations could also be read as a prerequisite in all matters to be approved. The aim was not to automatically replicate UN methods, clear majorities or voting. The preparations were for broad acceptance and consensus concerning the acceptability of solutions. For the main Western governments Europe's security concerns were the Vietnam War and the problems of relations between the two Germanies. These were concentrated specifically on the matter of Berlin.

"All countries responsible for the security of Europe, including the United States and Canada", were recipients of the Finnish memorandum. This gave a more realistic impression of tending to Europe's post-Second World War matters than earlier Soviet attempts to limit the conference only to the states of the continent of Europe. The memorandum spoke of countries and not governments. Finland did not want to take a stand on the German question.

The US now followed closely how the Soviet Union would behave on the basis of the Finnish initiative. In discussions held in New York on 12 September 1969 between Foreign Minister Karjalainen and Secretary of State William Rogers, the latter gave an assurance that the USA was interested in all discussions with the Soviet Union, particularly concerning European issues. Rogers wanted to know what the Soviet Union intended to deal with at the conference. There could be many views on the Brezhnev doctrine. Perhaps the Soviet Union wanted a new kind of activity to divert attention from Czechoslovakia. Matters of European security came up for discussion in NATO. Rogers affirmed that if the conference was going to be useful, the US would support it and the holding of it in Helsinki.

Risto Hyvärinen received a similar assurance from President Nixon's security advisor Henry Kissinger, when the two met in Washington on 24 October. The Strategic Arms Limitation Talks (SALT) were to start in Helsinki on 17 November 1969. Kissinger said that the US could not begin negotiations in any communist country or in a country that was under Soviet influence. "Finland was not – we just have to be sure that you put listening devices in our rooms for your use only!" Hyvärinen was left with the impression that Kissinger was not particularly interested in a conference on security. Only twenty minutes were set aside for their meeting.

In November 1969 President Kekkonen met with US journalists in connection with the SALT process. Speaking to Marquis Childs of the United Features Syndicate on 21 November he deliberated on the CSCE stance in the following way: the Russians' economic position was so much worse than the West's that they clearly had particular cause to strive for disarmament seriously. It remained to be seen whether American intentions were sincere.

Kekkonen thought that at first the Soviet Union had been especially keen about the initiative but had then become hesitant. It now seemed that Moscow was strongly pursuing the project. He thought that the main reason for this was that the conference should be held, even though at first it could only deal with very limited issues. Kekkonen characterised these as including the issue of the prohibition of the use of force and the reconciliation of discordant relations among different alignments. He said that the efforts might also fail. "In any case, we'll face that later."

Kekkonen told another US journalist, Chalmers Roberts, that even though the war in Europe had ended in 1945 a formal system of peace had not yet been made. The CSCE could be a matter of a series of conferences in which the two schools would continue to discuss different approaches. Kekkonen said openly that Finland did not want to specify publicly its standpoint concerning the agenda. This "would not accord with our position of neutrality."

At his meeting with C.L. Sulzberger of the New York Times Kekkonen crystallised the principle stand of Finland's CSCE line, according to notes taken by Matti Tuovinen, as follows: the opportunity for the coexistence of capitalism and communism now appeared to be in part possible. The systems appeared to be drawing closer to one another. It was recognized that the Soviet Union was interested in various market economy mechanisms in such a way, however, that the basic socialist structure would be preserved. Kekkonen did not think that it was possible that conditions of ownership in the Soviet Union would alter (in the direction of free market principles).

Kekkonen defined Finland's foreign policy and its attitude to crises in this way: "Finland seeks to pursue the sort of foreign policy that is suited to assuaging international tensions, that has a preventive effect on the outbreak of crises and conflict and that in the event of crises enables it to keep outside them."

The same two-part approach can also be seen in Moscow's attitude to the preparations for the CSCE. First there was the role of Deputy Foreign Minister Semyonov, referred to earlier. On 9 December 1970, Finnish Foreign Ministry head of department Hyvärinen visited Moscow to meet with the roving Ambassador involved in CSCE preparations, Lev Mendelevich. Mendelevich said that the over-emphasis on Finnish neutrality was causing irritation among "certain people at the top". The Soviet Union was a superpower and Finland was a small country. When they worked together for international peace and security Finland, accordingly, could not be neutral.

Mendelevich acknowledged Finland's neutrality policy. But if it were stressed too much it would cause irritation. "There were men in the Soviet Foreign Ministry who thought only bilaterally and were not versed in general political demands." Mendelevich said that he was more broadly familiar with international matters – in other words general political matters.

Finland ready to listen – neutrality's new terrain

President Kekkonen recognised in the Finnish initiative the scope to gain new terrain that diverged from Finland's cautious post-war foreign policy.

Wearing the hat of host of the conference's practical requirements the Finnish government had avoided having to take stands on disputes between the superpowers. Kekkonen felt that the CSCE initiative contained ingredients that appeared to run counter to the Treaty of Friendship, Cooperation and Mutual Assistance between Finland and the Soviet Union. His political antenna was tuned to possible comments of this nature from the Soviets, which were to come in due course.

When the Soviet mass media put out news of the CSCE initiative the part of it concerning the initiative's furthering the requirements of neutrality policy was censored. President Podgorny reiterated the same reservations during his visit to Finland in October 1969. In communiqué discussions Soviet officials showed no understanding of Finland's imperative intent that its neutrality would have a part to play in advancing the initiative.

Finland's diplomatic heavyweight, Ambassador Ralf Enckell, was appointed as roving ambassador on 23 February 1970 with the task to "find out and record the progress already achieved in the handling of European security matters". In this way Finland was able to remain in the centre of CSCE debates and to advance its neutrality policy. Finland had the fullest and most incisive understanding of the problems ahead and the possible sectors of consensus. It had gained an up-to-date view of all the priorities and problems facing the key countries.

Enckell made over fifty visits to the capitals of prospective CSCE countries for talks, starting from Bern, Dublin and Vienna. His intention was to treat all parties equally and his opening line contained three main questions: Why Finland, why a conference and why now?

All the visits offered the opportunity to assess sagaciously where the CSCE process might lead. The bilateral discussions with all possible participants separately created an extensive network in which to develop issues and promote the idea of the conference. The main aim of the consultations was to dispel doubts and exaggerated expectations. The conference preparations could not be pursued in a vacuum. Enckell told an Austrian colleague in April 1970 that unless there were results on the German question it would be very unlikely that the conference would have any chance of succeeding.

When Enckell met Andrei Gromyko in Moscow on 15 April 1970 the Foreign Minister asked him to pass his greetings to the Americans: "The knives are not being sharpened in Europe to bring down the Americans." Enckell met his US colleagues in Washington in early 1970 and conveyed Gromyko's greetings. Assistant Secretary Martin J. Hillenbrand considered that Finland's intense activity highlighted the significance of its careful preparations. "Finland knows how to separate its pragmatic activities from Eastern Europe's endeavours."

In November 1970 there was a careful changeover from purely bilateral preparations to the next phase. The Finnish Foreign Ministry announced that it was ready to hold consultations on arranging multilateral meetings in Helsinki. Enckell had in his bilateral meetings tentatively probed the opportunities for passing to this next stage. Such informal discussions between diplomats in Helsinki and the Foreign Ministry would advance efforts in mapping consensus.

With his experience as Ambassador to the UN and head of department at the Foreign Ministry Enckell was an excellent choice for the job. Many found his bearing so impressive that it took precedence over what he talked about in meetings. He said he was prepared to listen to everyone. It was an important gesture of confidence from the host country that everyone would be treated equally. He didn't have a mission, he would say, he was "on a mission". And the more he listened, the more interested became his interlocutors, who had yet to have the opportunity to present their position to him.

No written summaries were made of the bilateral discussions. A full survey of the general moods and aspirations ensured that when Finland was to eventually invite the heads of mission in Helsinki for preparatory talks there might be many matters of procedure and agenda problems to be solved.

Enckell visited New York on 2 June 1970, while on leave from the bilateral meetings, and met with Max Jakobson to discuss the situation. Jakobson described the current challenges facing Finland's neutrality policy and the security conference in a letter to Foreign Minister Väinö Leskinen:

For the Soviet Union the realization of the conference has an intrinsic value. The West on the other hand is seeking a sufficiently good price in advance for consenting to the conference. The NATO conference held in Rome on 27 May 1970 put forward the following: there should first be agreed mutual, balanced force reductions in Europe (MBFR). This was indirectly aimed at slackening the Soviet Union's political grip on Eastern Europe.

France's Foreign Minister Maurice Schumann had stated at the Rome conference that in connection with the prospective conference each country should have the opportunity to enhance its national identity. The conference slogan should be 'Détente – not the status quo!'

So, was the Soviet Union genuinely interested in results? asked Jakobson. There was some doubt about this particularly once there was a desire to shift discussion to the level of non-governmental organizations in the form of an organisation founded in Brussels in June 1972. Public forums were expected to be a power hub of citizens' activities. The politico-ideological antithesis and the economic competition between "imperialism and socialism" constituted, according to East Berlin, the dialectical totality of the class struggle.

A public committee was established in Finland too – the Finnish Committee for European Security. In Denmark the idea was mooted that parliamentarians should be included in the preparatory process. In Enckell's discussion with the Dutch on 15 June 1970 he did not support the idea, fearing that NGOs would only give the issue "propagandist overtones and complicate serious measures".

In Jakobson's view it was not cynical to say that for the Soviet Union the organisation of the conference was an end in itself, and for Finland the preparation of the conference was likewise an end in itself. For the Finns it meant opportunities to avoid taking a stand on matters of controversy and to continually maintain its neutral position.

It is at this point that Jakobson's and Enckell's speculations and aims parted company. Enckell had, on the basis of an abundance of bilateral discussions, identified a definite need to bring about a credible dynamic for continuing bilateral consultations. Already in spring 1970 many of the discussion partners had inquired during their talks how Finland proposed such bilateral meetings could continue. He presumed that Finland's activities would have clear visibility.

At the same time, the Soviet Ambassador Alexei Belyakov was putting pressure on Kekkonen for the Finns to speed up the convening of the conference. Kekkonen, however, kept closely to Finland's adopted principle: Finland would not make specific recommendations on starting the conference before there was certainty in Helsinki that the initiative would not be abandoned. He wanted the eventual solution and evaluation to remain in Finnish hands.

The germanies' tightrope dance

In a new memorandum concerning the conference, issued 24 November 1970, the Finnish government opted for gradual and cautious progress. It proposed that the governments mentioned would task their embassies and heads of mission to meet "with the Finnish Foreign Ministry for consultations, in arranged multilateral meetings, on organizing a security conference."

In a letter of 4 June 1968 to Foreign Minister Karjalainen, Jakobson said that Finland's stand on the German question was unique. There were no capitals in Europe apart from Helsinki where both Germanies had equal representations. Neither of them needed to feel that they were on enemy territory. Finland was therefore the only really neutral host country for a European security conference.

Some countries, including Spain and the UK, managed to change their regular representations in Helsinki in light of the new challenges.

Those chairing the practical work of the Soviet and US delegations were not their country's ambassadors to Finland, rather special envoys from their capitals: Deputy Foreign Minister Valerian Zorin from Moscow and George Vest, the US second in command at the NATO mission in Brussels.

Department head Risto Hyvärinen deliberated on the German question on 17 April 1968 in light of current pressures. He did not believe the official mantra coming from the GDR that the recognition of the two Germanies was the starting point for European security. The German question remained the most difficult superpower dispute in Europe and there was no sign yet of a solution. "The fact that Finland has not changed its policy has clearly been a fairly large foreign policy advantage." His recipe for the situation was to act in some respect or to remain in "thick-skinned silence".

In a memorandum written on 27 May 1968 Deputy Director General Keijo Korhonen stated that a change on the matter of recognition would be a heavy strain on the policy of neutrality. It would be reflected in international organizations, including the UN Security Council, and would not improve relations with the FRG, with whom trade was ten times what it was with the GDR.

In an interview given on 22 May 2006 Jakobson said that the initiative had several different aims. In addition to preventing recognition of the GDR it naturally sought to increase Finland's international visibility and strengthen its neutrality. Because it was an initiative aimed at multilateral action, it also sought to "crush the Soviet Union's traditional and continual bilateral policy in a pincer movement". In the strained atmosphere following the occupation of Czechoslovakia, Finland now clearly appeared as something quite different. "The Czechoslovakian road was not Finland's road." What was decisive from the viewpoint of both the process and Finland was that Helsinki became the starting place for the process. In that way Finland was able to continue with its efforts for strengthening its neutrality and securing it.

Recognition of the two German states was viewed in Bonn as an unfriendly action. The German question was not put on the conference agenda. The Federal Republic's Ostpolitik created a momentum, the clogged wheels were in motion. This was decisive from the standpoint of the process as a whole and starting the preparatory talks at Dipoli, near Helsinki. The initiative would not be allowed to collapse due to the dispute over Germany and between the Germanies.

There were clearly two participating countries that believed the speedy convening of the conference was in their national interest:

- Finland, and Helsinki, had the short-term aim of being the host and in charge of practical arrangements.
- From the standpoint of the issue of Europe's security, the ending of the division of Germany, the Bonn government was a central player in relation to the expected outcome. From the stance of the peaceful unification of the Germanies, there was already the estimation in Bonn, in connection with the preparation of new Ostpolitik agreements, that only an increase in peaceful cooperation and interaction in Europe would create the opportunities for it. Moscow received the 'Bahr letter' on 12 August 1970, concerning the signing of a treaty between Bonn and Moscow, and the Bonn's support in principle for the peaceful unification of the Germanies as a long-term objective. The Soviet Union rejected the letter out of hand, did not reply to it, or even confirm its receipt.

Egon Bahr, the main architect of the agreements with the East, visited Washington in spring 1972 for bilateral talks. He met with Henry Kissinger and Helmut Sonnenfeld. The Americans affirmed that the US did not oppose the convening of the CSCE. "If that's what the Germans want, the Americans are ready to attend."

Peter Steglich, the second in command at the GDR representation in Helsinki sent a message to East Berlin on 15 January 1971, which stated that the Finnish government appeared to have fully adopted the line of the NATO countries concerning the issue of West Berlin and coupling it with support for the position that only a solution to the issue of Berlin could further the practical preparations of a security conference.

The Finnish government's 'German package' contained a decisive key to the issue. Foreign Minister Väinö Leskinen leaked details of the package to the media in September 1971 at the time of the meeting of Nordic foreign ministers in Copenhagen. Helsinki had to act. The initiative was made public on 10 September. It proposed the establishment of diplomatic relations with both Germanies, prohibition of the use of force in bilateral relations and reparations for the damage caused to part of Lapland in the final stages of the Second World War as soon as could be agreed separately in negotiations.

The response in East Berlin and Bonn to the initiative revealed that the main aims were almost impossible to achieve equitably and simultaneously. East

Berlin welcomed the initiative. It was prepared for bilateral negotiations as soon as possible. The attitude in Bonn to the initiative was cautious. It was felt that the GDR clearly had more to gain from it. The GDR government's main aim would be realized: it would be recognised by one of the main Western governments in a situation in which the international conference was being planned to take place in Helsinki.

For its part Bonn arrived at the position where, for example, bilateral talks on the destruction in Lapland would be premature. There should first be clearance among the victorious powers. Diplomatic relations could be taken care of in due course without lengthy negotiations.

On the FRG's side, Chancellor Brandt and Foreign Minister Scheel had more pressing worries concerning Finland. The Christian Democratic Union (CDU/CSU) opposition in the Bundestag contained prominent politicians for whom the words CSCE and Finlandization were practically synonyms. The argumentation worked in Germany: as long as the ratification of the FRG's Ostpolitik agreements by the Bundestag remained open, and as long as the opposition had a handy hobby horse, indicating that the Brandt-Scheel government agreed all too easily, cheaply and credulously with the socialist countries' treaty compromises.

The CDU's long-term chairman, the Bavarian politician Franz-Josef Strauss drew an altogether different link with Finlandization in his 1989 memoirs. He said that on a visit to Beijing in 1975 Chairman Mao warned him of the Finlandization of Western Europe.

Such anti-CSCE views were like a gift from heaven for the ideologues of the GDR's Socialist Unity Party. As opponents of the CSCE process, the FRG's right-wing opposition could be pigeonholed as main proponents of European revanchism. This way, it was possible to orthodoxly show that the GDR and others of the socialist camp were on the side of peaceful coexistence, cooperation among nations, peace – and so were on the winning side.

The Bundestag ratified the Ostpolitik treaties and the four-power agreements concerning Berlin on 5 June 1972. The Finnish government's new German package of offers of negotiations was presented on 10 July. Negotiations with the GDR got underway in Helsinki on 30 July. The behind the scenes arm wrestling with Bonn continued on the challenges of equal treatment and simultaneous progress.

The CSCE preparations and the German question were now closely interrelated. Matti Tuovinen wrote in his diary in May 1972 that the convening of the CSCE now appeared to be on the horizon. Everyone thought that the holding of a security conference was necessary and that there were common positions on many subjects.

The actual achievements and existence of détente were indisputably linked to the FRG's concluding of its Ostpolitik agreements. On the other hand, in light of them how credible was it of Moscow to maintain the ideological trepidation, albeit within the political opposition and other "certain circles", following the preparation of the FRG's treaties, the locus of which was in Bonn? The bilateral agreements had dispensed with the threat of force and its use in bilateral relations, as well as in relations between the FRG and other socialist countries. In this situation, where the revanchist fear was without a convincing target, hadn't the principle of ideological absoluteness been watered down and its credibility with it?

In Prime Minister Karjalainen's talks with Prime Minister Kosygin on 19 April 1972, during the former's visit to Moscow, the view was offered that the Soviet Union did not approach European security issues in terms of power politics but rather international peace. The overriding tension, both political and economic, had to be alleviated. The US war in Vietnam would soon have to end. The Soviet Union would do everything in its power for the organisation of the conference of European states. There were various interests that opposed it, said Kosygin. "The United States clearly fears that it would bring about agreement on something that would not correspond with its interests."

At the time it had yet to be made certain that each participating country would have the right of veto on all decisions. Kosygin said that there was similarly a struggle for and against taking place in Germany. In emphasizing the importance of the FRG's, the Soviet Union's, Poland's and Berlin's agreements Kosygin guaranteed that in developing economic cooperation the Soviet Union could safeguard the good quality of life in Europe without the United States.

The GDR's starting point in preparing for the Dipoli talks was to emphasise the establishment of a collective security arrangement for Europe. It would be a gradual and long-term process. No single conference would be able to solve all existing fundamental problems, only create the bases for working on them. A major task would be ending the isolation of the GDR. Berlin expected the support of France, Finland and Switzerland on this.

The preparation of a bilateral agreement between the two Germanies was a final sign that Finland too would normalise relations with both Germanies. Bonn finally lost the last argument for putting the brakes on the process.

Tensions at home – CSCE or accommodating the soviets?

In addition to the German question, the second main pillar of Finland's policy of neutrality was its relationship with the Soviet Union. It was intended to agree on the sequel to the Agreement on Friendship, Cooperation and Mutual Assistance in good time before it expired. In this situation, it had to be asked whether the agreement would continue routinely as before, or would it be conceivable that Finland's current wishes would be introduced in connection with it.

Prior to the visit by President Kekkonen to the Soviet Union in 1970, Foreign Minister Väinö Leskinen called to Kalevi Sorsa, then secretary of the Social Democratic Party. The results of tentative probing by officials indicated that the agreement would remain as it was. The possibility was considered that in the sequel Finland would receive clearer recognition of its neutrality from the Soviet Union. It was natural for Finland, in connection with European economic integration, to look after its interests. The issue was whether Finnish neutrality and Western economic integration could be linked together in the same package.

When the matter was discussed with representatives of the Soviet embassy, the idea was rebuffed. If Finland were to come with such demands for additional conditions, the Soviet Union too would start talks on examining the contents of the agreement. In the context of his Soviet visit President Kekkonen issued a unilateral statement in which he announced that Finland would attend to its interests in connection with Europe's pursuit of integration.

Within Social Democratic circles the EEC was viewed differently from EFTA. It was a more political community, which also, according to a memo by Kari Tapiola, political assistant to Foreign Minister Sorsa, written on 27 November 1972, "directly represents part of the East-West antithesis". The political and economic challenge was real. At the beginning of 1973 the EEC would become a collective negotiating partner, also for individual CMEA (Comecon) countries.

On 28 January 1972 a new civic organisation was established in Helsinki whose main aim was to oppose Finland's membership of the EEC. The pressure mounted as the decisive point in Finland's EEC policy approached. If the EEC agreement could not be ratified, it would be a clear blow to Kekkonen's prestige and that of the factions of the Social Democratic and Centre parties.

In a letter to Foreign Minister Kalevi Sorsa, written on 11 November 1972, social democratic MP Erkki Tuomioja responded caustically to accusations that opposition to the EEC was merely supported by communists: "It seems that left wing thinking is being hounded," Tuomioja had affirmed. "EEC free trade would be dubious for Finland in terms of foreign policy and harmful to the working class in domestic policy."

In drawing up a statement for the Parliamentary committee on defence on 18 December 1970, Paavo Lipponen, research secretary of the Social Democratic Party, offered inferences on three matters of principle:

- the main task of foreign policy was to preserve the confidence of the Soviet Union by not haggling over the obligations in Agreement on Friendship, Cooperation and Mutual Assistance concerning political and military joint activity if needed. It had to be seen realistically, also in situations in which the agreement's mechanisms would really have to be carried out.
- The second major task of foreign policy – pursuing defence policy concerning outside military conflicts – had to be seen in light of the basic intention of the agreement. The neutrality policy's running into conflict with the opportunities for cooperative military activity must be avoided, if joint activity proved to be unavoidable.
- The security policy component of defence policy reinforced the direction of the foreign policy goal, or the "pursuit of national defence self-sufficiency" and was in contradiction with the Soviet Union's contact needs. In this way it "led to results at variance with those sought".

During the preparation of the Dipoli negotiations there was no intention within the Social Democratic Party's inner circles to consider that the CSCE process could have broader or more tangible impacts on the position of Finnish security policy or its room for manoeuvre in relation to the Soviet Union.

Jaakko Blomberg, an official of the Finnish foreign ministry, included similar theses in the April 1973 issue of the journal *Ulkopolitiikka* marking the 25th anniversary of the Agreement on Friendship, Cooperation and Mutual Assistance. If the position of neutrality were used in such a way that placed it in conflict with the agreement, with the goals of Soviet foreign policy, the consequence would be a breach of confidence. "The idea of neutrality as a leading principle of Finnish foreign policy would be alien because of the agreement's arrangement, if it were placed above the pursuit of peace policies."

The ambassadors' tea party and no overblown expectations

We cannot consider the CSCE in terms similar to UN membership, with permanent members of the Security Council and the separate classification of representatives of smaller states. Nevertheless, it was clear that the final decisions on the preparatory discussions for the CSCE started in Helsinki would be made in four powerful capitals: Washington, London, Paris and Moscow.

Contacts with these capitals and their representations had also intensified with the campaign for Finnish membership of the UN Security Council, and more recently in relation to the lobbying for Max Jakobson as a candidate for the post of UN Secretary General. The campaigns for the post of Secretary-General and for the possible hosting of the CSCE were regarded as having parallel impacts for Finland. Both were reflected in Soviet and Finnish bilateral relations. In part the aim of the campaigns was the same: to raise the visibility of Finland's foreign policy profile and extend operational latitude.

The contest for the position of UN Secretary-General ended in December 1971 in favour of Kurt Waldheim of Austria. The implications were analysed closely. The decision was also viewed in temporal terms in relation to the CSCE, even though it had not yet convened in Helsinki.

A Foreign Ministry memo of 28 January 1971 observes that the Soviet Union had by its veto let it be understood that it favoured the Austrian nomination for the post of Secretary-General. The affirmation of Austria's position of neutrality was viewed as bringing Austria closer to the Soviet Union. The emphasising of Finland's neutrality policy would, on the other hand, have been interpreted as drawing Finland away from Soviet policy. The incoming Secretary-General was considered "as being pliant and tractable". In this way the Soviet Union evidently wanted to ensure that there would be no re-entry of a Secretary-General of the independent Dag Hammarskjöld type.

During talks between General Secretary Brezhnev and President Nixon in Moscow on 24 May 1972 the Soviet side announced that on 31 May it would ratify the agreement concluded with the FRG and would be subsequently ready to sign up to arrangements concerning Berlin. Secretary of State Rogers suggested during the course of the talks that the two sides should do the Berlin part on 3 June, so that both would take effect simultaneously.

Brezhnev stressed that for the Soviet Union the convening of the CSCE was not an end in itself. "It would be one means by which a contribution to a discernable step in normalising and strengthening a durable peace for the European continent could be realized." This goal was in Brezhnev's view in everyone's interest. It would ensure that there would never again be war in Europe. In this way the European continent would be made peaceful more effectively than by seeking to use nuclear weapons or threatening to use them.

The two sides could not at this meeting agree yet on the convening of the conference. President Nixon stressed the need to consult his allies, as he supposed the Soviet Union would also do. At this point Kosygin asked the Americans a question: "Could you imagine a time when neither of us had allies at all and we were allies together?" Nixon replied: "Sure, but it'll take time." To which Kosygin said that that was "the objective we seek." "But for as long as you and we have allies we'll be at loggerheads."

On 1 June 1972 Matti Tuovinen, the new head of the Foreign Ministry political department, was tasked with exploring a definite timetable for the conference among the ambassadors in Helsinki. Over lunch with the British Ambassador Bernard Ledwidge on 19 July Tuovinen asked whether the British would agree to 22 November 1972, for instance, for the start of multilateral meetings. The French and US representations were asked the same question by phone. State Secretary Richard Tötterman put the question to the Soviet Ambassador Viktor Maltsev. The US and British ambassadors replied on 31 July that they would have to consult with their allies before giving a definite answer.

Before Helsinki had received an answer through official channels, the Washington Post reported on 8 September that Assistant Secretary of State Walter Stoessel had let it be known in a Congressional committee that the US was prepared for a CSCE meeting at the end of November. When Foreign Minister Karjalainen met Secretary of State Rogers on 29 September at the UN General Assembly session in New York, Rogers said that Finland could assume that the meeting would go ahead "perhaps right on 22 November" as had been proposed. Rogers added that he believed that the meeting would not take long or be complicated. The main thing was that it would adopt the agenda of the conference. The conference could presumably be held in 1973 somewhere other than Helsinki.

Henry Kissinger's memoirs reflect the main line of activity in Washington's diplomacy: the dialogue between the superpowers and relations with other major states, including China. Washington was concerned about the west Europeans' unilateral and bilateral initiatives with Moscow. Kissinger writes in his memoirs for 1982 that he was also concerned by the thinking of some European leaders in which the process of European integration and Atlantic solidarity were seen to be mutually competitive. In these circumstances the multilateral CSCE process was a local and hopefully passing disturbance. Washington was forced to take it into account in the name of solidarity with its allies.

In discussions between Foreign Minister Karjalainen and the FRG's Foreign Minister Walter Scheel in New York, on 4 October, Scheel confirmed that the CSCE would begin in Helsinki on 22 November. Diplomatic relations between the FRG and Finland could be established in half an hour. Concerning the CSCE agenda, Scheel reiterated the FRG's position on the division of Germany: the FRG could not accept a divided Germany. "The organisation of its peaceful unification must be strived for by rational consensus."

The Soviet Union's representatives, Ambassadors Maltsev and Mendelevich vitited Matti Tuovinen in Helsinki on 18 October. They too had positive greetings. Foreign Minister Gromyko, who was in Washington in connection with his trip to the UN, had said that "Finland will get the CSCE, while the Central European Mutual Balanced Force Reduction negotiations will go to Vienna." At the time the Soviet Union thought of integrating the processes more closely. Moscow announced its support for Finland's heading the international secretariat, which would act as a bridge and channel of contact between the two processes.

There was now sufficient clarity on the positions of the main decision-makers. After this the approval of the main recipients would be negotiated orally concerning the contents of the invitation. Once this was achieved, with the positive feedback from NATO's council, on 23 October, the final invitations to multilateral consultations in Dipoli were sent out on 9 November 1972.

Even after the invitations had been sent the Soviet side disclosed to the Finns that they would possibly have a representative higher than an ambassador heading their delegation. President Kekkonen was worried by this possibility, fearing that some might use it as an argument for not attending the meeting.

In order that the main participants would be treated equally at the start of the conference, the government foreign affairs committee decided on 17 November that Finland would announce its recognition of both Germanies on the evening of 19 November. This happened to be an election day in the FRG, and so the news did not dominate the headlines. The GDR's Consul General in Helsinki Oelzner announced that his country took a sympathetic attitude to the timing of the recognition and also of its linkage with the CSCE.

Preliminary 'treaty' between the alliances

There had been an intense dialogue between NATO and the Warsaw Pact since the 1967 Harmel report. This was a factually based dialogue not just on issues concerning military but also humanitarian relations. The Vietnam War had burdened the US position both abroad and at home. The presence of US troops in Europe was a key issue when it came to solidarity and credibility among NATO states.

On another issue, discussion of the occupation of Prague had focused on the Brezhnev doctrine, posing the question of how the lives of citizens of small socialist states, and their contacts with Western Europe, could be made easier by strengthening international cooperation. "The freer movement of people, ideas and information", was the objective as described for the first time in the declaration of the conference of NATO foreign ministers in December 1969.

After this, the approximately simultaneous start of the CSCE and MBFR talks formed an acceptable solution, particularly in discussions between Moscow and Washington, concerning preconditions for the convening of the CSCE. The parties reached an agreement on this in autumn 1972. The CSCE assembled in Dipoli on 22 November and the first meetings of the MBFR negotiations began in Geneva on 31 January 1973. At the same time, the main parties agreed that the official opening of the CSCE would take place in June 1973 without the venue being confirmed. The MBFR talks proper started in Vienna at the end of September 1973.

At a seminar on the CSCE held in Helsinki on 16-17 November 1998 US Ambassador James Goodby noted that the concurrency of the CSCE and the MBFR talks had been the result of two things. Washington indirectly recognised the inviolability of the Soviet Union's power and sphere of interest as a result of the Prague events. On the other hand, Washington saw that the Soviet Union was, due to the CSCE process, ready to recognise the US presence in Europe, both militarily and politically. Simultaneously, the tussle in Washington between Congress and the administration on the content of Soviet policy continued. Senator Jeffry Jackson's presentation to Congress in October 1972 set out conditions for US trade policy. The Soviet Union was granted favoured status and advantageous credit terms. The condition was a more permissive attitude by the Soviet Union to the emigration of Jews.

Henry Kissinger's stance was that this sort of pressure would yield more effective results if it were applied in secret, through private diplomatic channels rather than publicly. The Soviet leadership may well have agreed: an agreement made publicly could appear humiliating. On the other hand, this kind of bilateral 'horse trading' eroded the general significance of the political commitments that all 35 participating countries made in signing the Helsinki Final Act.

The man in charge of the practical work of the US delegation, George Vest, was asked how he would be able to get the work started in Dipoli properly taken care of. He replied to Secretary of State Rogers "by keeping one hand on the shoulders of the French and one on the shoulders of the Germans". In other respects, he considered that the US had no cause to behave aggressively and to criticise Soviet policy openly. US diplomats preferred to keep in the background and leave the centre field to others.

This suited the French, among others, perfectly. Within the EEC they launched the initiative for drawing up a common political concept and the start of political consultations in connection with the CSCE preparations. The main protagonist in this was Ambassador Jacques Andreani, a long-term CSCE expert, who participated in coordinating EEC work from Paris.

There had been significant simultaneous changes to Europe's and Washington's political map during 1969: de Gaulle was replaced as president by

Georges Pompidou in April of that year. Pompidou took an appreciably more favourable attitude in considering the opportunities of the multilateral European conference than his predecessor. At the same time, the French continued to stress the importance of the East-West dialogue as an alternative only to having closer contacts between the military alliances. France's stance continued to be strict: the military negotiations and the CSCE meetings must be kept separate, including geographically. This position ended only with the break-up of the Warsaw Pact and the end of the MBFR negotiations.

In Bonn, the Christian Democrat Chancellor Kurt Georg Kiesinger was succeeded in October 1969 by the Social Democrat leader Willy Brandt and the new coalition of the Free Democrats' Walter Scheel. The FRG's new Ostpolitik broke down taboos. It also made it easier for other West European states to have contacts with Eastern Europe. As Ambassador James Goodby noted, West European governments are actively putting out feelers in a new way, by which each can pursue its own interests eastwards and not leave the field exclusively for Bonn.

In Washington, President Richard Nixon took over at the White House in January 1969. His security advisor was the German-born Harvard professor Henry Kissinger. James Goodby stated that President Nixon talked of the Warsaw Pact's Budapest appeal and the Finnish government's 5 May 1969 CSCE initiative during a hiatus at the 10 April NATO ministerial conference in Washington and set in motion an assessment of general prospects for East-West negotiations.

James Goodby was involved in this work from the start from the US representation to NATO in Brussels. Positions of power became complicated, not least at the top in Washington, between the Department of State and the Pentagon. The White House and Henry Kissinger were key players in this.

For Goodby, in terms of work progress it was decisive that the Department of State's bureau for European affairs was the primary source of guidance for the US representation at NATO. It conducted various negotiations in the sphere of the NATO political advisory committee. The instructions resembled President Nixon's message: of the discussion frameworks, the CSCE conference must be a consequence of the importance of its content. "European security is not an abstract concept. We must be aware of the causes for uncertainty and how to eliminate them. Conferences are useful if they are able to deal with concrete questions. This is why they must be prepared carefully."

French Foreign Minister Maurice Schumann's visit to Moscow in October 1969 signified a decisive step forward in the conference preparations. In a joint statement the two sides said that the European security conference would facilitate the end to the division of Europe into blocs. This was quite a far-sighted pronouncement. The same month the Warsaw Treaty's foreign ministers meeting in Prague received Moscow's blessing for beginning bilateral discussions with Western governments for bringing about the conference.

NATO's ministerial meeting of 5 December 1969 recorded that the prospective agenda of the conference would not only deal with technological and economic matters but also "issues concerning cultural exchange and the free flow of people, ideas and information between East and West." According to the Western alliance, the conference would be more plausible to arrange if at the same time existing open questions of European security could be solved in other forums, thus ensuring the opportunity for all member states of the Western alliance to take part in the conference, to prepare it with care and have the assurance that the conference results would not mean a strengthening of the prevailing division of Europe, but on the contrary endeavours to deal with the causes of the division.

At the end of 1970 the Western alliance was in a position to be more precise about the themes of free movement and information exchange. They would concern in particular the easing of travel restrictions placed on the citizens of socialist countries, an end to the jamming of foreign radio transmissions, the freer availability of foreign books and publications, an improvement in the working conditions of foreign journalists and more freedom for citizens to make transactions at foreign representations. The reunification of families and the reduction of the number of areas closed to foreigners were put on the list at a later stage.

The French were active initiators of the development of the EEC's six-nation consultative mechanism. The CSCE preparations offered an excellent tool for this. The first CSCE working group of EEC countries was held in Paris on 1 November 1971. The first item on the agenda concerned the procedural matters of the conference preparations. The harmonisation of human rights policy in relation to the socialist countries took an increasingly important position in the course of the negotiations.

Much serious attention was paid within the alliance to specifying the main objectives of the negotiations. There also arose a discussion on how different capitals view and estimate other parties' – in this case Moscow's – readiness to accept sensitive subjects as matters for negotiation. When the Bonn government was the first to receive a decision on bilateral discussions with Moscow, it could calmly represent the Western alliance in the discussions. Even in 1971 Bonn proposed that the area of human interaction be limited to cultural exchanges. The Americans considered this a completely insolent tactical notion. In their view, Moscow's primary objectives, prohibition of the use of force and as clear as possible confirmation of prevailing national borders, were arguments against which there had to be credible demands from the Western standpoint.

In October, NATO's political advisory committee had its recommendations ready. The US representation reported to Washington that more than two months of negotiations had produced a satisfactory result. The committee proposed to the ministerial conference that the freer movement of people and ideas would be closely tied to the Warsaw Treaty's well-known aims for prohibiting the use of force and the principle of the inviolability of borders.

The French, particularly Ambassador Andreani, clarified the stance of the community in proposing that the preparatory conference, the Dipoli meeting, should give priority to drafting mandates for different subjects in more detail to be dealt with by the working groups in the negotiating stage proper, in Geneva. The preliminary division of labour for the working groups had within the Western group been four-part:
- principles guiding inter-state relations
- the freer movement and contacts of people, ideas and information, and cultural exchange
- matters concerning economic, scientific and technical cooperation, and
- environmental protection.

At the 23 April 1973 annual conference of the Associated Press, held in New York, Henry Kissinger delivered a speech in which for the first time he publicly provided a sketch of US policy on Europe. 1973 was being celebrated as Europe Year. The time of decisions taken by the previous generation was coming to an end, and there were new challenges ahead. Kissinger stressed that Western Europe's recovery was a new fact. Likewise, US military superiority had shifted to an almost "equal military balance, which required a new kind of consensus on common security".

A decade later 'common security' was the new buzzword of the Palme Commission. Kissinger added that the period could be characterised as a "reduction of tensions". He supposed that the prevailing line of division of the previous decade would dissipate and the needs of national identity would be emphasised in a new manner. "The dramatic change of atmosphere in the West had presented Western leaders with a fundamentally new challenge." Kissinger nevertheless adhered to the global responsibility of the US: "The United States has worldwide interests, our European allies have regional ones."

Kissinger had to admit in his memoirs that the timing of the speech had been a failure. In the next meetings with his European colleagues Nixon had, because of events such as the Watergate scandal, become a defendant. Western Europe's political leaders had no opportunity to coordinate their response to the new situation. Its reception remained vague.

Détente accelerates dialogue

The FRG's *Ostpolitik* agreements, particularly the 12 August 1970 treaty concluded with Moscow, formed the new creative dynamic of their influence on the European situation. Superficial impressions and images disintegrated, new kinds of contact and cooperation opened up between the West and the East. The resourcefulness of the FRG was remarkable. It sparked a lively debate in the FRG on domestic policy, in which the primary criticism concerned the mutual relationship of bilateral agreements with the East and the unification of the Germanies. The opposition in the FRG followed with particular concern the talks on relations between the FRG and the GDR. Treaty relations notwithstanding, the GDR was not ready for inherently comparable 'foreign relations' with other foreign powers.

In the Soviet Union's use of language détente for the most part meant peaceful cooperation and interaction between states with different social systems in the interests of both sides, based on the principles of strengthening and stabilizing peace in Europe. The policy of détente was therefore limited to Europe. The intention was on the one hand to confirm the status quo of the borders created as a result of the Second World War, and on the other to cross the dividing lines according to agreements carried out in different sectors, acknowledging different social systems, employing new forms of cooperation.

Détente in Soviet terms was also often seen as risky from the West's standpoint. The idea couldn't be avoided of being lulled into a false sense of security by the more open atmosphere of the other side that could contribute to the erosion of the alliance relationship and solidarity in the Western camp without reciprocal and corresponding effects being observed in the Warsaw Pact. Henry Kissinger stresses in his memoirs (1982) that the socialist countries seemed to have the upper hand in exploiting détente. "Détente rhetoric could lead to rapture and notions reminiscent of psychotherapy." Kissinger's memoirs, published in 1999, also stress the new kinds of challenge involved: the Soviet Union shows the sort of flexibility that is cause for deep suspicion and uncertainty.

As the former socialist GDR representative, Ambassador Siegfried Bock wrote in a 2005 article that it became apparent in the negotiations that the Western alliance's individual members had noticeably greater latitude than the Warsaw Treaty's member countries. The Soviet Union wanted to keep a firm hold on things within its own camp, and at the same time exploit the West's disunity.

EEC countries did not want to consider that the Cold War was officially ending, "because the results gained have not yet become a reality." It was for this reason that the EEC states were from the start fairly sceptical of the idea of holding the final phase of the CSCE at summit level: "It would awaken the illusion of a period of collective security."

In February 1975 the British government drew up its draft defence budget for the following year. The text stated that the Soviet Union appeared at that time to be establishing, together with the socialist countries of Eastern Europe, a more secure and productive system of relations in the framework of the Geneva conference, so that the neutral and non-aligned countries would take part in the process. The British were also prepared to make a full and cooperative input in the work in Geneva and the MBFR talks in Vienna. But progress in talks required that both sides were ready to negotiate in a "constructive spirit".

Détente came to mean the realization of long-term, fruitful and mutually beneficial cooperation among governments regardless of their political, economic or social system, based on equality and mutual respect. Only such progress could assure those who feared that détente was an instrument of the

Warsaw pact. Its objective would be to break up and placate the West while the East continued to strive gradually to turn the balance of power to the advantage of the Soviet Union. The ongoing East-West negotiations were therefore a test of each side's determination to transform the rhetoric of détente into reality.

The British government's assessment of the situation stated that progress had been slow on many central issues. Many of them had not been dealt with before in multilateral conferences. On the other hand, the majority of negotiators were not ready to approve results and measures in a purely declaratory form without being accompanied by practical consequences. If satisfactory solutions were able to be brought about concerning existing open issues, in the view of the British government it would be proper for the final stage of the conference to be organised in the form of a summit meeting in the near future. This might ensure that the decisions made would be implemented.

The British ambassador to Helsinki, Thomas Elliott, also headed the British delegation in Geneva. He wrote his findings in a wide-ranging report at the end of February 1974, when President Nixon's national security advisor, Henry Kissinger, had visited Geneva to meet with the Western delegations. Kissinger had impatiently criticised the over-detailed nature of the indefatigable aims of the negotiations. Instead, he had thrown in the idea that the West should present some minimal objectives to speed up the talks. Ambassador Elliott said that Kissinger didn't seem to understand the character of the CSCE talks or the West's basic interests in them. Elliott feared that pressure from the Americans and Kissinger might even become fateful in terms of the West's coherence.

The neutral countries strict underlying principle was that all participants in the talks were equal. They could also prevent progress if they were challenged in the wrong manner. Elliott wrote that Dr Kissinger had misunderstood the importance of the CSCE to the West. He gave the impression that détente would work only as an adjuster between governments and that humanitarian viewpoints were secondary.

Kissinger admitted in discussions with Foreign Minister Genscher, in Bad Reichenhall on 11 June 1974, that the Europeans and Americans had different views of CSCE matters.

In bilateral discussions with Ambassador Jaakko Iloniemi, held on 19 November 1973, Ambassador Mendelevich of the Soviet delegation stressed that for the Soviet Union the principle of the inalterability of frontiers was especially important. On the other hand, détente appeared to be a markedly more serious phenomenon than some years before: the Soviet Union was on the way to becoming a more open society and it valued this goal. But a too rapid development towards unimpeded information exchange could bring about destabilising side effects on the road of détente. Therefore a certain reserve in Third Basket issues would support the policy of détente in practice."

The Soviet leadership continued with high-level bilateral meetings and summit level conferences with the main Western powers throughout the period of the Geneva negotiations. The end of 1974 was an especially intensive time, as recorded in the summary of NATO's 12-13 December conference in Brussels. The Soviet leadership had wanted as clearly and conclusively as possible to make sure in its meetings with the Germans, Americans, French and others that their pursuit of the policy of détente would continue regardless of changes of government.

The same aggregate was linked to their interpretation of the results of the US-Soviet summit meeting in Vladivostok: the Soviet Union was prepared to accept the exclusion from the SALT negotiations of US tactical nuclear missiles, as well as Britain's and France's nuclear weapons. Here, too, the explanation was that the Soviet leadership wanted to emphasise the continuing importance of détente in its relations with the United States.

The new French President, Valéry Giscard d'Estaing, played a role in creating the Franco-Russian draft preamble to the disputed Third Basket, in connection with General Secretary Brezhnev's visit to Paris in December 1974. This introduced the main parts of development, promotion and implementation in relation to détente.

The Finnish side gave up on achieving a more specific and defined détente during the negotiations. It was soon realised that détente was a serviceable concept in many ways and in a certain manner synonymous with the entire CSCE process. It was both an activity and an objective, an instrument of national policy in many directions. This flexibility and diversity of interpretation was more useful than seeking a uniform concept. Just as politics was a matter of will, détente was a like-minded assurance of good will to one another.

The aim of the Finnish government's CSCE policy was the general promotion of the development of détente from the stance of the various parties involved. This was stated in the subsequent foreign policy sections of the government programmes. How it was best to be realized was left up to Ambassador Iloniemi and the Finnish CSCE delegation.

In January 1975 Iloniemi examined the CSCE's "basic philosophy of détente" from the perspective of the different parties. To some Western representatives it meant new possibilities to recover from the wounds of the Second World War, opportunities to reunite families and meet relatives. Others saw in it a new opportunity opening up for the West, which the East already had: to present and defend its philosophy in another's territory.

From the viewpoint of the socialist countries, the CSCE process was an intermediate stage, a transitional phenomenon, which levelled the road to an objective process, to a scientifically inevitable development. Based on these differences of basic perception, it was clear that there would be a wealth and variety of interpretation attached to CSCE decisions.

Finnish and Swiss attitudes to these sorts of gross accrual approaches differed markedly from one another. During his discussions with Iloniemi, the head of the Swiss delegation, Professor Rudolf Bindschädler, had characterised these sorts of complex solutions as "sly and dishonourable".

The final resolution of the content of the concluding document was linked to the Soviet Union's notion of the "irrevocability" of détente. This was an interesting aim, which was regarded with suspicion in Western delegations. It could be supposed that in this way the Soviet Union wanted to increase the authority of its own interpretation of the CSCE, and use it in public and political discourse as an instrument of the "umpire of détente" when its original CSCE goals met with opposition. In the end there was a compromise on the nature of détente. Among all the 35 countries the hope was expressed that it would "become continuing and lasting".

The Dipoli arrangements

At the initiative of the Foreign Ministry head of department, Risto Hyvärinen, Ambassador Joel Pekuri was put in charge of the CSCE's practical arrangements. Pekuri was supported by a secretariat, which included Lauri Korpisaari, an architect whose key role was to modify the design of Dipoli, the main building on the campus of the Helsinki University of Technology, in line with the novel requirements of the conference.

The diplomatic tea party in Helsinki became the CSCE preparatory meeting. The opening of the meeting took place on 22 November 1972 in Dipoli, under the chairmanship of State Secretary Richard Tötterman. (Photograph: Lehtikuva)

Thirty-five delegations comprising about 350 delegates took part in the Dipoli consultations. The biggest difficulty facing the secretariat was to get the interpreters for the various languages to Helsinki. UN practice was adopted for the CSCE's official languages, with Italian and German added. The foreign ministries of Italy and the Germanies were ready and willing to hire interpreters. In fact as recently as June in East Berlin the idea had been abandoned that Russian, English and French would suffice as working languages. In the end both Germanies supplied the secretariat with interpreters, to the extent that in the German language booths there were two, one from East Germany, the other from West Germany.

In an interview given in 2002, Switzerland's CSCE Ambassador Brunner described his country's role in the inclusion of Italian and Spanish. Switzerland, not Italy, presented a motion that Italian, one of its national languages, be included. Switzerland was responding to the FRG's appeal that German be a CSCE working language. This would have prevented the German delegations from using different languages, the GDR Russian and the FRG either English or French, which would have only further emphasised that the countries belonged to different camps. Switzerland naturally supported the inclusion of German, an official language in Switzerland, but expected that the FRG would support Italian as a CSCE language.

Joel Pekuri's strength was his ability to improvise. The CSCE was also enough of an exceptional and prestigious challenge that Pekuri didn't have to wrestle with the foreign affairs administration over tricky demands. It was usually enough for him to say that he had agreed on matters in principle.

His role was extremely diverse in the Dipoli preparations – "He constituted a multifaceted focal point". Pekuri's even-handedness and experienced diplomatic finesse were his own positive influences on the success of the conference. For their part, some of the main Helsinki embassies' successful staff selections contributed to the smooth cooperation. The Spanish embassy's Javier Ruperez, had had a long and distinguished career both in diplomacy and domestic policy. The young diplomat Hans von Ploetz, working in the FRG's Consulate General, became the 'adopted son' of the Finns and another young diplomat, Kerstin Asp of the Swedish embassy, later became her country's ambassador to Finland.

The chairperson's, State Secretary Richard Tötterman's office included his first deputy, special advisor Jaakko Iloniemi and the office's General Secretary

Paavo Keisalo, as well as specialists. Matti Tuovinen, the head of the political department, headed the Finnish national delegation.

The shared view of the parties involved was that State Secretary Tötterman carried out his duties as advisor very correctly and diplomatically. The same can be said of the work of the secretariat, under Joel Pekuri's leadership. His team comprised sixteen of the Foreign Ministry's youngest officials plus the heads of the UN's Geneva office and its interpretation services, Francis Veillet-Lavallée, Andre Courtoit and Rowe Ginrich, and their expertise.

Speaking at a lunch for newspaper editors on 17 November 1972, Foreign Minister Karjalainen stated the Finnish line of operation: "Finland has not become the mouth and head of the Dipoli conference." As the organising country Finland had kept aloof in matters of substance – in all matters it sought only to support the chairman.

At the close of the general discussion stage, on 5 December 1972, Finland was the last to speak. Tuovinen touched on the proposals of the NATO countries concerning the free flow of ideas and people – the rapprochement of people and nations. He announced that Finland was also prepared to host the CSCE.

The preparations for the Dipoli consultations were carried out carefully. There were even expectations in the discussions that the CSCE negotiations proper would start in Helsinki. Procedural practices could be adopted immediately. The German delegations were able to sit side by side. On the initiative of deputy head of department Keijo Korhonen the conference decided to use the Francophone alphabetical order.

The matter arose again in January 1973, when the UN Secretariat had confirmed the use of the Anglophone seating order. Jaakko Iloniemi confirmed to Finland's UN Ambassador, Aarno Karhilo, that the French seating order used for the Dipoli consultations would remain unchanged. In the Francophone list of diplomatic representations in Helsinki the Germanies were together.

Soon after work started, the notion of a genial tea party of heads of embassies working in Helsinki changed fundamentally. The GDR's Foreign Ministry and party machinery hastened to invite specialists from various fields to assist the delegation in Dipoli. It was no longer a matter of tea and biscuits, but something more serious, including matters concerning GDR society.

The search for a balance of interests

The CSCE's four 'baskets' were a product of the Helsinki meeting of foreign ministers concerning the adoption of the CSCE agenda. The original range of subjects of the Soviet Union and other socialist countries had emphasised the principles of clarifying state and interstate relations and scientific-economic cooperation. The Western countries wanted people-to-people contacts and an easing of information exchange included in the discussions.

Ten principles were selected as subjects for negotiation. The aim was to eradicate causes of tension, promote peace and security, and at the same time disarmament, which would complement political détente. The main subjects in the basket on economic cooperation concerned exchanges in the areas of economy and services, industrial cooperation, science and technology and environmental protection. The complexity of the economic and social systems and the advantages and reciprocal nature of advantages and obligations set pressing challenges for developing trade and cooperation.

The novelty of the CSCE process was the use of negotiation to develop cooperation in the humanitarian sphere. In the context of people-to-people relations the goals were to be the examination of contacts between family members "in a positive spirit and mutually acceptable conditions" for permitting them, the removal of barriers to international marriages, the improvement of opportunities for both private and official travel, freer and more extensive exchanges of information, improvement in the working conditions of journalists in participating countries and the improvement and expansion of educational and cultural exchanges. Special mention was made of national minorities and the recognition of their cultures.

The preamble to phase III puts these in a different order. The objectives were recorded as strengthening peace and understanding between nations and the spiritual enrichment of people regardless of race, gender, language or faith and irrespective of the political, economic or social system to which they belong. The working groups and subcommittees were given the task of investigating the possibilities for creating better circumstances "for increasing cultural and educational cooperation and exchange, a broader dissemination of information and contacts between people and the solution of humanitarian problems."

The participants did not limit their work to prevailing forms of cooperation, but pledged to draw up new solutions for achieving the objectives. The second paragraph of the introduction to basket III of the Blue Book points out, in addition, that in drawing up recommendations the principles of interstate relations will be followed and respected, as was agreed separately in the basket I phase.

The formalities concerning follow-up of the conference were still very general in nature. References were made only to the requirements by which the participating states could promote security and develop cooperation in Europe "on the basis of progress made". Proposals for future negotiation could also be "organizational in nature". In agreeing on the follow-up, the efforts of existing international organizations had to be kept in mind.

It was agreed in the Dipoli recommendations that the participants would share the expenses. The six largest countries – Britain, Italy, France, the FRG, the Soviet Union and the United States – committed themselves to paying over half (52%) of all mutual costs. The Finnish share amounted to two percent, the figure also set for Denmark, Norway and Switzerland.

In issuing a review of the international situation, on 11 September 1973, the Parliamentary foreign affairs committee characterised the goals of the main parties highly appositely. The Soviet Union's underscoring of the policy of peaceful coexistence was stated to be still based on ideological struggle and the promotion of the worldwide victory of socialism. Because of this, socialist ideology had to be kept "clean of harmful influences coming from the West". The socialist countries appeared to be striving, in the context of the CSCE, for politico-legal confirmation of the status quo. The aim was to safeguard the socialist system and its ideology from the pressure directed at it as a consequence of peaceful coexistence. In payment, the Western powers wanted more mobility for human and ideological as well as spiritual influences.

The aims of the neutral and non-aligned countries was seen as developing the circumstances that would give small countries outside military alliances continued security without the danger of external interference. The CSCE offered an opportunity for launching initiatives and making compromises. The committee stated that the prerequisite for achieving results in the CSCE concerning the basic political situation depended on the one hand on US-Soviet relations and the level of interaction between the US and its Western European allies, and on the other on the development of relations within the socialist countries. Because the main parties' goals were at that point still to be specified, the negotiations in Geneva were expected to be laborious and lengthy.

Prior to the first Helsinki conference of foreign ministers, General Secretary Brezhnev paid an official visit to the United States, from 18-25 June 1973. The two sides signed bilateral agreements on several issues, including the prevention of nuclear war and limiting strategic arms. A fundamental principle of both parties was that the CSCE should reach decisions as soon as possible. Progress in the work of the conference made it possible to achieve this at a high level politically. The common aim of the two countries was "the stability and security of Europe".

In April 1974 Iloniemi returned to the results of Dipoli and Finland's resumption of scheduling. In the past year international affairs had experienced various setbacks and crises: the war in the Middle East, the oil crisis, the Watergate scandal, disunity in the Atlantic community, Chancellor Brandt's problems, and the recent death of President Pompidou. Although the Blue Book negotiated in Dipoli was only a detailed list of subjects, "it had proved to be a durable basis for work and an already valued partial result. It had become especially popular for codifying the international situation and the parties' binding work programme". Even though the international situation had not developed in a positive direction since the summer of 1973, the participating states hardly had the chance of disassociating themselves from what had been set as a common objective in the Blue Book. It is entirely conceivable that, in the spring of 1974, reconvening the Helsinki consultations in Dipoli would no longer be possible.

Consensus and agenda

The fruitfulness of international negotiations hinged essentially on which party was able to write the aims it considered important into the results. Under Helsinki recommendation number 69, the CSCE adopted the principle of consensus decisions. This did not mean that such decisions were somehow weaker than those adopted by qualified majority. Consensus could be said to have been achieved when there were no requests to speak after the chairperson had asked if there were any objections. The consensus principle ensured that all 35 participating countries were equally involved in all decisions.

Group photograph of the first foreign ministers conference, 1973, hosted by Foreign Minister
Ahti Karjalainen. On the back row, third from the right, is the Prime Minister and Foreign
Minister of Malta Dom Mintoff. This was the only time he took part personally in a CSCE meeting.
(Photograph: Lehtikuva)

The Dipoli consultations did not end with delegates going home for Christmas carrying some sort of communiqué with them, a few weeks after they had
convened. The talks continued through the first half of 1973 so that they would
reach agreement in time. The Dipoli, Helsinki, recommendations, the Blue
Book, comprised a noticeably different negotiating document than the CSCE
participants originally invited to the Dipoli tea party had expected. In practice,
the tea party was a preparatory conference.

The Final Recommendations, the outcome of the negotiations, were
adopted at the final session in Dipoli on 8 June 1973. The recommendations

were meant to be presented to the governments of the participating countries for their approval. It was hoped that by 25 June they would notify the Finnish government of their approval of the organisation of the conference and of the decisions on the list of subjects. They were also asked to confirm their attendance at the first stage of the conference.

The first meeting of CSCE foreign ministers, on 3-7 July 1973, was the largest international event to take place in Helsinki since the 1952 Olympics. Some 1,400 people took part in the conference arrangements. The event was followed by 500 journalists, 300 of whom were from abroad. The cost of the three-day meeting was 4.8 million Finnish markka. In line with the cost sharing agreed in Dipoli, Finland paid two percent of this.

The CSCE was to be a longer gathering. It was decided that the conference would be organised in three stages: the first stage in Helsinki at foreign minister level, the second stage in Geneva, and the final stage once more in Helsinki.

Due to the FRG's Ostpolitik treaties the socialist camp faced a political difficulty. The treaties had endorsed at bilateral level prohibition of the use of force. The GDR authorities feared that on the basis of these treaties, the Western alliance could assert that the ban on the use or threat of force would now be unnecessary within the framework of the CSCE. The principal aims of the socialist camp remained, firstly, to bring about recognition of the regional status quo and, secondly, a multilateral agreement to prohibit the use of force.

In his speech in Finlandia Hall on 3 July Soviet Foreign Minister Gromyko stated emphatically that the negotiated outcome must be based on the recognition of existing regional and political realities. "It must not feed dangerous illusions". He did not recommend anything that would require changes to the social or political system or the breaking of relations with allies or friends. Regional integrity and the inviolability of borders were, according to Gromyko, central principles based on the experiences of the Second World War. He said that a lesson could be taken from the agreements concluded between the FRG, the Soviet Union, Poland and the GDR and they could be used for improving the situation in Europe. He attributed the end to the isolation and political boycott of the GDR to the FRG's Ostpolitik.

The participants in the first Helsinki CSCE foreign ministers conference put forward both general and detailed objectives for the expected talks in Geneva. In their interventions, the socialist countries reiterated the importance of the principle of peaceful coexistence and the role of détente in promoting security and cooperation. The speeches did not define détente precisely. Its role and significance appeared somehow self-evident and a consistent feature of the general foreign policy of the socialist countries.

Détente was the central theme of the speech by the FRG's Foreign Minister Walter Scheel. All participating states would like to be involved as active elements in the policy of détente. Ten years before there had not been enough détente for it to characterize European politics. According to Scheel, the recognition of European realities, and with them the existence of the two military alliances, were preconditions for advancing détente. Because of it Berlin could for the first time take part in its good results. The FRG's Ostpolitik agreements recognised European realities. "From this basis we can promote security, co-operation and détente. Ordinary people, too, hope to benefit in their everyday lives from the fruits of détente. The removal of obstacles in the way of this interaction was now the task of the negotiations ahead."

An enduring public impression of the 1973 conference of foreign ministers is that Foreign Minister Scheel performed at it as a super power representative. He stayed at Haikko Manor, east of Helsinki, and travelled from there to Finlandia Hall by helicopter, for which the nearby Hesperia hotel had a helipad on its roof. On the final glorious summer evening of the conference, he hosted an outdoor reception at Haikko Manor for all the participants. The food and service were all flown in by air force freighter from Germany.

In the view of US Secretary of State Rogers, the recommendations adopted in Dipoli did not merely comprise a list of subjects, but also a detailed working programme, the aim of which was the promote peaceful development in Europe. Rogers reiterated President Kekkonen's message that "security is not a matter of putting up fences, but of opening gates". The US expected tangible progress and practical improvements. It wanted to eliminate the antitheses from all divisions affecting the negotiations. Washington also did not rule out the possibility of agreements concluded between states for the peaceful transformation of frontiers.

The Dipoli recommendations had already confirmed universal respect for human rights. Basket III obligations had, according to Rogers, a unique significance: the participating states were committed to reducing obstacles to the free flow of people and information. "Care must now be taken that these regulations do not merely remain footnotes in history books, but that they affect the daily life of the ordinary person."

The last to speak was Finland's Foreign Minister Karjalainen. He saw that in the discussions all the participants had shown good political will. "Taking into account the difficulties and risks expected in advance, the preparatory conference produced a good result." Everyone was expected to be decisive and ready for compromise at the coming negotiations, if they wanted to steer the development of Europe towards reducing tension and increasing cooperation and mutual confidence on the basis of equality and equal rights.

The main aim, in Karjalainen's view, was to bring about security. This should set the tone of the forthcoming negotiations. He considered that there was a danger of "exaggerated expectations and empty reiteration". This must be avoided by finding the means to genuinely improve political security. Karjalainen thought that all of the participants must be able to attend to security in such a way that national identity was preserved. "In the view of the Finnish government this was a key ingredient of European security."

He also referred to the fact that Europe's group of neutral countries, though numerically small, must not be disregarded. The right of the neutral countries to remain outside disagreements between the superpowers must be contained in the results of the negotiations. "The policy of neutrality was a peace policy."

Karjalainen said that Finland supported Switzerland's proposal for the peaceful settlement of disputes. Finland proposed that during the second stage of the negotiations the idea of a Nordic nuclear weapons-free zone should be examined from a new basis. Economic cooperation must chart rapid growth and the conditions set by a changing world – earlier recommendations and guidelines aged quickly and became unnecessary.

When speaking of the subject matter of the Third Basket, Karjalainen set out Finland's attitude closely to the familiar demands of the socialist countries: "The sovereignty of every country must be the basis and starting point when making decisions and recommendations on issues of cooperation in human interaction." The Finnish government was satisfied that the Dipoli consultations were able to agree already on very detailed objectives in this area. "We have been by no means unaware of the differences in opinion, arguments and risks that the participants had, stemming from their different social and political systems, and the roles and responsibilities of states on these matters." Finland was an open society. In this context the Foreign Minister wanted to emphasise Finland's Nordic reference group. "We have also had positive experience of the cooperation of countries representing different social systems, particularly our neighbour the Soviet Union. He was encouraged to predict that "this kind of experience would become a help when new opportunities to develop contacts and practical means of cooperation are mapped out."

At the end of his speech, Karjalainen affirmed the Finnish government's political support for the continuation of the conference: "It is difficult to imagine that a conference such as this could be a one-off event or that its work will have been completed when the final recommendations and decisions are adopted. This development was put on track due to the CSCE and therefore its continuity must by necessity be made certain."

The negotiations also showed the Finns new kinds of opportunity there were to take part in and exert influence for the prize of positive results. The Soviet Union appeared to be ready for new concessions once it was assured that the European security conference would achieve visible progress. From the standpoints of both the Soviet Union and Washington the conference of foreign ministers in Helsinki was perhaps originally meant to be the main event. For a great many other participants it was just the start of proper, intense negotiations for which no time limit had been set.

Iloniemi's team

The participants in the Geneva phase of the negotiations were unable to return home for Christmas. In this respect, and with the launch of the negotiations in autumn 1973 in Geneva's brand new international conference centre, Ambassador Jaakko Iloniemi had good preparations in place. On 9 July 1973 the government had presented in its supplementary budget new mandates for eight posts: one ambassador, four legation counsellors, and vacancies for a couple of junior legation secretaries. The government had decided to set up a CSCE special representation in Geneva for the negotiations.

During talks held at the administrative department of the Foreign Ministry in July 1973, Iloniemi thought that the coming phase of negotiations would last "from six months to two years". He had already predicted that following the negotiations a permanent presence would perhaps be needed in Geneva. It was important that Finland's activity was planned for the long haul.

When the delegation was finally appointed, on 24 August, Iloniemi was given free rein by Foreign Minister Ahti Karjalainen on its composition. Iloniemi was chairman of the delegation and Paavo Rantanen vice-chair with responsibility for Basket II, on issues concerning economic, technological and environmental cooperation. Counsellor Esko Rajakoski was transferred from London for the Basket I talks. In addition, counsellor Leif Blomqvist came from the Foreign Ministry's trade policy department to be Rantanen's assistant. Attachés Markku Reimaa, with the representation in East Berlin, and Jaakko Laajava were mandated to assist Ministerial Counsellor Klaus Törnudd with Basket III, on human contacts, exchange of information, and education and culture cooperation. The delegation's general secretary was counsellor Paavo Keisalo. During the negotiations, experts on various issues were brought from Helsinki to assist for short periods. The specialist on military matters was initially the Finnish military attaché in Bern. The task was then performed from Helsinki alternately by Colonels Pentti Laamanen and Pentti Lehtimäki.

Offices were reserved for the CSCE special representations on the second floor of the Hotel Royal.

In the rotational hosting duties it was agreed that during the Geneva phase of the work Finns would work for the international secretariat.

Helsinki's self-esteem grows

The Finns gained valuable self-confidence for the coming ordeal from the experiences of Dipoli and particularly the conference of foreign ministers.

On 2 June 1973, during the final week of the Dipoli work, the participating states agreed that phases one and three would be arranged in Helsinki and phase two in Geneva. The Dipoli consultations ended on 8 June 1973, when Malta finally dropped its demand for the possibility of Arab countries to participate in the conference.

The conference of foreign ministers decided that the negotiations proper, CSCE II, would start on 18 September 1973. No date was set for its completion.

Representatives of the socialist countries issued a statement at their conference in Crimea, on 31 July 1973, which proposed "with the good will of the participants the negotiations could reach an agreement by the end of 1973." They included their frequently repeated stance that the final result should at the conclusive stage have the blessing of a higher political level.

Even a few weeks after the work this hope appeared to be a pointless and even damaging tactic. It was often the case in CSCE negotiations that those who hastened to reach an agreement during a negotiating stage would reveal indirectly that they were prepared to be more flexible and willing to compromise than other participants.

The decision in principle on the arrangements for phase three fully met the hopes of the Finnish government and President Kekkonen, as well as the civil service staff working in the CSCE. Finland now had a definite fix on the future, politically impressive European happening.

A new kind of neutrality

The Geneva negotiations, 1973–1975

Helsinki and Bern attached very different significance to the adoption of the three-stage CSCE conference. Switzerland was interested in participating in a multilateral European conference for reasons of principle. It was not involved in the UN organization, as all other European countries were. Its need to highlight its international profile expressly in the CSCE was very limited. The chairman of the Swiss delegation, Rudolf Bindschedler, had, in accordance with custom, put forward a proposal on the peaceful settlement of disputes, which Switzerland pursued during the Dipoli and Geneva negotiations.

At Switzerland's initiative, the four neutral European countries held their first meeting in August 1973. Switzerland asked the group to support its proposal. Liechtenstein posed a new challenge for Switzerland, as it wanted to be involved in the CSCE as a separate nation. This deviated from previously followed practice according to which Bern represented Vaduz abroad. The CSCE showed the way for Liechtenstein's active 'foreign policy' in its progress towards UN membership before Switzerland's.

In a report on the start of the work Iloniemi wrote in October 1973 that as the host Switzerland acts differently from the way to which Finland was accustomed. The Swiss general secretary of the conference took an active role in explaining the standpoints of the Swiss delegation. The hosts were also very conspicuously active concerning the media, and the Swiss press was always aware of the Swiss input on decisions made. On a practical level, Bern had not been active on getting the negotiating round to Geneva. A private enterprise project, the Geneva international congress centre in the heart of the city, was ready on time by the beginning of autumn 1973.

The Swiss secretariat carried out its tasks routinely and professionally. Those working in the Finnish secretariat felt the CSCE talks were "the Finns' own thing". The results would in the end be adopted in Helsinki. This is why the representatives of the Finnish secretariat took an interest in the substantive content of the work, the progress of the negotiations and the schedules of the months ahead.

There were altogether twenty Finns serving in the secretariat of the Geneva phase, of whom seven were civil servants. Lea Virtala, who had handled interpretation services for several decades, was in charge of those of the conference.

Getting organized

The coordinating committee of the participating states, the body responsible for the conference's general arrangements, convened on 28 August 1973, for an organizing conference. Three head committees and twelve subcommittees were created for the work. The head committees dealt with security policy, economic cooperation and questions of humanitarian cooperation, according to the division of the baskets.

Discussion of the conference follow-up started in two stages: first in the form of follow-up meetings separately agreed in the coordinating committee. Not until the beginning of spring 1974 would a separate subcommittee be created for more detailed work.

The division of labour of the first committee's subcommittees was as follows:
- Principles guiding relations between participating states
- The peaceful settlement of disputes
- Military issues

The second committee's subcommittees dealt with:
- Trade
- Industrial cooperation
- Environmental matters
- Other forms of industrial cooperation

The third committee's subcommittees concerned
- Human contacts
- Information
- Cultural cooperation
- Cooperation in education

On 11 December 1973 the Parliamentary foreign affairs committee was reported on the start of the work. It was emphasised to Parliament that the matter
was not of three head committees and 12 sub committees involved in separate
negotiations, but of a single entity, the parts of which were in mutual interaction. The autumn session had mainly heard the presentation of principle positions, had made written proposals and had explored the general requirements
of the negotiations.

There was more scrutiny of policy in Finland's activity in Geneva than during the Dipoli discussions. Finland expressed its national viewpoint and interest
in the aims of the conference and in the issues more emphatically and actively
than previously. In its addresses to the different committees Finland presented
its positions on the goals of the Blue Book, adopted in Dipoli, and commented
on the proposals of others.

In Helsinki, Finland's activities were followed with interest. Head of department Matti Tuovinen was sent the list of speakers in mid-November
1973, when the proceedings had been underway for two months. There had
been ten addresses given in the coordinating committee, nine in the first
committee, 16 in the second committee, and 22 in the third committee. By
mid-December the total of interventions from the Finnish side had risen to
70. Specialists from various ministries in Helsinki took part in many of the
discussions.

Finland delivered an address to the committee dealing with military aspects
of a Nordic nuclear weapons-free zone based on President Kekkonen's 1963
initiative. Finland also proposed that the issue be discussed in the CSCE. Only
Romania, Yugoslavia, the Soviet Union, the GDR and Spain considered the
idea a good one and worth supporting. But even they did not consider that the
issue should be discussed within the CSCE framework. Sweden and Denmark
reiterated their previously publicised announcement that the realization of the
proposal would require the backing of the superpowers.

In line with the principle of rotation, the Finnish delegation chaired proceedings in the various working groups some twenty times during the autumn session.

Intermediate report of december 1973

The first autumn of the Geneva stage of the conference was in many respects still an exploratory period. Ambassador Iloniemi wrote in his 'Autumn Harvest' report of 19 December 1973 that all participants had the same understandings and sense of the overall objectives, namely to improve international relations and increase security. But these understandings diverged greatly from one another on the matter of how those objectives should be achieved. The starting point of the socialist countries was that a declaration should be swiftly drawn up, a general declaration of principle that the heads of state would sign in the final stage of the conference. "Its declaratory and moral strength would bind the participants." More detailed regulations would be agreed following the conference, in the work of an "advisory committee", which would be convened.

The EEC countries were still in the midst of clarifying their goals. They had prepared efficiently for the conference. Iloniemi thought that their coordination even worked "strikingly well". Concerning security questions, the EEC countries considered that the form of a declaration might be correct "but according to the EEC it is necessary to reach a more legally binding programme of work on matters of cooperation, particularly on the freer flow of people and information." Only then could the conference prove its worth and justify its existence. It must first be seen what could be achieved and only then could it be decided what sort of final document there should be.

Iloniemi said that the time following the conference was "bound to the same network". In the view of the eastern bloc the application of detailed proposals would be taken care of by an advisory committee. Possible differences of opinion over the application of proposals would be handled through bilateral government negotiations.

Iloniemi said that, along with other non-aligned countries, Finland backed the creation of a functional multilateral negotiating powerhouse. It would the best guarantee that the interests of the small and non-aligned countries would be taken into account, more so than the bilateral period preceding the conference.

In the committee on economic cooperation much of the time was taken up by discussion between the socialist countries and the EEC. The socialist countries considered the EEC's treatment of non-member countries discriminatory and illegal. The EEC had to grant the socialist countries most favoured nation treatment without counter concessions – as renouncing an "illegal" practice did not warrant counter concessions. The EEC countries adopted the practice during the CSCE negotiations whereby the delegation of each country responsible for the chairmanship included a representative of the commission. When the socialist countries protested against this, the Danish delegates stated that they were entitled to determine who was included in their delegation. The EEC countries criticised the socialist countries' practice whereby the intentions of state administrations could be easily measured in trade policy terms by their original commitments.

Iloniemi said in his first interim report that Finland had no reason to intervene in the dispute between the EEC and socialist countries. Instead, Finland focused from the outset on questions such as environmental cooperation and made its first cooperative proposal immediately during the autumn session. In its address in the second committee Finland focused on the need to increase and exchange financial information.

From the start, the Basket II discussions reflected the extent to which work of the CSCE would duplicate or overlap that of the Economic Commission for Europe. The same issues had been dealt with for years already.

From the outset, issues concerning Basket III took the form of a high level dialogue. General Secretary Brezhnev himself said in a statement that the Soviet Union would not accept the West's proposals "under any circumstances". Interference in the internal affairs of another country should not be permitted under cover of the free flow of people and information. The spread of propaganda and anti-culture against the laws and customs of another country were forbidden.

According to the Western delegations, the situation was precisely the opposite: the CSCE's general objectives could only be accomplished if the free flow of people and information could be guaranteed. "Security is not based only on the absence of war but on the individual's awareness of what happens to his neighbours and what they think."

"Negotiations are not yet taking place with an eye to the final document. The negotiating positions were being sought with next spring in mind," Iloniemi wrote in December 1973. The proposals presented were designed from tactical starting points. Because of this, the objective has not been, at least not yet, the feasibility of proposals or recognition of prevailing realities.

The arm wrestling was also going on at the level of principle, concerning what adherence to the Helsinki proposals meant in practice. The Soviet delegation tried at the first meeting of the subcommittee to dismiss the West's proposals on the basis that they went beyond adherence to the Dipoli recommendations. It was therefore unrealistic to adopt them.

Iloniemi stressed that the differences in standpoint were based on diverging value judgements. "They will not be easily altered." These value judgements crystallised into two entities: on one hand international principles, on the other the free flow of people and information. The West challenged the East and the socialist system within sight of the latter's own citizens, at an individual level, to compete with the West's system. This was why, said Iloniemi, the East responded in expected fashion, by emphasising the priority of national and collective issues.

Détente, Iloniemi believed, was only able to effect a narrowing of these divergences to a limited degree. "If the direct threat to security is felt to be diminishing, a greater degree of flexibility might emerge. " But in the final assessment, Iloniemi opined, the general expectations of the CSCE "should be fairly modest."

Inter-governmental relations

Could communism be spread by publicly presenting the methods of Lenin and certain other Soviet leaders without violating the principle of the non-interference in the internal affairs of other countries? This was the question put by a British delegate in the committee dealing with principles, in mid-November 1973. Ambassador Lev Mendelevich replied that Lenin's remark of 1923, when Winston Churchill was the Minister of War in the British government and the British had executed 24 People's Commissars, might be appropriate. Lenin had said that the day would come when the Soviet Union would be so powerful that it would be able to seize capitalists by the throat.

Generally speaking, according to Mendelevich, the transition to socialism was a "historically objective process, which proceeded naturally under by its own accord and there was no need to interfere in the internal affairs of other states."

The Soviet Union did not consider that revolution was an export commodity. It therefore did not accept any attempt to export counterrevolution to the socialist countries. General Secretary Brezhnev had said in his speech of 26 October 1973 that in the climate of détente the conditions for establishing communism had improved, "because in the occurrence or threat of war, efforts were put into strengthening security and this took resources away from building communism."

Mendelevich admitted that naturally the class struggle continued, "but it was not directed against any state. Peaceful coexistence had given improved possibilities for competition between the different economic and political systems, to determine which of them would win."

The discussion of principles soon turned to a key question: were similar countries within the socialist system entitled to conclude mutual relations other than those based on the current principles now being mediated among the 35 countries? Iloniemi explained in his December 1973 report that the socialist countries proceeded from the position that this should be possible in the future. The name of this sort of principle was "proletarian internationalism", the maxim of socialist internationalism. In the context of the Prague occupation of August 1968 it acquired a new epithet, "the Brezhnev doctrine".

On the one hand, at the Geneva CSCE negotiations, there was detailed demarcation between already confirmed legal principles, particularly the international declaration concerning friendly relations, and the current principles to be applied in state relations among the 35 CSCE participating countries. From the standpoint of the socialist countries the principles of socialist internationalism and peaceful coexistence were now, for the first time, the subjects of detailed analysis. Alongside the freedom and equality of citizens, the socialist states' "necessary defence of unity, friendship and mutual assistance" was also a major demarcation in the CSCE. Should they now struggle against imperialism or direct their gaze to the altar of closer cooperation?

The predominant socialist conception of justice required harmonisation of the interests of the socialist countries with the interests of the whole community, "fraternal mutual assistance and cooperation in all areas of life". When the demands of communality were seen coupled with "rebuffing the threat of

attack from imperialism and the forces of reaction", the notion of fraternal assistance in connection with the Prague events extended to cover forcible means
of assistance.

The second focus of the socialist countries was to emphasise the integrity of
frontiers and the principle of non-interference in internal affairs. The integrity
of frontiers meant, according to the Soviet interpretation, the permanence of
current frontiers. They could not be altered under any circumstances, not even
by agreement between states.

According to a proposal presented by France, on behalf of the EEC, the
principle of proletarian internationalism could not be accepted as a new precept. The EEC countries wanted to hold fast to Western Europe's preconditions
for integration. They also wanted to reserve the possibility for peaceful change
to frontiers and agreements between states. By stressing the principle of the
right to self-determination and the equality of nations, delegates of the EEC
countries believed they could gradually weaken the collective cohesion of the
socialist countries.

Another subject in the discussion of principles was the question of how
agreed ground rules should be observed by countries outside the conference.
The socialist countries emphasised the organization's separation from the UN
and countries outside the CSCE. The EEC countries on the other hand wanted
to avoid isolation of outsiders and the impression that the CSCE would act
against them.

The content of the principle concerning the inviolability of frontiers was
initially ready before the start of the Easter recess, in March 1974. The text
was agreed upon without differences of opinion, but the FRG had a provision.
It required that before the final adoption of the principle, there should be
agreement on the content of the sentence on peaceful alteration of frontiers,
its exact phrasing, the reciprocal nature of the principles and the final German
language version.

From the FRG's stance the key demand was that reference to the possibility
of peaceful change should be attached to the principle of sovereignty and not
to the principle of the inviolability of frontiers, as the Soviet Union required.
Foreign Minister Hans-Dietrich Genscher met Secretary of State Kissinger in
July 1974 and said that he wanted a further condition added to the binding
nature of the principles, namely that nothing in the principles would have an

effect on the possibility of peaceful change. Kissinger hesitated. Genscher said that the FRG could drop this condition from the proposal if it was clearly stated in the declaration of principles that all ten principles carried equal weight and that they must all be considered as parts of a whole.

From Finland's position there was no problem with incorporating principles on international relations in connection with the CSCE. The texts of the UN Charter and the 1970 agreement on friendly relations further strengthened the internationalization of the European colloquium. From the outset, the countries involved in the discussion of principles included both Germanies, Liechtenstein and Switzerland, all of which at that point were not yet UN members.

The reference to the principle of neutrality made in connection with the principle of the right to self- determination was a specific accomplishment of the neutral countries. Their identity was clarified and their practical activity in the CSCE process received equal recognition alongside the various alliances. Finland's support for Switzerland in making the proposal was confirmed by the President of Finland. Finland worked on the assumption that neutrality was in this context understood as a general term. It was a symbol uniting the position and policies of all neutral countries regardless of how they themselves defined their roles. Finland spoke of its policy of neutrality. Switzerland stressed the legal nature of its neutrality.

Switzerland's proposal for compulsory methods for the peaceful settlement of disputes became a long-term issue. From the outset, the socialist countries opposed the compulsory nature of the mechanism and considered the debate a waste of time. "Compulsion would only complicate and slow the reduction of tensions," the Soviet delegates stated. The parties to a dispute should have the chance to choose appropriate means of resolution without outsiders – that would be in the spirit of détente. The issue was further dealt with several times, including at the CSCE countries' conference of experts. Of the neutral and non-aligned countries, Yugoslavia and its representative Professor Achimovic were particularly active in the discussion concerning the principle. The main points of contention were, as expected, the human rights principle and its relationship with human contacts dealt with in more detail by the substance of Basket III, and the principle of the sovereignty of states.

The text of the principle on non-intervention in internal affairs was adopted preliminarily in connection with a solution package on 26 July 1974. The main remaining sentence in brackets was the qualification that ran: "regardless of the mutual relations of states". The Soviet Union had previously accepted this but now expressed reservation. The stance of many delegations was that the adoption of the sentence would mean the abandonment of proletarian internationalism, or the Brezhnev doctrine.

The legal department of the Foreign Ministry also gave an opinion on the principle of non-interference in internal affairs. It considered that the formulation adopted in Geneva was based for the most part on the 1970 UN declaration on the friendly relations of states. In accordance with this, the participating states refrained from direct or indirect interference, separately or jointly, in the internal or external affairs of another participating state's sphere of jurisdiction, regardless of the bilateral relations between the states.

This was illustrated in the final document by three examples: the prohibition of the use or threat of armed force, the prohibition of military, political or economic sanctions and the prohibition of terrorist activity and other subversive contributory activities. But the memorandum stressed that the decisions were only binding on the activity of state and government or their authorised representatives. The positions of the press or non-governmental organizations of another country were not listed as interference. Only accountable governments can have the power to speak for their nations.

When head of department Tuovinen paid a fact-finding visit to Geneva in December 1973 he wrote that the significance and role of Basket I principles was emphasised more than before as the negotiations proceeded. The Brezhnev doctrine was a subject of controversy given that the Soviet Union's repeated demand that the socialist system must not be affected by the decisions.

Spring 1974 – temperance or trumps?

In his March 1974 assessment, Iloniemi considered that progress in drafting a final document was proceeding slowly. The proposals on the text were often far apart from one another in content and character. Work on them would take time and effort. On the other hand psychological pressure had built up over the spring session to the extent that the conference's final stage had to be organised before the coming summer break. Iloniemi attributed the slow pace of progress in part to the aims of the EEC countries, whose cooperation and cohesion had weakened.

Originally, before the guidelines for the negotiations were provided, it was more difficult to achieve the required modifications and flexibility demanded by the situation. Faith in achieving a noteworthy result and breakthrough appeared to be wavering. There were voices in EEC circles expressing the view that the current negotiations would only start up important processes. They would be developed only after the closing stage of the conference.

Iloniemi had to say that by March 1974 the least progress had been achieved in the working group on the principles generally regarded as essential. The touchstone appeared to be the principle of the inviolability of frontiers. The Soviet Union's and the FRG's views on the peaceful transformation of frontiers were now completely at loggerheads. Iloniemi characterised the FRG's stance on the matter at that point as still "a fantasy".

He thought that with the US behaving fairly passively, the neutral and non-aligned countries had an opportunity to keep a higher operational profile than earlier. This was so in particular in the working group on confidence-building measures. The prior notification of major military exercises had proved possible. The details of the scope of the exercises, the prior notification of timeframes and areas of application remained open. Agreement on practical notification of movements of large bodies of troops appeared difficult.

Finland's efforts to get at least an indirect mention of the nuclear weapon-free zone in the stage dealing with disarmament ran into strong opposition. "Clearly, this will have to be dropped from the proposal or it will be reduced in the future to being investigated on a conceptual level," Iloniemi wrote in March 1974.

The Basket III issues concerning contacts between people and access to information were the conference's ideological focal point. The doctrinal dispute over what should be the mutual relationship between the goals of measures and détente had only partly been resolved. The parties agreed that a separate introductory part should be added to Basket III, before more detailed recommendations. Iloniemi doubted the readiness of the socialist countries to agree to such detailed proposals as those presented by the Western delegations. "The concessions would be ideological," Iloniemi noted.

Foreign Minister Kalevi Sorsa revealed his expectations for the Geneva results in his talks with Willy Brandt in Bonn, in December 1973. Sorsa thought that results would not be reached if the "West's objectives were very ambitious." "The socialist countries cannot be forced into changes of principle from out-side. The issue is not just that of the communist system but also the traditions of those countries." For this reason Sorsa thought that there was a chance of achieving more in the area of economic cooperation.

Brandt replied that real progress was needed "so that the conference could fulfil General Secretary Brezhnev's desires for a summit." Economic coopera-tion and the easing of tensions without changes in the societies of the socialist countries was not in Brand's opinion acceptable.

There were appreciable differences in the West's points of political empha-sis. Henry Kissinger's starting point was that the Soviet Union should not be pressured "too much". But his European colleagues expected that the CSCE process had the aim, in one way or another, of increasing the freedom of action of the smaller socialist countries and of loosening their direct dependency on Moscow. In this sense the multilateral forum continually put the effectiveness of the Brezhnev doctrine to the test in practice.

Preparing a package deal

Issues of economic cooperation could be partly separated in the conference into their own entity. Agreement on them had no direct linkage with the other baskets. This was why Basket II issues could for the most part be ne-gotiated by summer 1974, and so the staff of the Finnish delegation could be reduced. Minister counsellor Paavo Rantanen was transferred to the post of ministerial advisor at the Finnish Foreign Ministry's department of trade policy.

From Finland's standpoint, promoting economic cooperation fitted natu-rally with the country's endeavours to secure the requirements of economic interaction in all directions. Ambassador Leif Blomqvist has said that the main challenge of Finland's policy with the eastern bloc during President Kekkonen's term in office was to promote economic and commercial interests. Finland sought to limit commercial interests to a separate, close political dialogue with the Soviet Union. Commercial relations with the West developed regardless of the structural limitations in force under the Treaty of Friendship, Cooperation and Mutual Assistance.

According to Blomqvist, the definition of the practical application of the West's key demand for effective reciprocity and the main aim of the socialist countries for reciprocity, particularly in commercial sales of high technology, remained open until the final outcome. In the West thousands of commercial and economic decisions were made at various levels. In contrast, the centrally planned economy of the socialist camp had only one political source that made decisions. The problem appeared insoluble, although eventually it found a solution in the final text that was acceptable to all.

The complexities of matters of principle were noticeably intricate. This was one of the CSCE's special features. The CSCE was the first international conference to deal with matters of security and cooperation also from the standpoint of individual citizens. Their freedom to travel, meet relatives abroad, marry foreigners and reunite families had dissolved as a result of the Second World War or for other reasons

This body of subjects, from which the CSCE human dimension later developed, formed a clear dividing line between the East's socialist, state leadership and the West's free market visions and aims. The Soviet and the socialist countries' representatives emphasised logically that at issue was "an intergovernmental conference and general increase of cooperation at government level". The further possibilities of their cooperation were now being discussed, so that under détente everyone could feel that their security was growing. By emphasising the principle of non-intervention in internal affairs the socialist camp sought to show that the alteration of state systems, bringing pressure for such change, or internal activities to promote it, were not acceptable.

Soon after the start of the Geneva negotiations General Secretary Brezhnev delivered a speech in Moscow to the world congress of peace forces, on 26 October 1973, in which he dealt widely with the Soviet Union's peace policy and the methods and aims of peaceful coexistence. He emphasised that the policy of the Soviet Union and socialist countries had brought about a watershed in world politics, having moved from the Cold War to détente. He guaranteed that this process was irrevocable. Concerning the CSCE, he reiterated the Soviet Union's fundamental aims for regional integrity, inviolability of frontiers and non-intervention in internal affairs.

But there were other signs too on the horizon. Brezhnev considered that in some circles the Cold War campaign had shifted to a psychological war against the socialist countries "under the guise of defending human rights". There were some who claimed that détente was not possible unless the socialist countries carried out changes to their internal system. Others set out openly to market the goal whereby the socialist system would be weakened and finally overthrown. The liberalisation of the socialist system was dressed up as concern for human rights. Talk of freedom, democracy and human rights in reality aimed only at the common imperialist goal, namely interference in the internal affairs of the socialist states. The West talked of liberalisation, but in reality the aim was the destruction of socialism's achievements and the crushing of the socio-political rights of the socialist countries.

Brezhnev said he had no intention of avoiding discussion of human rights. He was always ready to defend the rights of workers to life, education, social security and employment. In the non-socialist countries there were over a hundred million unemployed people lacking basic rights. The socialist revolution also guaranteed fundamental rights to national minorities. "If the socialist countries started to call for corresponding changes in capitalist countries, it is unlikely that the healthy development of intergovernmental relations would be possible."

The Western delegations, including the European neutrals, started from the assumption that the realistic goal was gradual progress. Due to this, although some initial proposals happened to contain a demand for "free" movement, the text soon changed in the drafting phase to refer to "freer" access to information and "freer" movement. Nevertheless, it was supposed that the commitment to concrete action on citizens' living conditions, freer movement and freer access to information were necessary precondition for the adoption of a balanced result in Geneva. Only credible progress in deciding on the Basket III issues would open the way to a serious debate on the arrangement of the CSCE's final stage, its date, the level of the participants and the manner in which the results would be finally adopted.

Actual drafting work on the final document started in Geneva in February 1974. When there was preliminary consensus on a small part of the text or on a wider body of it, it was entered as a common outcome in the secretariat's record book. The text was registered. All delegations had the possibility to present reservations over the final form of the text by demanding that certain words or phrases were bracketed. In most cases, the final place of the text was left to be decided separately.

When writing his report to Foreign Minister Karjalainen in April 1974, Iloniemi estimated that the work had progressed fairly satisfactorily by the Easter break, "the penultimate session of the second phase". The planned timetable for reaching agreement in the Geneva phase could still be considered realistic. By mid-June numerous night sessions were held. The majority of the delegations seemed prepared to for these.

Finland seeks a negotiating profile

Iloniemi's overall work in Geneva was directed at securing Finland's neutral and constructive mediatory role and its role as anticipator and at strengthening Finland's credible operative profile. Naturally, it had not been only a matter of Finland's 'neutral' work in Geneva, but more generally strengthening the practical value of the neutrality of Finland's foreign policy. At the initial stage of the negotiations Finland had to quickly adopt a principle the circumstances of which would constitute the main elements of Finland's operational profile, how it be in proportion to the rest of the negotiating setting. The delegation did not receive more specific guidance on this from Helsinki.

And so Iloniemi also wrote from Geneva at the beginning of November 1973 to Sorsa's head of information, Tom Grönberg, confirming that there was an "information struggle" in relation to matters concerning information. This expressly concerned the attempts by Western delegations to influence the internal developments of the socialist countries using the CSCE's mutual decisions. Iloniemi thought it embarrassing that President Kekkonen's message to an international conference on communications, held in Tampere on 21 May 1973, was widely quoted in the speeches of the socialist countries.

Concerning the role of the mass media, Kekkonen had said in his Tampere speech, clearly with the help of professor Kaarle Nordenstreng, an expert on the media, in preparing the text, that they are used to promote the goals of peace, friendship, international understanding and cooperation. "These goals are best promoted in such a way that as equal a balance of information exchange among states as possible is sought, so that then we can escape from the prevailing disparities to equal cultural exchange. We need to keep an eye on factual information about the conditions of other countries." It was evident that from the stance of the negotiations there were two highly contentious notions linked to Kekkonen's speech: the "equal a balance of information exchange among states" and "factual information about the conditions of other countries".

It was clear that Basket III comprised the ideological focal point of the conference. Some matters had been agreed upon. It was unlikely however, wrote Iloniemi, that the socialist countries would agree to the unregulated, wholly free exchange of information. On the other hand, the West's representatives considered that definite progress was important, such as improving the working conditions of journalists when they worked in another participating country.

In its Basket III presentations Finland stressed that in connection with contacts between people those who had tabled proposals and were particularly interested in the matter would focus on it among themselves in a closer dialogue on the basis of the proposals. In connection with the exchange of information, Finland stressed, logically enough, particular problems facing small states and language areas, and described its own experiences with information exchange and cooperation. A proposal by Canada for a sub-committee on contacts among people dwelt on matters to do with emigration and exit visas. In its speech, Finland took in the overall picture of immigration practices. The processing of permits concerning such matters must take place in a positive and humanitarian spirit.

At the beginning of March 1974, Iloniemi returned to the central issues of the negotiations. The importance of the immutability of frontiers as a negotiating point was stressed by the Soviet Union, but in another form in English: the inviolability of frontiers. The FRG adhered closely to the idea that the peaceful alteration of frontiers should be generally accepted in the CSCE. It was supported in this by the EEC. In the opinion of the latter, the importance of frontiers would change and diminish with the progress of integration. Ireland too took the view that the possibility of altering frontiers in Northern Ireland should be kept open. Iloniemi still characterised the FRG's goal of the peaceful change of frontiers as a "Wiedervereinigung fantasy". EEC members Ireland, Spain and the FRG justified the need for this sort of principle on their own national grounds. The preliminary text was able to be entered and registered on 2 April 1974. The precise location was left open.

In spring 1974, the neutral and non-aligned countries made a comprehensive and fairly detailed presentation on measures to increase confidence in the area of military security. In his report to Karjalainen, Iloniemi justified Finland's involvement from two angles. First, involvement in this group made it possible to present Finland's ideas for dealing with the nuclear weapon-free zone in conjunction with the CSCE. Second, Iloniemi confirmed in writing that there were considered to be four CSCE neutral countries: Austria, Sweden, Switzerland and Finland.

Switzerland had made a proposal for the recognition of neutrality as part of the principle of sovereignty. Unfortunately, Switzerland and Austria had not given their reciprocal support to Finland's Nordic NWFZ suggestion. They considered that under the current circumstances it was not a neutral submission.

Excitement was mounting in Geneva as the negotiations had run for well over half a year, from September 1973 to May 1974. It was generally assumed that if the final phase of the CSCE were to be arranged that year, it would be realistic to hold it in July-August 1974. In order to provide enough time for texts to be finalised, decisions in principle were required by the start of summer 1974.

Foreign Minister Karjalainen reported on the international situation to the Parliamentary foreign affairs committee on 14 May 1974. He confirmed Finland's desire to see the CSCE final phase organised during the coming summer. On the other hand, there could be surprises in store and delays over decisions. The international situation was pretty tumultuous as a result of the Middle East and the oil crisis, tensions between the EEC and the USA, the resignation of Chancellor Brandt, President Pompidou's death and President Nixon's resignation.

On 9 May 1974, during a brief visit to Helsinki, Iloniemi confirmed Finland's position that July would be held to as the date of the third phase until such a time as it would seem impossible.

On Henry Kissinger's initiative, 1973 should have been a European theme year and 1974 marked the 25th anniversary of NATO. As a result of the aforementioned events and the Carnation Revolution in Portugal in April 1974 uncertainty and the economic crisis only deepened. Franco's Spain also appeared to be moving towards instability. The Spanish delegation made use of its official speech at the meeting of the coordinating committee on 13 June to express concern about the holding in Switzerland of a conference of the Communist Party of Spain. The danger was that it would set up a government in exile in Switzerland. There had yet to be any breakthrough on the main issues. It was roughly estimated that over half of the drafting work on the actual text was still unfinished. A situation assessment found that the closing phase was being approached in two different ways: some considered the timing to be important, others put sufficient content as the condition for the closing phase.

The Finnish delegation had a special interest in following as closely as possible how and when decisive compromises would come about. Ambassador Iloniemi had acquired a genuine and broad credibility for the educative baptism of fire of the Dipoli consultations. He and his delegation could be relied on when sincere problem solvers were needed. During spring 1974 the trio of Jaakko Iloniemi, Klaus Törnudd and Esko Rajakoski were among the groups that attracted the most attention in the Geneva CSCE negotiations. A key position in their work was occupied by Finland's Basket III novel proposal concerning the introductory section. The proposal was divided into three parts: aims, means and the application of political principles. At the informal consultations, Finland had tried to put these three overall themes on paper as the structure of the preamble, but at the beginning of May 1974 the Soviet Union was still not ready to deal with more than one subject at a time, namely the political provisos of Basket III.

During the spring there was an attempt to speed up the work on Basket III by putting each sub-committee under the coordination of a representative of a neutral country. Austria took on human contacts and Switzerland information exchange. Finnish legation secretary Jaakko Laajava coordinated the sub-committee on culture and Sweden the sub-committee on education.

Iloniemi versus Stepanov

To Iloniemi's surprise the Soviet Ambassador to Helsinki, Vladimir Stepanov, became a key player in leading the series of events for the aforementioned package deal. Iloniemi's Soviet counterpart in Geneva, deputy minister Kovalev, was also in for some novel surprises.

Ambassador Stepanov and his deputy, first secretary Yuri Deryabin, tried to influence the Finnish delegation through the Soviet embassy in Helsinki. At first the aim was for Finland to be active so that it would still be possible to hold the third phase in summer 1974. During a private sauna on 14 March 1974 with counsellor Arto Mansala, a Finnish diplomat familiar with the direction of Moscow's diplomacy, Deryabin clearly set out his wishes with respect to Finland. Why doesn't Finland start operating in Geneva on a third front, by focusing on finding a solution to the principle of the inviolability of frontiers, formulating a preamble for the delicate part concerning human contacts, and so that Finland would already at this point in time raise the matter of the timing of the final phase.

The UK's Ambassador to Helsinki, Anthony Elliott, who was also chairman of the British delegation in Geneva, discussed the West's view of the state of the negotiations with head of department Matti Tuovinen, on 30 April 1974: unless there was progress on the Basket III issues within a couple of days and a breakthrough on the other issues within a couple of weeks, the current phase of negotiations could not wind up by the mid-June, and so the third stage could not be arranged before the start of the holiday period.

The Soviet appeals for Finland's active input were such that President Kekkonen himself considered seeking a quick solution to the disputed issues through a publicised appeal.

On his return from Moscow on 14 May, Ambassador Stepanov requested prompt contact with President Kekkonen. The Soviet leadership was prepared for Finland to make a new proposal for the highly sensitive matter of the preamble to Basket III. "The Soviet Union had all the arguments to give President Kekkonen so that the said proposal would be received with understanding also by the United States." Iloniemi was called to Helsinki and met with Kekkonen on 17 May. Kekkonen gave him the proposal received from Stepanov. In the context of the regulatory principles of international relations and Basket III, there was a desire for more explicitness concerning the phrase "respecting the laws and government regulations of each participating state." This way the principle of non-interference in internal affairs would be more emphatically linked to keeping a watch over contacts between people and implementing the recommended measures dealing with information exchange. This way too it would be possible to ensure that Basket III recommendations would not by

President Urho Kekkonen, Ambassador Jaakko Iloniemi and Foreign Ministry Head of Department Matti Tuovinen – the Helsinki CSCE decision-makers of 1972–1975.
(Photograph: Archive of the Finnish Foreign Ministry)

themselves require measures that were separate from the respective conditions of détente. The socialist countries would reserve the right to estimate when there were appropriate preconditions for applying recommendations concerning the freedom of action of individuals.

Iloniemi immediately expressed doubts that the proposal would be widely acceptable. Kekkonen made use of Ambassador Stepanov's assurances that the Soviet Union and the US had agreed on the matter between themselves.

The discussions between Ambassador Stepanov and President Kekkonen considered in great detail different forms and alternatives of proposals. The

discussions gave the impression that the state and schedule of the Geneva negotiations could have been managed by fine-tuning and remote control by those
concerned. There was perhaps too much trust in the mutual understanding of
the superpowers.

When President Kekkonen's wishes were sent to the Finnish delegation in
Geneva, Iloniemi responded in clear language by phone and cable on 28 May.
If Finland were to make a proposal with such content, it would immediately
lose its good reputation and the position of a credible intermediary it had had
until then. Just to be sure, Iloniemi copied the message for the attention of his
Soviet counterpart deputy minister Kovalev. Kovalev concurred with Iloniemi
and also saw that the proposal would not have been in line with the Soviet
Union's interests. A proposal of similar content made by the Soviet Union had
been rejected at a previous stage of the negotiations, in July 1973, when the
Dipoli recommendations were adopted.

Department head Tuovinen and Iloniemi agreed by phone on 31 May
that the proposal conveyed by Stepanov should not be made from the Finnish
side. Tuovinen wrote: "We were relieved that the matter could be dealt with by
mediation and hygienically" President Kekkonen asked that Iloniemi's cable
mentioning Kovalev be shown to Ambassador Stepanov so that the matter
could be finally taken off the agenda.

The next day, 1 June, after having made a quick trip to Moscow, Stepanov
once again called on the President with the same instructions. He now pleaded
that "General Secretary Brezhnev himself had personally proposed an appeal
of this kind". Stepanov confirmed that a message along the same lines had gone
from Moscow to deputy minister Kovalev in Geneva. Stepanov tried several
times to assure the Finns in Helsinki that the Americans were prepared to agree
to such a text. But in some meetings Stepanov had to moderate this claim.

President Kekkonen wrote in his diary of his astonishment at Stepanov's
behaviour. The order from the Kremlin amazed him "a hell of a lot". "Had
Gromyko and Kissinger agreed on the matter?" the President asked himself.

With such pressure from the highest political level in the Soviet Union,
President Kekkonen no longer had the possibility to withdraw from the initiative. Iloniemi was given instructions on 31 May to present the original proposal. But Iloniemi could not let the matter rest there. He pleaded that merely
the presentation of a Soviet proposal would in the future irreparably damage

Finland's image and possibilities of operating. He asked for and was granted the opportunity to present a package deal on 5 June 1974, and in a separate address he presented a Finnish interpretation that clearly deviated from the Soviet stance.

The implementation of the Basket III decisions must be examined from a broader viewpoint than merely the principles of sovereignty and non-interference in internal affairs. It must cover all principles, and therefore also human rights, and the commitment to implement adopted decisions in good faith. Iloniemi had the approval of the Parliamentary foreign affairs committee for this, conveyed by Tuovinen, in the hope that it would help the supposed US-Soviet teamwork.

As a preliminary package deal the Finnish proposal appeared to achieve two aims. By its activity and original manner Finland was able, with the package, to raise crucial questions for discussion. At the same time the EEC countries, among others, considered that the connection with Basket III in Finland's proposal was now sufficiently loose. On this basis it would be possible to prevent an excessively restrictive interpretation of the obligation to implement the decisions.

Finland's proposal did not produce an unambiguous, readily acceptable decision. But the package deal suggested by Finland did now offer in a constructive spirit a fresh overall view of all the special features that would have to be taken into consideration when new, more sensitive matters were drafted to be adopted by everyone. It was still some weeks before the formulations were finalised.

Washington and Moscow shake hands

Henry Kissinger and Andrei Gromyko had decided in good time that the way towards the package deal would be sought in highly confidential bilateral talks. The countries' two delegations in Geneva were not included in the preparatory stage of this process.

In April 1974 a close dialogue was started between the US Ambassador to Moscow, Walter Stoessel and Deputy Foreign Minister Georgi Kornienko on the form and content of the package deal. In the central position regarding principles and the contents of Basket III was a reference to domestic legislation and prevailing practice. If a common understanding regarding the issues was to be found between Moscow and Washington, the decisive detail was who would make the proposal. The key question was how the Americans would get their allies to back it. The Soviet representatives realised early on that it would not be tactically fruitful if the proposal were to come from the Soviet delegation. They saw that it would be preferable if it were to be made by the US delegation. "If it was done by a neutral or Western delegation, the impact would be remarkably greater. The text would be considered easier to adopt.

The next US-Soviet talks on the CSCE situation took place in Nicosia, Cyprus, on 7 May 1974. The presentation of the package deal was again central to the agenda. According to Kissinger the only functional impediment was which delegation would present the proposal to the conference. Kissinger called it 'Country X'. Gromyko asked if Kissinger had a definite proposal. Kissinger answered that their thinking was that the country in question could be Finland. "Yes maybe! All right, maybe Finland," replied Gromyko. Someone only had to approach the Finns on the matter.

The head of the Soviet delegation in Geneva, deputy minister Kovalev, had discussed the issue with Helmut Sonnenfeldt and Arthur Hartman and dealt with more complicated scenarios. They had considered gradual progress. The first proposal had been less favourable to Soviet goals and it would be at first rejected. But if Country X were chosen to present the proposal, it would have in practice to give the same text almost unaltered.

In practice, the text agreed by Moscow and Washington for the preamble of Basket III and the reference to international principles was a take it or leave it proposal. It was no longer meant for negotiation, simply to be adopted.

Now that it was agreed in principle that Country X was Finland, Kissinger proposed to Gromyko that the Soviet Union take the initiative and approach Finland. "The US supports this procedure and the content of the proposal in the form that it is in, although the US delegation in Geneva could not do so openly right away. The US could not give the impression that it was bringing pressure to bear on its allies." Throughout the whole process of the negotiations the US showed great understanding towards the Soviet Union's wishes.

The assurance of Finland's key role in the secret talks between the two superpowers was in part a confirmation of what was already evident in the Geneva negotiations. There was trust in the Finnish delegation's role as a mediator and in its ability to offer useful compromise proposals. Ambassador Iloniemi personally, and the Finnish negotiating team as a whole, acquired a conspicuous role in the operations. Helsinki's behaviour in strengthening Finland's role was perfect for highlighting the exceptional nature of the operation. It was not just a routine matter in Geneva.

The package proposal was presented in Geneva on 5 June 1974 without consultations with the Western alliance, the EEC or neutral countries. It was now the turn of the Americans to ask their Soviet colleagues to show understanding. It would take them time before their allies and friends came round to supporting the package deal. They had been told nothing of it beforehand.

In the view of the British, Finland's original proposal, which later on the other neutral and non-aligned countries also backed, established a sensible balance. The connection between Basket III and the principles was realized by general reference, and not in such a restrictive way as the socialist countries had initially proposed. They obtained the definition which respected the rights of others and their own right to determine their internal affairs.

According to Iloniemi, the initial responses to Finland's proposal were encouraging. "People had learnt to trust the authenticity of Finland's aims during the CSCE. Finland was commended for its initiative and activeness. Positive comments had come from the sphere of the US delegation, which was a slight surprise. For the time being the view of the Nordic countries was still cautious."

Iloniemi summarised the basis of Finland's effectiveness in a memo of 7 June. Finland had displayed its proactiveness in its efforts to perform a service and build compromises. Concerning principles, Finland had spoken out strongly for the unreserved recognition of the principle of human rights. Finland had not revised its line on this matter, but had continued its resolute stand.

Human rights and non-interference in internal affairs were often counterposed with one another. Because Finland had emphasised the peace-strengthening and confidence-building nature of respect for human rights, the exceptional occurrence of it in the context of the principle of non-interference in internal affairs could be credibly made, based on the pursuit of common compromise and consensus. At internal meetings of the Finnish delegation Iloniemi had advocated his personal view that Finland should not have made a package-deal type of proposal. Other delegation members were ready to follow suit. Finland had no national need to make the proposal, especially since it was not in the situation of being a plaintiff concerning the main issues of Basket III and had not been a player actively representing the proposals concerning them. There were great risks that there would be no positive results. However, Iloniemi had to announce to the delegation on 5 June: "The order from Helsinki is to table the proposal". He characterised Finland's role in finishing the operation as that of a photographer. What was written in the proposal was what others wanted to see in consensus.

The package contained Basket III's preambular reference to national legislation and national practice in connection with the relevant principle's (on non-intervention) reference to all regulatory principles of international relations, and therefore also to the human rights principle. The Finnish proposal did not, however, immediately receive straightforward support, particularly from EEC countries and the neutrals. The informal comments heard around the corridors the next day could be summed up thus: understanding in relation to the package method; reservations in relation to its content. It was nevertheless significant that no one dared openly oppose the operation.

Iloniemi's earlier observation on the internal cohesion of the Western group was proven correct in this sensitive detail of the negotiations and the whole balance of the final result: "It could be an arrangement of two superpowers against the other 33. Moreover, the EEC countries were as a separate group emphasising the West's experience." Instructions sent on 8 June by Henry Kissinger to the Geneva US delegation stressed that the US would not publicly comment at that stage on Finland's proposal. The solution lay with the Soviet Union. It must show a definite readiness to agree on Basket III's open questions. The US delegation at the internal meeting of the NATO group was prepared to give general, low profile support to the Finnish proposal.

President Nixon and General Secretary Brezhnev swapped impressions of the Geneva negotiations when they met for talks in the Kremlin's Catherine Hall on 29 June 1974. Nixon said that the Americans had found it hard to get their European allies to support the plan worked out jointly with the Soviet Union. The US had no difficulty in supporting the package proposed by Finland, which "meant an extremely constructive step forward in the negotiations."

Kissinger added that, apart from the acceptable decision on the Basket III issues, measures to increase confidence remained a major open issue. The

US would now try to resolve the relationship of humanitarian matters to the principle according to Finland's proposal. "But we have had immense problems with our allies," said Kissinger. In his opinion the only way out was first to agree on the more detailed content of Basket III and then to integrate it with the Finnish proposal.

Informal discussions continued for several weeks in an intense atmosphere, particularly as the Americans had to conceal their official and open support for a proposal drawn up with the Soviet Union. At the beginning of July, the US delegation stated that Finland's original package proposal required certain additions. The neutral countries had considered these and proposed, clearly with the assistance of the Soviet Union, that there should be added the principle of fulfilling the commitments made in good faith, in accordance with international law.

This reference was roughly from the original Soviet demand that all implementation must only follow international legislation and practice. This phrase was transferred to the principle of non-intervention from the context of the sovereignty principle, which is what the Americans' allies had advocated.

The US delegation, headed by Ambassador Sherer suggested to Washington that together with the allies they could express their support for the broader package deal that was now under consideration. In this way the neutral and non-aligned countries presented the supplemented package proposal to the other participants on 11 July.

The package deal was adopted in its final form at the last meeting of the summer session, on 26 July 1974. The last remaining problem had to do with a translation issue: how to translate "legal obligations" into Russian. Once this had been cleared up, the delegations were able to leave for the summer break in buoyant spirits and a good atmosphere. Ambassador Iloniemi was personally commended for finally bringing the package deal happily to harbour after the intense two-month period.

Jack Maresca, a US expert on the CSCE, provides a sincere acknowledgement of Ambassador Iloniemi's role in bringing about the package deal in his 1985 account of the Geneva phase of the history of the 1973-1975 negotiations. He writes that Iloniemi succeeded in defending Finland's neutrality at the CSCE forum and in creating the preconditions for the results in the negotiations on the package deal that were acceptable to all. "Iloniemi was one of the diplomats who can be counted on the fingers of one hand who not only understood the nature of the CSCE but helped make it functional."

President Kekkonen also saw fit to write of the Geneva result, on the basis of a cable sent to him on 26 July. "Following the deal, France, Switzerland and the Soviet Union especially thanked the Finnish delegation and Ambassador Iloniemi for their work on the package. The break therefore began in high spirits. The work started again in a good atmosphere after the break."

In his report of 22 August Iloniemi took stock of the results achieved so far. He noted that since the Dipoli consultations and the advent of the Blue Book the differences in viewpoint between the Soviet Union and the West had crystallized around a few questions of principle: the impact of the regulatory principles of international relations on the Basket III issues of contact and information, and the practical procedural matters concerning them. The Soviet Union sought to get the regulatory means it needed in the area of implementation. Such interlaced, binding agreements did not enable problems to be solved as isolated issues. The package deal was the only way.

Iloniemi considered that the role of being the active architect of the package deal fell fairly naturally to Finland. In 1974 Finland had already drawn up the first written proposal for the preamble to Basket III. At the same time, Finland had prepared a full text on non-interference in internal affairs, which was based on all the existing proposals. This was intended as a compromise, but only in relation to the text of Basket III's preamble. This approach gradually lost support, first in the East and then in the West. Because the parties required progress primarily on the issues they considered priorities, the idea emerged of putting a package deal on paper.

"The negotiations did not move forward without measures from the neutrals, because of the inflexibility of the alliances," said Sherer.

1974 ended in some respects on a positive note. In its report to the Parliamentary foreign affairs committee the Foreign Ministry considered that US-Soviet relations, as the cornerstones of détente, had developed in the form of the summit meeting in Vladivostok, on 23-24 November 1974. The CSCE talks in Geneva had achieved their first significant compromises on Basket III matters. Texts had been approved by all on the possibility to reunite families and solemnize international marriages. The discussion on principles had proceeded in a constructive spirit. The textual parts of eight of the 10 principles were

already prepared. Progress in the subcommittee on military matters and confidence building measures had been sluggish. The issues were sensitive and this
was the first time that they had been the focus of broad multilateral discussions.
On the peaceful settlement of disputes, it was decided to move the question of
the compulsory presence of a third party to a dispute to be dealt with later in
the follow-up to the conference. In the area of economic cooperation the text
was for the most part already prepared. A number of difficult issues remained
open, such as most favoured nation treatment, reciprocity and treatment of
developing countries.

Dutch cabaret in Moscow

There was in addition an intense US-Soviet dialogue taking place in their respective capitals. The country delegations working in Geneva were usually deliberately excluded from these deliberations. At talks held in the Kremlin on
March 26 1975 General Secretary Brezhnev told Kissinger that they appeared
to be achieving a common understanding in relation both to matters of substance and procedure, "our joint mode of action". Foreign Minister Gromyko
thought that it was now a matter of how to put this consensus into practice.

By Brezhnev's reckoning the conference had already lasted for three years.
It was time to bring the negotiations to an end. In Gromyko's view there was a
close connection between President Nixon's visit to Moscow and a prompt and
successful conclusion. "If President Nixon was in Moscow while the substantive content of the Geneva negotiations hung in the air, the general view of the
Soviet people would be incredulous." However, Kissinger did not think that
the President's visit could be made contingent in this way – the visit was in the
interests of both sides.

For the Soviet leadership, the matters of the peaceful change of frontiers
and the inviolability of frontiers were the most crucial unresolved questions.
Contrary to what was required by the initial consensus among countries, US
allies Belgium and the Netherlands had ahead of others made new proposals
dealing with the military sector that sought to open up all of Soviet territory
to outside inspection. Washington did not support this. Kissinger was in some
difficulty to explain simply how Belgium and the Netherlands could withdraw
the proposal. He nevertheless promised to find a way.

For Gromyko, it was Basket III that was proving a nuisance. It involved a whole cluster of documents, which in the view of the Foreign Minister were mainly "waste paper". Kissinger had gone along with his counterpart in this impression when he admitted that he had never read the documents. "I didn't believe that the Soviet system would be affected by opening a Dutch cabaret in Moscow."

According to Kissinger, there were two unresolved Basket III principles: the provisions of the principles governing international relations, and the provisions of the substantive content of Basket III. Some European countries considered that the question of content was important for national reasons. From the Soviet stance it was important to attach to the provisions of the basket the national right to decide on legislation. Kissinger believed that it would probably be possible to find an acceptable solution. "The United States will try to use its influence so that the Soviet Union is not embarrassed by these matters and not asked provocative questions." But, as Kissinger had already made plain, he was unfamiliar with the Basket III documents and the US had not proposed anything definite in these areas.

General Secretary Brezhnev had often said that the Soviet Union was prepared for extensive cultural cooperation, provided it took place in line with national legislation. The same applied to humanitarian issues. "The conference was about European security, not the possibilities for foreign states to open restaurants in the Soviet Union or for printing plants under foreign ownership." This would be contrary to the principle of non-interference in the internal affairs of other countries.

A background memorandum drawn up in connection with President Nixon's visit to Brussels in June 1974 relates that Finland's 5 June proposal for a decision on the central relationship of Basket III and the principles initially received a negative reception from Western delegations and the neutrals. It was nevertheless possible that the Western delegations would eventually accept the proposal, and that the Soviet Union would demonstrate flexibility on the formulation of the as yet unresolved details concerning the free flow of people and the exchange of information. The remaining threshold questions concerned improving the working conditions of journalists, increasing the availability of foreign publications and the opening of reading rooms, freedom of internal travel, with the reduction of the number of areas closed to outsiders, and increasing freedom of religion. This was by no means a modest list of key objectives.

The US position was that "the Soviet Union must make concessions in each of the sub-areas, if the West's opposition to the importance of the role of domestic legislation were to be relaxed. At the same time, the Soviet Union would get the Western alliance's agreement on convening the final phase."

It was stressed in the memorandum that the US had struck a deliberately low profile in the conferences, but had consulted closely with everyone on finding compromises and achieving progress. The US had backed Moscow on the issues that the Soviet Union considered important, and the Americans had also given support to the proposals of its allies. The memorandum stated that acceptable decisions concerning freer movement and freer information exchange were the only remaining negotiating assets that the West had. It was because of this that the West and the neutral delegations had not been prepared to submit to a closer discussion on the timing of the CSCE's final stage or on its level of participation until an agreement on these issues was acceptable to them and confirmed.

Nixon's and Kissinger's talks in Brussels were music to Finland's ears. The Italian Prime Minister, Aldo Moro, openly praised the neutral countries' active and constructive role. Kissinger responded by saying, "They were good boys but in Geneva there was too big a gang fiddling with matters too insignificant."

Before the spring 1974 Easter recess the Soviet position had suggested that after the adoption of the principle on the inviolability of frontiers, the Soviet Union would be more flexible on those issues the West considered important. According to the Western delegations, this promise had not been kept during the June work phase following the Easter break.

Foreign Minister Gromyko reiterated the Soviet Union's support in principle for the conference and the Basket III issues. The main thing was to reduce the danger of war and not to focus on matters of secondary importance. "The Soviet Union is prepared to allow Mr Smith to marry Miss Jones," but in this regard it was important to respect national laws and practice, in line with UN principles.

Brezhnev took another example, that concerning the recent talks with President Pompidou in Pitsunda. The French President had been surprised that France was continuing to demand the acceptance of the Third Basket provision, on the basis of which the French could for example open cinemas on Soviet territory under French management and French jurisdiction. According to Brezhnev, an astonished President Pompidou had demanded that the French delegation immediately withdraw the proposal.

The Soviet Union had been busy with the US on a package model, and they had found a third country – Finland – to propose the compromise, which it had volunteered to do. Brezhnev observed: "I can't say we were happy with the Finnish proposal, but on the basis of it we could perhaps achieve a consensus."

It was apparent that everyone felt that the conference was approaching its decisive phase, because following acceptance of the Finnish proposal they started to set new conditions. The FRG initiated a discussion on the principle of the peaceful alteration of frontiers. Moscow had expected that after the Finnish proposal the US would have seized on the matter purposefully. But this was not to be. Gromyko said that the US must use its influence on its allies more effectively. Gromyko thought that it was now important that those who had supported the Finnish proposal should stand closely by its original design.

The talks between Brezhnev and Nixon ended with Nixon saying that he would submit the text to experts to be finalised and to see where the points were that were more important to America's Western allies so that the conclusion of the conference did not stumble over a "quibble over language".

Why were the soviet leaders in such a hurry?

Since the first conference of foreign ministers the speeches and statements of Soviet and other socialist countries' leaders kept repeating the aim of reaching the conclusion of the conference as soon as possible.

In mid-February 1974, Ambassador Iloniemi said at an internal meeting of the Finnish delegation that there did not at that stage seem to be any urgency in reaching a speedy end to the conference. The earliest possible final stage had been mentally shifted to early July.

The events that led to the spring 1974 package deal showed that the Soviet political leadership wanted to bring about a quick decision in Geneva. The declarations of intent of top decision-makers were used as means of bringing pressure via Finland in realizing the operation. Too much was evidently made of the combined operation of the two superpowers, as the multilateral forum and the equality of the 35 participating states was, after all, the CSCE standard. It could not be ordered around by the leaders of the two big powers, and in this respect the Geneva phase of the negotiations must have brought both surprises and disappointments to each. The prestige, importance and influence of the superpowers were nothing like what had been expected. Perhaps their authority had become weaker as a consequence of the Geneva talks.

When Gromyko and Kissinger met on 28 February 1974 Gromyko repeated General Secretary Brezhnev's hope that the Geneva talks could be concluded as soon as possible. "The second phase of the CSCE negotiations must reach a conclusion in May." At the same time a decision should be made on the timing of the third stage at summit level, preferably before President Nixon's visit to Moscow, from 24 June to 1 July. Kissinger said that the President could not link his Moscow visit with the closing stage of the CSCE. He must be able to return from Moscow to Washington. Kissinger stressed that these decisions required the consent of America's allies. They would come to the final stage at summit level, "if the decisions of the conference make it possible."

One of the main aims of the Soviet Union's CSCE policy was to get the exercise to a rapid conclusion. This tactical stance reflected a variety of things. Just as the US delegation was crucially concerned about preserving the West's solidarity and operability at the Geneva negotiations, Moscow may have had similar worries about the Warsaw Treaty Organization. The longer the negotiations ground on, the harder it would be to maintain solidarity and unity and to develop new and credible positions.

Repeated compromises eroded discipline. The impatience and irritation of the smaller socialist countries was more palpably visible. The exception was the GDR. Ambassador Siegfried Bock, its head of delegation in Geneva, wrote in a 2005 article that his delegation had the fewest opportunities to stray from the Soviet Union's instructions. On the other hand, he admitted that the hurry to bring about a result was an end in itself for the upper political echelons. As a negotiating tactic it lacked wisdom.

In a speech to the Geneva coordinating committee on 2 May 1974 Professor Marian Dobrosielski, long-time head of the Polish CSCE delegation, tried to repudiate the dominant Western perception that the Soviet Union wanted a speedy end to the conference: "The urgency is not based on the notion that the socialist countries would be prepared to make the biggest concessions".

The second most pressing challenge may have been the inner workings of the Soviet decision-making machine. In June 1974 Foreign Minister Karjalainen discussed the CSCE situation with Ambassador Stepanov. Stepanov referred to the approaching elections to the Supreme Soviet, due on 15 June. For this reason President Brezhnev clearly had a personal interest in registering progress at the Geneva talks. Progress towards the Helsinki summit would have been the clearest indication of the Soviet leader's political success.

In June 2007 Ambassador Yuri Dubinin confirmed that the success of the CSCE process was a personal political goal for Brezhnev. His dream, rooted in experiences of the Second World War, was that "He could shout out to the world from the Eiffel Tower that all wars were now over!"

In his report to Iloniemi of his discussions with his Polish counterpart Marian Dobrosielski in Geneva, in early July 1974, US Ambassador Sherer stated that Dobrosielski had said that the Soviet Union's obstructiveness following the Easter break had been due to a policy dispute among the Soviet leadership. Brezhnev's policy of détente had come up against criticism and doubt. Dobrosielski was of the opinion that Brezhnev had eventually prevailed, but as a result his room for manoeuvre had been curtailed. The struggle had shifted to the Soviet delegation in Geneva. The delegate in charge of Basket III, Yuri Dubinin, had links with the anti-Brezhnev forces. To Sherer's surprise Dobrosielski said that Dubinin did not always follow the instructions of the Soviet head of delegation Anatoli Kovalev.

On the other hand, Dubinin had a partner in Basket III matters, General Sergei Kondrachov, who enjoyed the confidence of famed KGB leader Yuri Andropov. He was far more sociable than Dubinin, and had extensive personal connections due, not least, to his excellent language skills. Kondrachov was called to Geneva in spring 1974, when the questions of the key principles and, from Moscow's angle, the sensitive matter of the free movement of people had to be solved. He was not one to keep a low profile. While other delegation members were chauffeur driven or brought by minibus, Kondrachov would drive himself to the conference centre in a large, white BMW.

According to Kondrachov, "Andropov coordinated everything." Kondrachov played a crucial part in matters concerning information, internal security and military preparedness. Foreign Minister Gromyko, on the other hand, did not always want to perform in the foreground. Formally, all instructions went through him, but on a personal level he preferred to stay in the wings. Nonetheless he clearly had momentous ambitions. He always knew how to choose the winning side, formulate his sentences precisely and clearly and, in the opinion of many of his contemporaries, was "the country's best diplomat", Kondrachov explained in a conversation in Moscow in June 2007.

During the talks between Brezhnev and Nixon in Moscow in June 1974, Brezhnev said that various excuses could always be made for concluding the negotiations. Increasingly, Soviet diplomats would characterise the setting of conditions as merely obstructive tactics and delays lacking credible reasons. This was why the Russians hoped that the Americans would come out more strongly in favour of the speedy arrangement of the summit meeting.

Gromyko spoke of his recent discussion with one of the US's "most difficult allies", The Netherlands. "Ah, the cabaret," Kissinger added. But the two believed that a few small states could not prevent the realization of a high level final stage. For many West European governments the solution to the matter hinged on the contents of Basket III. The US did not share this view to the same extent.

During the 1974 Easter break, Iloniemi described in writing the current international problems that could make difficulties for finalising the Geneva talks: inter alia war in the Middle East and its resulting oil crisis, the Watergate scandal in Washington, the EEC's internal problems, disunity within the Atlantic alliance, Chancellor Brandt's problems, the death of President Pompidou There was nevertheless reason enough for the CSCE to proceed "because it would be an encouraging indication of the long term vitality of détente and the correctness of Finland's thinking on the (original) initiative."

In July, the Soviet delegation threatened to raise a political dispute unless the Western delegations were prepared to carry the talks forward to a negotiated settlement without a summer break. By the beginning of the month, the design of Basket III and the human rights principles in connection to the package deal remained unresolved. The EEC in particular considered that the only remaining means of bringing pressure was to threaten the Soviet Union with a summer break or an even longer break in the Geneva talks. On 1 July the US representation concurred – a summer break in the negotiations appeared to be the only realistic option.

In August, Iloniemi observed that the public appraisal of the end of the second phase of the conference and the timing of the final phase interested the media and the wider audience remarkably more than the latest deliberations in Geneva over matters of content. Around the time of the previous Easter it was still thought that July would be a feasible date for starting the third phase. August was out because it was part of the holiday season in much of Europe. September was unsuitable because of the start of the UN General Assembly. These arrangements posed a political problem for Finland. Finland could not unilaterally block preparations for phase three, because it would then be guilty of taking a biased stand in opposition to its role as host.

In order for Finland to resolve this dilemma, on 27 June Iloniemi presented an overview of the arrangements as chair of the coordinating committee. He announced that Helsinki was technically ready for the conference to be held in July. With three weeks warning Finlandia Hall could be got into the shape required for the summit meeting. There were altogether 3,200 technical and security specialists on alert. For reasons of cost there was a six-week limit for reserving hotel accommodation. Many of the top representatives could be accommodated in their embassies. But unless unclaimed reservations were cancelled in time, the state would face "massive costs" in the autumn.

The socialist countries considered that the organisation of the third phase in July was still "objectively possible." The Western countries stated in their addresses that it was no longer "realistically possible". Finland was able to state that the coordinating committee was not ready to proceed with the organisation of the third stage on a consensus basis. This was interpreted as an announcement that the July conference was abandoned for the reasons explained. Finland had to pay dearly for the summer 1974 dress rehearsal.

The prior scheduling for the conclusion of the Geneva talks was not realized that year. The efforts made in the spring and summer to resolve the main issues did not yield final results. In the autumn the process shifted to a new stage. According to Iloniemi, the socialist countries had drawn their own conclusions on this. They moved from running out of time to playing for it. Though certain key points of the final document had been reached, in connection with the package deal, the decisions on secondary questions and the entirety were still open. This offered the chance to play for time. Deputy Minister Kovalev told Iloniemi at the end of September that he was glad that a key misunderstanding was now out of the way. The Soviet Union was not in a hurry to bring the conference to a close. "That will be decided by the results."

The new target deadline for the third stage was now announced publicly as the end of 1974 and early 1975. The longer the work continued on the second stage the greater was the danger that daily political matters would become linked with the conference business and so complicate its long-term work. According to Iloniemi, "Efforts should now concentrate on possible achievements, without forgetting that this conference is just the first step in the policy of easing tensions by organised cooperation."

Foreign Minister Karjalainen visited Geneva on 27 September 1974. During his most recent conversation with Gromyko, in New York, the latter had given the impression that from the Soviet viewpoint the Geneva talks were going well. Concerning the schedule, Karjalainen thought that it seemed as if the impatience in NATO circles to bring about a quick conclusion to the talks was greater than that on the Soviet side. He thought that one reason for this was that the trump card for measuring the success of the conference had now been given away. Western leaders had at many top level meetings been prepared to decide on having a summit at the highest political level.

Summit and citizens

The West's attitude to the conclusion of the negotiations crystallised around the notion that only results should determine the timing of the closing stage and its level of participation. According to Iloniemi, the main adherents of this strict line were the FRG, Canada and the Benelux countries – Belgium, The Netherlands and Luxembourg – each of which had conditions of their own. In his view, this also indicated that the EEC countries' common line, in the form that it had during the Dipoli stage, was now "just a husk".

The close dialogue between US and Soviet representatives continued in both nations' capitals and in Geneva. It was natural to assume that the Soviet leaders drew their own conclusions about the West's actions. It is not inconceivable that the shift towards playing for time was a consequence of their American contacts. Iloniemi met with US Undersecretary of State James Loewenstein in the presence of Ambassador Mendelevich during the former's visit to Geneva. Loewenstein said at the start of the autumn session, in late

September, that the US could accept very minor results from the round of negotiations. The problem was their allies; they would not agree to this. If the negotiations were unreasonably prolonged, it could, according to Loewenstein, be detrimental to the general development of détente and be "a burden on the Vienna arms reduction talks."

Mendelevich used the occasion to rebuff the efforts of the Western delegations to demonstrate the superiority of their system. "We can't go along with that," Mendelevich said. Western conceptions of, for example, Basket III were not universally applicable. Mendelevich admitted that the Basket III issues constituted a new area in relations between states. And in this area the partial results obtained were important in themselves. "With the continuing development of détente and in the light of experiences attained we could perhaps go further later on."

At a discussion on the general situation, held in the Oval Office of the White House on 15 June 1974, under the supervision of President Gerald Ford, the CSCE situation was also touched on. Kissinger said of the CSCE that the US had never wanted it. "We followed Europeans' wishes and went along with them." Kissinger said that the Soviet position on the expected result was more ambitious. It wanted it to be a replacement for the lack of a peace agreement. An open issue in the negotiations continued to be the mechanisms concerning the free movement of people. Kissinger characterised these as "insignificant". It was as though it was an exhibition match for the satisfaction of the [European] left."

When it came to the final act, Kissinger said the Europeans would resolve its conclusion at a summit meeting. The US had already defined its position with the Soviet Union on the matter of a summit meeting. Washington had been faster than the Europeans in this. When the President asked when the summit could be expected to take place, Kissinger said perhaps in March 1975. If Ford was to meet with Brezhnev in December 1974, the Soviet Union would not want a CSCE conference beforehand.

Kissinger was again in Moscow on 24 October 1974 to meet General Secretary Brezhnev and Foreign Minister Gromyko. Kissinger openly expressed his frustration with the negotiations. They had become absorbed with deliberating on placing various phrasings before or after something. He said candidly that the exercise should be brought to a conclusion. It was impossible to maintain a credible negotiating process. "It violates the rules of logic." Perhaps March 1975 would be a sensible point to wind up the conference.

Now Brezhnev too expressed his annoyance with constantly hearing about new times for concluding the conference. He had expected it to happen in 1972, and then it should have happened in 1973, and then 1974, and now the talk was of March 1975. Gromyko said that March 1975 had been put forward only because some people wanted to prolong the work of the conference artificially. Kissinger assured them that there were no problems in the two countries' bilateral relations due to the conclusion of the CSCE. He proposed that both countries try over the following two months to assure their allies of the need to wind up the conference. The leaders of both countries were soon to meet the French and FRG leaders. In January 1975 either Gromyko or deputy minister Kornienko would visit Washington, at which time it would be possible to see how things stood.

Sonnenfeldt and Hartman then quickly met with Chancellor Schmidt and Foreign Minister Genscher in Bonn, on 27 October. Moscow's greetings were briefly conveyed. The main issue in the discussion concerned the challenge of a unified Western stance on unresolved issues, such as the level of participation at the final conference. Schmidt saw that the Americans had already agreed with the Soviets on having the highest level. The Americans replied that Brandt and Pompidou had already committed themselves to a summit meeting in a joint statement.

Schmidt considered that a key question from the FRG's side was the principle on the peaceful alterations of frontiers. The Americans reiterated what their Soviet counterparts had said, that they would accept whatever formulation was agreed by the FRG and the Soviet Union.

Active diplomacy towards Moscow was not confined to the Americans, Germans or French. The British too were busy. In his memoirs Final Term Harold Wilson highlighted the importance of his visit to Moscow in February 1975. "The talks covered the basic quality of bilateral questions more widely than any post-war meeting since Winston Churchill's visit to Moscow." Brezhnev and Wilson issued a joint communiqué on 17 February dealing with both bilateral contractual relations and international matters. It lauded the development of détente and peaceful cooperation, and resolved to "strengthen the firm basis of détente worldwide". They were convinced that there "were the preconditions to conclude the Geneva stage of the negotiations and hold the third stage at the highest level in the near future."

The Soviet leadership used high level visits, meetings and the whole diplomatic machinery efficiently to emphasise the importance of quickly arranging the third stage of the CSCE. At the meeting in Pitsunda between General Secretary Brezhnev and President Pompidou, in March 1974, Brezhnev had stressed the matter of holding the third stage at a high level. Pompidou's response had been in principle positive, providing that the results could be classified as historic. A high level of participation would then be in order.

From time to time it appeared that the holding of the final stage of the CSCE at a high level was an end in itself for the Soviet Union. Described by Iloniemi as an excellent and experienced political negotiator, Ambassador Lev Mendelevich had often said that having the final stage of the CSCE at the highest political level would mark the end of the post-war period and the start of a new era. There would no longer be a place for concepts such as a second or third world war. "The summit meeting would be the symbol of a qualitative change in relations among the European states."

In a message sent to Helsinki on 10 April 1975, Iloniemi wrote that it appeared to him as if the Soviet delegation had put itself under time pressure in stressing getting the work in Geneva concluded by the end of June 1975, with the aim of arranging the final stage in Helsinki in July. In May, deputy minister Anatoli Kovalev reiterated these objectives. He also asked that the matter be noted by the Finns so that the question of time pressure would not be used against the Soviet delegation in the final negotiations.

It seemed to Iloniemi as if some of the key partners in the debate had insufficient contacts with their decision-making levels back at home. He gave the example of the FRG delegation, whose guide was sometimes the Federal Chancellor's Office and sometimes the political leadership of the Foreign Ministry. Particularly, when it came to the question of the peaceful transformation of frontiers and the possibilities for German unification, responsibility lay with the Ministry of Justice in Bonn. There were many actors involved in the Ostpolitik, Iloniemi thought, not least those whose gaze was directed at the fact that the process would in no way be conducive to strengthening the position of the GDR.

Speaking in June 2007, the former US Ambassador to the OSCE, John Kornblom, said that the haste in bringing about the CSCE summit affected both superpowers. Washington and Moscow were experiencing major difficulties in their operations abroad – the US in Vietnam, Russia in its relations with China. Both were showing signs of weakness, and this was also reflected in domestic policy. They also had to recognise indirectly that détente was having an effect on the world, changing it. This was why Moscow was in a hurry to get the status quo confirmed in the shape in which the Second World War had left it. This of course indicated that the Soviet Union's attitude to the CSCE process was primarily defensive.

The Soviet and Russian Ambassador Deryabin encapsulated the same point in an interview in October 2006. In the early 1970s, Moscow did not look ahead but backwards.

Polishing up the general settlement

The high level shuttle diplomacy continued throughout the late autumn of 1974 and the early part of 1975. At the start of the autumn session of the negotiations, 12 September 1974, the Finnish delegation estimated that shuttle diplomacy on the part of the socialist countries in capital cities would increase. Soviet representatives had by that time made consultative visits to all the Nordic countries except Iceland. Among the Western delegations there appeared to be a certain discrepancy growing between their work and instructions from their capitals. Was it that the CSCE's attraction was losing effectiveness as the broader perspectives of détente were being left the background in discussions?

The EEC countries held their own summit meeting, as did the Warsaw Treaty countries. FRG Chancellor Helmut Schmidt visited Moscow, General Secretary Brezhnev went to Paris and both Brezhnev and President Ford met in Vladivostok. Referring to these meetings, according to Iloniemi, was justified as the discussions involved CSCE-related problems, either indirectly or directly. An outsider would felt obliged to ask whether in relation to them the possibilities of new concessions and counter-concessions were discussed, so that the Geneva negotiations could really move forward.

Iloniemi again repeated his general observation that opinions varied greatly over the importance of the CSCE at the highest political level. For the socialist countries the CSCE was a vitally important project of political activity and public diplomacy. We can suppose that they wanted their responses to be heard elsewhere than across the negotiating table in Geneva. Iloniemi admitted that the long-lasting negotiations, from the Dipoli conference of winter 1972-1973, had left the negotiators to see only their own working environment. "You couldn't always tell what sorts of change in background linkages had been brought about, or could be brought about, on the wishes of political leaders." But in this work the diplomats carried out the tasks that concerned them – namely the basic construction of the different parts of an acceptable whole.

Alongside expressions of frustration at the top political level, the Geneva negotiators had for a year deliberated on issues for which decisions had to be reached under the consensus rule – one way or another. In an assessment of the negotiations in autumn 1974, Iloniemi's delegation considered that when finalising the texts, and examining the main unresolved issues, in the background was the question of how the development of détente would affect the current European situation and how the finished texts would finally be understood.

An example is the seventh principle and coverage of the discussion concerning human rights. This had been addressed in committees from July to November in altogether 56 meetings. The consideration of the principle was divided into eight separate questions for analysis. The key questions concerned an acceptable relationship of the principle with the commitments already adopted in the UN. The treatment of these commitments had progressed very unevenly among the participating states. Freedom of religion and the rights of individuals from national minorities to know of their rights and responsibilities, and to act in accordance with them, were the themes of the most difficult negotiations in finalising the text. The text was initially in an acceptable form by mid-November 1974. Still awaiting deliberation were another three principles and the preamble, as well as a second reading of all the principles.

Among the group of principles dealt with earlier was the still-disputed question of the text on the peaceful alteration of frontiers. Apart from the content, the placing of the text was argued over: should it be placed with the principle on the inviolability of frontiers, as the Soviet Union proposed, or with the first principle on the sovereignty and right to self-determination of the participating states, as the FRG suggested?

This issue drew attention to the collective solidarity of the EEC countries in political questions. Iloniemi noted in his report to Foreign Minister Karjalainen on 21 January 1975, that the EEC-nine could easily fall apart when relations with a single Germany had to be defined. The Bonn government required the rejection of a principle in which the 'dream of reunification' could be nullified as an outcome of the CSCE. At the same time, the main partners had to be sure that Bonn's dream would not come true.

The relationship between the political substance of the principles and their implementation was directly reflected in the issues of Basket III, particularly those concerning proposals on human contacts and information exchange. In September 1974, France tabled a proposal that all Basket III issues be dealt with simultaneously, arguing that it would not be possible to decide on any of them separately. It repeated the practice adopted concerning the earlier "package deal", attempting with a broad package to make the detailed texts acceptable for all the main parties.

France's mini package comprised extracts from the preambles of the sub-committees, the operative text on the unification of families, the operative text on international marriages, the possibilities for promoting travel, the possibilities for establishing libraries and cultural centres in other participating countries and the magic conditional phrase, already adopted for the Dipoli Basket III text "under mutually acceptable conditions."

On 10 October the first compromise was reached on the issue of the dissemination of printed information. It was decided that the number of sales points for foreign publications would be increased and the possibilities to subscribe to publications made easier. Still a matter of dispute was how "all kinds of information" should be defined. The West's interpretation was that it meant diversity of content and that content criteria could not be gone into. The interpretation of the socialist countries was very pragmatic: information spread by all methods of dissemination should be made more easily available.

The first concord was reached on the issue of international marriages, on 9 December 1974. The commonly agreed text would also be useful concerning contacts between people.

Deputy minister Kovalev told Iloniemi on 25 October that as far as the Soviet Union was concerned the conference could reach an agreement before Christmas, as all concessions had been made. Issues concerning international marriages and family unification had been resolved better than the Western delegations could ever have imagined.

Mounting stress and effort in Helsinki

At the beginning of April 1975, Iloniemi emphasized that Finland should have all the practical preparations in place for organising the final stage of the CSCE under all eventualities. "If Finland is unable to host the conference at the earliest possible date, the political fallout could be considerable." The decision was taken at the Foreign Ministry, under State Secretary Tuovinen's direction, and based on Iloniemi's suggestion, to "create the necessary state of readiness" for the CSCE's final stage.

Finland had to be prepared to take financial risks in case of alternative options. Earlier in the year General Secretary Brezhnev had proposed the date of 30 June 1975 to four Western counterparts. This had to be taken into account, because it had not been rejected. Even if the date of the final stage were to be postponed, Finland would have to bear political and financial responsibility for the change. For this reason, Iloniemi proposed that all possible practical work get started in Helsinki, including hotel bookings, so that Finland could meet its responsibilities as host from the beginning of July. The hotel reservations were made on 4 April in readiness to receive guests from 27 June.

In another development, President Kekkonen gave a written assurance on 5 April to both the Foreign Ministry leadership and to Ambassador Iloniemi that possible elections in Finland would be purely a matter of domestic politics and would not affect the CSCE schedule.

In an interview given to the Finnish broadcasting company, YLE, on 6 April, President Kekkonen said that in light of current information a summit level meeting would be organised in Helsinki at the end of June and early July.

On 22 May, Iloniemi said he estimated that the final stage of the CSCE could be scheduled from the end of June up to early September. The first half of September, before the session of the UN general Assembly, was the last feasible option, otherwise decisions reached on the most important questions would start to "decay" and consensus would disintegrate.

Iloniemi appeared before the Parliamentary foreign affairs committee on 29 May. He told the committee that the nearly two-year round of negotiations in Geneva had created "the sort of sense that we are now at a decisive point and that the final stage of the CSCE has to happen during the summer." It was in this spirit, in Geneva in early May, that Finland had taken the initiative of starting the main discussions on the organisation of the final stage.

Iloniemi had met with the heads of the US and Soviet delegations, and based on these meetings had described the situation as "hopeless". The two sides no longer believed in a July-August schedule for the summit. The West's full proposal on contacts between people and information exchange had received a negative response from the Soviet representatives. They had objected to over 60 items. The registered texts were under revision and new content was being added to them. The confusion in the negotiations was in part caused by the coordinator for contacts, Austrian Ambassador Helmut Liedermann, and the coordinator for information, which had been the Swiss delegation, particularly the ever active Edouard Brunner.

US Ambassador Sherer estimated that the Soviet Union was being driven into a considerable predicament. It had tried to make a lot of impressive compromises to the West on key issues. Alternatively, it would make a new appraisal on the basis of the concessions it had already made. Deputy minister Kovalev seemed nervous and distraught. The delegation's Basket III specialists seemed almost in a state of shock. Iloniemi reported on 4 June that the mood swung this way and that. "At times, it seems that nothing can be ready by July. But at others it looks as if July is home and dry, certain." "In just the last few days there has been so much fundamental progress that once again a July final stage looks fairly possible." To this end, Iloniemi requested instructions for announcing in Geneva that Helsinki was ready to arrange the final stage at four weeks' notice. Finland stepped up its readiness for July and appointed Ambassador Joel Pekuri as general secretary for the final stage arrangements. The Finnish news agency STT was sent a press statement to this effect on 5 June. At the same time, Iloniemi announced in Geneva that Helsinki would need about four weeks notice before the start of the final stage.

In February, Iloniemi's delegation received information via Helsinki, based on a reliable communication, stating that President Ford's schedule would be booked for the CSCE from the week beginning 28 July. Such information was priceless for obtaining the firm resolve of the other superpower on bringing the negotiations to a conclusion. The message could also be read another way: it hinted that the Americans no longer had any important objectives left unattained. They trusted that their minimum expectations would be fulfilled. President Ford could prepare to take part in the final stage at summit level. The

British, on the other hand, stressed to the Finns, even at the end of June, that before they would agree to confirm the schedule for the third stage there would have to be agreement with the Soviet Union on confidence building measures, their area of application and troop levels.

It was known that Henry Kissinger was constantly active with respect to Soviet relations. He also, somewhat reluctantly, had to get involved with and take a stand on the problems of the CSCE's Geneva talks. The head of the US delegation in Geneva, Ambassador Sherer, told Iloniemi in April that there was still strong opposition to the CSCE in Congress. It was therefore important for the US that the final result would be adopted in Helsinki at the highest political level. The issues of improving the working conditions of journalists and promoting contacts between people came to be the Americans' clear priorities.

Kissinger and Gromyko met in Vienna from 19-20 May. This spurred the idea in Geneva that the Soviet Union would show new flexibility on Basket III and measures to increase confidence in military matters.

Exceptionally, deputy minister Kovalev's substitute, Ambassador Mendelevich had in part to amend his superior's messages to the Finns. Kovalev had repeatedly appealed to the Finns to make groundlessly optimistic pronouncements about the timetable. This was partly due to a misunderstanding. It was now possible to calculate the warning time in two ways: either that it was calculated from the actual end of the second stage or from the time when the holding of the third stage was decided.

Among the delegations in Geneva there were daily attempts to reach agreement on the final problems concerning subject matter. The moment of reckoning, including the possible date of the final stage, was unavoidably approaching. Time pressure started to be one of the main negotiating assets. And it wasn't surprising that various guesses were leaked from Geneva to the world media on the timing of the final stage. One such option, 28 July, was misleadingly included in the Journal de Genève on 17 June as a proposal supposedly from the Finnish delegation. The Foreign Ministry had to issue a press statement the next day denying that Finland had made such a proposal. The matter had not begun to be formally discussed and so there were no proposals yet on the table. The press release corroborated the Finnish government's announcement of 16 May, according to which Finland was ready to organise the third stage of the

CSCE at any time, as long as the starting day was agreed about four weeks in advance.

In early July there was uncertainty in Finnish delegation circles over the organisational responsibility of the host country. This was because no one appeared to be fully responsible for the order in which the unresolved issues should be decided. For France, it seemed to be most important that the rights of the four victorious powers would continue to have undisputed recognition in Europe. The FRG focussed on ensuring that the peaceful alteration of frontiers would continue to be possible by joint CSCE decision – in other words the peaceful unification of Germany. The head of the FRG delegation, Ambassador Klaus Blech, confirmed on the basis of discussions with Foreign Minister Hans Dietrich Genscher that this issue would become a key weapon in attacks against the government by the opposition in the FRG. The Netherlands appeared to be raising the stakes concerning clauses on military confidence-building measures and contacts between people.

The dispute between Turkey and Cyprus continued to be a threat to finalising the schedule. The dispute at the talks concerned the right of Archbishop Makarios of Cyprus to sign the final document for Cyprus. Turkey's position was that the signatories should include Rauf Denktash President of the Turkish part of Cyprus. Iloniemi remarked, "It seems there's neither a government nor an alliance in charge of the situation."

Iloniemi supplemented this analysis in a separate assessment of the activity of the EEC countries. Such activity was disjointed. The FRG and the Netherlands in particular supported slow progress unlike, for instance, France, Italy and Denmark.

In early July, the prime Minister of Malta, Dom Mintoff, paid an official visit to Bonn. According to German sources, he was satisfied with the general reference to the development of cooperation in the Mediterranean region (including many Arab countries). Although this was a positive signal with respect to Malta, deputy minister Kovalev indicated that he was almost desperate concerning the schedule. "The situation was in the hands of political hooligans in the West."

In line with the wishes of Iloniemi and the general secretary of the third stage, Ambassador Pekuri, an appeal and guidelines were sent to the capitals of the EEC countries on 30 June: unless a decision could be reached by 3 July on the date of the third stage, the possibilities of meeting the wishes of the EEC countries would be lost and Finland would have to seek new proposals on a deadline.

At this point the Nordic countries came to the aid of the Finns with a concrete suggestion. On 26 June, Sweden proposed at a meeting of the coordinating committee that the CSCE's final stage could aim to start in Helsinki on 28 July, requiring that the work in Geneva be brought to a successful conclusion in good time. Now Finland's original four-week advance notice was being turned into a means of pressuring the actual negotiations. Formally, the adoption of this decision at the end of June, such as at the 28 June meeting of the coordinating committee, would meet Finland's original demands.

In the evening session of the coordinating committee on 7 July, Iloniemi announced that he had received instructions in Helsinki that the starting date of the third stage could not be 28 July because it was less than three weeks away. "Some four weeks is not three weeks!" Iloniemi said that each day taken up from now onwards would postpone the start of the summit by a day.

Now the Americans too were becoming edgy. The schedule of President Ford's visit to Europe had already been confirmed. Furthermore, the Geneva delegation knew that Ford was scheduled to meet the Japanese Prime Minister in Washington on 5 August. If the Helsinki summit was to last two and a half to three days, the leeway started to look slim. The CSCE meetings had to be wrapped up as soon as possible.

A vivid example of this attitude had been already given in the spring, when the US State Department official in charge of Finnish affairs, Paul Canney, visited Helsinki, on 17 April, and conveyed greetings from Washington to the Foreign Ministry head of department Matti Tuovinen. It appeared that Malta and Cyprus were playing an active role in the final stage of the Geneva talks. Canney said "No political Mickey Mice could disrupt the CSCE's third stage from gathering in Helsinki, probably in July." Canney also said that according to the political movers (Kissinger) "The CSCE has already taken up too much of the State Department's resources that it should be got rid of as quickly as possible."

The conference groups in Geneva were squeezed, with sessions in the evenings and at weekends. The coordinators dealing with the main subjects were permitted to arrange unofficial, open meetings without the services of the secretariat and interpreters. Decisions increasingly required the presence of delegation leaders and possible instructions from the capitals to be used flexibly, and so the coordinating committee was reserved the possibility to hold meetings each day and in the evenings at short notice.

Relations between the Western alliance and the EEC countries sharpened into outright squabbling when on 8 July the EEC representative at a meeting of the coordinating committee announced that he was not prepared to accept even a conditional date for the final stage before questions concerning the content of the document had been decided upon. This position was particularly in line with the demand of the FRG government that the text of the final document had to be made ready before the date of the final stage could be confirmed.

Deputy minister Kovalev described this sort of attitude as "provocative". The US too said that it was a "completely unrealistic stance". The conference had spent the last few weeks specifically concentrating on resolving the schedule issue with a two-level option: a final stage at the end of July, providing that the work would be ready by a certain date. According to Iloniemi, now 29 July was also out of the question. The Americans told Iloniemi that 31 July was the last possible starting day for the final stage. If it were to be moved to August then the US representative would be Vice-President Rockefeller and not President Ford.

Feelings were becoming heated and in the meetings of the coordinating committee accusations flew against individual delegations. On 3 July the FRG apologised for its previously inflexible stand in blocking consensus on the confirmation of the date of the summit meeting. Belgium took over the FRG's tough line, announcing that the matter still could not be agreed. Later that evening, at the start of the 21.00 meeting of the coordinating committee, the Polish delegation officially apologised for having characterised the behaviour of the Germans as "irresponsible". Intense negotiations continued over the following day, during which there were altogether eleven separate meetings. The fourth of July was a Friday and the conference prepared to continue into the weekend without breaks.

Canada's Ambassador Delworth received strict instructions from Prime Minister Pierre Trudeau to deal with the issue of the final stage's timetable. He announced this at the meeting of the NATO group. He said that he had come to propose a solution whereby the CSCE final stage would begin on 30 July, requiring the work in Geneva to be completed by 15 July. Trudeau had other arrangements in August.

At this point Malta's Prime Minister Dom Mintoff caused added problems, particularly for the superpowers. He demanded that the superpowers cut their armed force levels in the Mediterranean. At the time, 10 July, Gromyko and Kissinger were having a working dinner in Geneva. Deputy minister Kovalev interrupted them. He proposed a solution whereby the conference would consider a decision without Malta. In US Ambassador Sherer's view the consensus rule was so strong that the Americans and Russians had only to stand squarely behind Canada's proposal on the schedule. They could then see how Malta would react.

Malta held fast to its demand that the superpowers must reduce their military presence in the eastern Mediterranean. For its part, Turkey kept a grip on the specialists of the group on military matters, as the issue was one of defining an area for applying confidence-building measures that was in its European part of the region. The EEC and Soviet Union were still battling it out in mid-July on the precise application of most favoured nation status and reciprocal treatment: were they general policy lines or just principles to be applied to trade? Concerning Basket II, all open questions had been laid to rest by midnight on Friday 18 July. In the Finnish delegation the decision was seen as a draw from the standpoints of the main parties.

The next day Malta announced that it was ready to adopt the agreed texts and also that the text concerning the reduction of armed forces in the Mediterranean was meant to have consensus approval and was not binding in relation to reducing the schedule.

The location of the CSCE follow-up meeting led to some last minute arm wrestling between Belgrade (then Beograd) and Helsinki. Finland did not actively announce itself as a candidate as Belgrade had. Helsinki would have been ready as the venue of the first follow-up conference, if its friends had proposed it. The final evening at the conference indicated that of the EEC countries only the FRG and Denmark were clear supporters of Helsinki. France supported Belgrade. The Romanian Ambassador Lipatti said that the principle of rotation and a kind of geographic balance was important among the conference venues.

The Geneva phase of the CSCE negotiations reached a successful conclusion on the morning of Monday 21 July at 02.42. In the Finnish delegation the last routine daily cable was prepared for despatch to Helsinki. This explained all the preparations needed for holding the summit meeting in Helsinki. The cable was sent to Helsinki at 04.40. At the suggestion of Ambassador Iloniemi, the whole delegation relocated to one of Geneva's 24-hour restaurants for a good sized breakfast. There was then time for a few hours rest before returning to clear up other practical matters at around mid-day at the Rue Lausanne offices.

The Swiss secretariat had a tough job to get the document in all six languages ready in time for signing. The Finnish delegation translated the document into Finnish on the Finnjet ferry from Travemünde to Helsinki.

Between a rock and a hard place – what sort of document?

Specialists from a range of fields worked day and night in summer 1975 to achieve a credible outcome to the high level diplomatic exercise. The FRG and its representatives paid particular attention to ensure that the result in no way resembled the missing peace settlement of the Second World War and that it could not be characterised as a substitute for it. Also, the outcome was not to take the form of an internationally legal, juridical document, and not interfere with the rights of the four victorious powers with respect to Germany and Berlin, nor open up debate on demands for its ratification by national parliaments. Acceptance by the Federal parliament in Bonn of the FRG's Ostpolitik had come about by a narrow margin. The attitude of the political opposition to the CSCE during the Geneva stage of the negotiations had by no means relaxed.

There were lengthy debates on the nature and structure of the CSCE's final document. These had started in connection with the Dipoli consultations in a situation where, on 1 August 1973, in Helsinki, the foreign ministers of the participating states had commissioned specialists to devote themselves to drafting more precise proposals on various general subjects. The more exact structure and character of the final document were deferred for later decision. It was clear that the division into baskets would be the probable framework used in the final document.

The Soviet Union had already reiterated in Geneva, in a variety of contexts, that the principles guiding relations between states must be given priority. In summer 1974 the Americans discussed the nature of the final document with their closest Soviet counterparts. The Russians said that at the closing ceremony the representatives of the participating states should sign only a "general declaration" containing all the principles. There would only be a brief reference to other items and recommendations. More detailed and practical proposals could be contained in the final document's annexes.

In February 1974, the Netherlands made the first proposal for the structure of a comprehensive final document. What should be signed should be a single, integrated document.

Later in the negotiations the Soviet representatives adapted their original outlook. Deputy minister Kovalev proposed that the outcome of the conference should be four separate documents, one on each basket and a fourth on the follow-up to the conference. All four would be signed at the final stage at the highest political level. Western analysts interpreted the proposal as indicating that General Secretary Brezhnev would sign only the declaration concerning the principles. He would leave the rest of the signing to his subordinates.

The Americans' allies thought differently. The Western delegations starting point was that all recommendations concerning the list of subjects should be of equal weight. In this they would naturally be comparable to the Dipoli Blue Book. This did not differentiate between principles and other recommendations. The Dutch had been the first to propose the outline of the final document: it would have a short preamble that would be signed and the actual documents would be appended to it. One signature would in practice signify the high level adoption of all CSCE decisions.

There was not such a detailed discussion in the Finnish delegation on a more precise design for the final document. On a brief official visit to Helsinki at the end of April 1975 Ambassador Jaakko Iloniemi said that it would be in Finland's national interest if the conference prepared four separate documents and that each would be signed.

The Swiss adapted this idea in a form that was eventually accepted. All the texts would be combined as a uniform document, and all the signatures of the highest political representatives of the participating states would come at the end of the document. In a discussion with President Gerald Ford, Secretary of State Henry Kissinger said on 15 August 1974 that there were not yet any rules of implementation attached to the current draft of the CSCE agreement.

In the end there were less than two weeks left for preparing the original final document for signing. This creditably accomplished task exemplified the services of the Swiss secretariat. It was ready in time. The original copy of it is kept in the national archive in Helsinki.

The freer movement of people

Following protracted and persistent discussions, the Third Committee arrived at an important decision on 8 February 1974. It began drafting the preamble of the text of the basket on humanitarian issues. The political nature of the phrasing of the preamble was generally seen as an attempt by the socialist countries to put practical measures under the umbrella of political consensus decisions. In the view of the Finns these types of decisions had various ramifications.

Pressure increased to give the texts a structural uniformity. According to some, this fundamental change to the structure of the Dipoli recommendations weakened what the Western delegations had achieved in Dipoli. None of the key issues were conclusively resolved in Dipoli. The struggle continued in Geneva up until the final days of the talks.

At an internal delegation meeting, held on 6 March 1974, ministerial counsellor Klaus Törnudd observed that the lack of symmetry in the work of the conference was most glaringly reflected in the efforts on Basket III. The discussion on the preamble showed that there were differing expectations attached to its significance and authority. In the Finnish view the starting point had to be increasing confidence, which would make possible the attainment of positive follow-up measures.

The biggest tussle at that stage focused on deciding with what degree of emphasis the measures now agreed should serve the general development of détente. Would they be applied only on condition that they served détente or because their implementation alone would contribute towards it?

The Soviet writer Alexander Solzhenitsyn was taken from his home for interrogation on 13 February 1974. Two days later, on 15 February, he arrived in Zurich, from where he continued to West Germany. The cynical comment of one American diplomat to Matti Tuovinen was: "This could help with the negotiations in Geneva."

No delegations at the CSCE conference took a "neutral" attitude to the Basket III issues concerning interaction between people and the release of information. This was what Michael Alexander, responsible for the Basket III work of the British delegation, wrote of a remark by a Soviet delegate to him. Austria's Ambassador Helmut Liedermann added these impressions to the text.

It is precisely the part of Basket III concerning contacts between people that is cited when one wants to highlight the special nature of the CSCE compared with other international, multilateral negotiations. This was also the case during the various stages of the talks. The attention and interest shown by the 35 participating countries to Basket III issues varied considerably. Mostly, the actual wrangling took place between the Soviet delegation and the delegation representing the EEC countries.

Pressures to bring about significant and positive results, in terms of everyday life, were maintained in Geneva as a precept particularly of the EEC countries' negotiators. Törnudd fretted that the EEC countries had far-reaching instructions confirmed at ministerial level to demand significant concessions from the socialist countries. On the other hand, he got the impression that the situation assessments and most recent reports on possible progress in the work of the negotiations were not met with sufficient interest at ministerial level in the nations' capitals.

Notions differed greatly within the Western alliance on what the practical significance would be of the accepted decisions resulting from the Geneva talks. Some negotiating objectives were mainly formalities from the standpoint of the alliance's cohesiveness. Others departed from the idea that they should have a palpable effect within the socialist community, at least in the long run. Once the final decisions on contacts between people had been achieved, ministerial advisor Esko Rajakoski was the only member of the Finnish delegation who predicted that eventually there would be queues outside the offices of the OVIR visa and emigration permit authorities in the Soviet Union. He forecast that Soviet citizens would be lining up enthusiastically to apply for foreign travel and emigration permits citing the CSCE decisions.

Human contacts, meetings, family reunification and international marriages were not in numerical terms special problems for Finland. People from the territory ceded after the Second World War had all resettled in Finland.

There were no families divided on either side of the border as in Central Europe. This was the actual reason why Finland did not consider it relevant to profile such matters in the negotiations. The bulk of unresolved issues centred on Central and Eastern Europe, particularly Germany. The CSCE became an important safety net in the context of handling bilateral relations between the Germanies. It was possible to conclude bilateral agreements in accordance with the general goals and spirit of the CSCE, and not merely as a result of negotiations between Bonn and East Berlin.

Under Soviet pressure, State Secretary Tuovinen presented compromises to the Soviet Union that required flexibility. At the time of the Dipoli negotiations the Finns were asked precisely on what issues the Soviet Union would show enough flexibility for decisions to be reached. The Finnish side had specified matters relating to human contacts, freer information exchange and improvement of working conditions for journalists working abroad in other participating states, particularly the socialist countries.

At the end of May 1974 Tuovinen warned that unless the Soviet Union soon showed corresponding flexibility towards compromise the EEC countries should seriously consider a break in the Geneva negotiations for two or three months "or maybe even for a couple of years". It would have been the surest guarantee that possibly prevailing momentum in the negotiations, serious determined efforts to produce a breakthrough, would vanish into thin air.

In a conversation in summer 2006 Tuovinen emphasized that he had had lively contacts with Soviet Embassy representatives in Helsinki right up to the 1975 summit. He had often pleaded with the Russians not to drop out of the CSCE talks under any circumstances. A constant struggle over Moscow's policy was clearly reflected at the Embassy in Helsinki.

The Americans too, in connection with the spring 1974 package deal, had to define more precisely the Basket III issues that required definite results. Consensus on these issues would have assured the Soviet Union that the final stage could be organised at the highest political decision-making level of the participating states. A paper approved by Deputy Secretary of State Hartman and special advisor Sonnenfeldt mentioned, in the sphere of human contacts, meetings between members of families, family reunifications and an easing of travel regulations. Concerning information exchange, the improvement in working conditions for journalists, improvement in the dissemination of newspapers and books, an end to the jamming of radio broadcasts and the facilitation of religious contacts.

In August 1974 Iloniemi was still maintained that the demands of the Western delegations would be "beyond the East's possibilities."

During talks with Romania's Foreign Minister Macovescu, held in Bucharest on 3 November 1974, Kissinger reiterated his position on the challenges of Basket III. He said that some representatives of the participating states had got the idea that it was possible to erode the political structure of other countries with the help of international agreements. "This was naïve in the extreme," said Kissinger. By assuming that present political structures would remain, it was possible, he believed, to agree on some concrete action. Kissinger affirmed that the US was flexible. The only limit was that the US could not pay too high a price on behalf of its allies.

The meeting between General Secretary Brezhnev and France's President Valéry Giscard d'Estaing in December 1974 showed a clear limit in squeezing Basket III concessions from the Soviet Union. The French President "understood" the broader framework of the results to be achieved. He personally put a stop to the demands of the French delegation in Geneva that Moscow should establish reading rooms on French legislative terms.

When the Geneva talks were at their most intense the Finnish government prepared nationally for such matters as dealing with aeroplane hijackings. On 18 June 1975 the Parliamentary foreign affairs committee approved a bilateral Finnish-Soviet treaty on such hijackings. Under the agreement, Finland would not have to extradite its own citizens. An additional protocol also contained the clause that if national interest so required, citizens of a third country need not be extradited.

Controlling exchange of information?

Apart from freer interaction of people across borders, the second taboo-breaking theme of Basket III concerned matters of information exchange. The western media closely monitored the handling of these issues. Progress on them was very close to being a decisive yardstick for whether the CSCE would achieve anything definite that would benefit ordinary people.

These were times when although television and radio were daily staples TV transmissions via satellite across borders were not. The jamming of foreign radio broadcasts played an important role in "protecting the citizens" of the socialist countries. On the other hand, Radio Free Europe and Radio Liberty, like the broadcasts in various languages directed at Eastern Europe from the largest West European and American radio stations, harked back to the early years of the Cold War.

The reception of the Finnish broadcasting company's radio and TV programmes on the north coast of Estonia was an exceptional arrangement. Knowledge of Finnish opened a window on the Western world. The subtitling in Finnish of foreign films and documentaries made it easier (for Estonians) to follow events.

Professor Kaarle Nordenstreng, a Finnish media expert, was distinguished in matters concerning press responsibility. It was he who had evidently drafted the speech delivered by President Kekkonen at a conference on communications held in Tampere on 21 May 1973. In his speech, Kekkonen made a number of observations concerning free competition and freedom of speech. In his view the Finnish print media in no way corresponded to the opinions represented by the democratically elected Parliament. Almost 90 percent of the bourgeois press were backed by a slim conservative majority.

In this context, the President referred to work carried out in Unesco where, he said, "Declarations on behalf of an abstract freedom of speech had been reduced." "Instead," he continued, "They (the UN and Unesco) have moved in the direction of planing down the lack of balance in international communications."

This objective had also been included in the recommendations of the EU-ROCULT conference, held in Helsinki in summer 1972. The aim was that "the mass media would be used to promote the objectives of peace, friendship, international understanding and cooperation." In his speech in Tampere the President drew the following conclusion from this:

"As I understand it, these aims would be best promoted by trying to achieve a "balance of payments" in communication between states to the largest degree possible, and by achieving an equitable cultural exchange in place of the present disparity. I think a measurement could be information based on facts about conditions in other countries." At the end of his speech, Kekkonen stressed that democracy would not function properly unless original critical thinking became prevalent among the general public.

There were vigorous communiqué negotiations on the preparations for visits linked to discussions on the content of the CSCE and the state of Finnish-Soviet relations. At a lunch given for Helsinki newspaper editors on 15 January 1971, Prime Minister Karjalainen had appealed to them to avoid "imprudent articles on the upcoming 24th congress of the Communist Party of the Soviet Union."

Issues to do with information also had other links with current issues, in addition to the CSCE negotiations, including the finalization of the EEC agreement by Parliament and the polemic aroused by the allegations of Finlandization (Finnlandisierung) in the FRG. A German parliamentary delegation visited Finland in 1973. Its members said that the term had been used above all because there was dislike in the FRG of the German package proposal put forward by Finland.

During Kekkonen's visit to the Soviet Union in October 1974 a communiqué was drawn up with President Podgorny that referred to the role of the mass media. This was a return to the form of 1973. The two sides agreed to promote the work of the mass media. They were important. There was no desire on the Finnish side for governments to start being guarantors of the media.

In the 1970s the network of Finnish newspaper correspondents abroad was meagre. For this reason the Finnish delegation proposed, on the initiative of the Finnish Union of Journalists, that the use of multiple entry visas be extended to travelling journalists. This facilitated professional travel to the Soviet Union.

Increasing commercial cooperation

In its official positions, since the Dipoli negotiations, Finland had emphasised the importance to it of matters of commercial cooperation. European integration was at a stage of strong development at the time of the CSCE Geneva talks. Important decisions were expected of Finland, including decisions based on foreign policy. The leaking to the press of President Kekkonen's talks in Zavidovo, NW Russia, raised the issues of President Kekkonen's activities in relation to Soviet policy and European integration. The debate on the domestic front became so heated that even the foreign delegations that had been in Dipoli, could not stay out of it.

There were different displays of strength by the Soviet and socialist system. Many believed that competition between the two systems would intensify, level out or even turn in favour of the socialist system. In some East German documents a view expressed was that a new Member of Parliament of the Social Democratic Party, Dr Pekka Kuusi, was one of the leading Finnish economists. He was considered to be an impressive exponent of the convergence theory. There lay a possibility between the systems of the free market and socialist planning to create functional co-existence. Some economists in Finland presumed that Finland could belong to such a development as a winner. It already had "functional" commercial links in effect with the socialist countries of Eastern Europe. Membership of EFTA ensured a presence in Western markets and there were special arrangements pending with the EEC countries in Brussels.

Work on Basket II progressed in relatively normal circumstances. Executive secretary of the United Nations Economic Commission for Europe (ECE), Janos Stanovik of Yugoslavia, attended the initial stage of the negotiations to report on the ECE's possibilities to act as a future channel for discussion of Basket II. Drafting of the texts progressed gradually. The main issue in the talks on industrial cooperation concerned how international agreements pertaining to it should be emphasised. The US and Canada were notably inflexible in their opposition to Soviet proposals. The standpoints of the EEC countries were at that point highly disparate. The French even considered that the European Commission did not have the authority to enter into serious discussion on industrial cooperation.

In his report of August 1974, Iloniemi stated that in the CSCE economic issues could be basically dealt with on their own terms. The section on environment was practically ready. The principal open question involved the EEC countries' general assessment of the situation when deciding on the recommendations to be included in the text. No revolutionary new Basket II discussion transpired. The same issues had been dealt with for years in the ECE. The ECE's work was now getting a new boost for the promotion of varied European economic cooperation.

According to Ambassadors Paavo Rantanen and Leif Blomqvist, the aim of the socialist camp was to access the West's technological market on a reciprocal basis and to obtain for the CMEA countries a more visible international operational role, and to concentrate in the CSCE on three main themes: environment, transport and energy.

For the West the aim was to obtain recognition of the EEC's coordination of and responsibility for the sphere of Basket II. There was an open political squabble over this during the 1975 summit concerning the the right of Italy's Prime Minister, Aldo Moro, to sign the final document as both the Italian representative and in the name of the EEC's presidency country.

Finland agreed with the practical objectives, such as improving information concerning commerce and promoting business contacts. On the f ormer, there was acceptance of Finland's proposal for research by the ECE on the notification system of laws and regulations concerning foreign trade. Finland proposed, together with Hungary and Bulgaria, concluding bilateral free trade agreements, but this idea did not provide an impetus for more detailed discussion.

In other respects the West's objectives were as specific as they could be: improving the possibilities for business travel, increasing the comparability of statistical information and facilitating business-to-business contacts. On the principle side, the main question was how reciprocity could be managed in practices between the different economic systems.

Increasing commercial cooperation was a timely issue in many ways for Finland. It was vital to strengthen the development of Western trade and to achieve an agreement system with the EEC. These aims had been lacking in recent decisions. There was also the matter of how the Soviet Union and socialist countries would be able to preserve a commercially effective level in trade. Foreign Minister Karjalainen told State Secretary Tuovinen that Finland could make a definite proposal on this problem in connection with the CSCE.

The government foreign affairs committee took a principle decision on 27 April 1973 for Finland to propose active expansion in the development of East-West commercial relations. The point was to try to take care of the EEC decision and CMEA agreements simultaneously so that tariff relations of the small CMEA countries would be handled with the protective laws. As Kari Holopainen observed in his book on trade with Eastern Europe, Finland-CMEA interaction was implemented in practice by establishing a new organ, the cooperation commission, under an agreement signed in Moscow on 29 May 1973. Practical activity had nevertheless to continue on a country-specific basis, via decisions on different tasks involving nine socialist countries.

Finland presented a relatively high profile on the part to do with environmental protection. Environmental issues had come into international discourse on a new level due to the first major international conference on the environment, held in Stockholm in 1972. This lent a wholly new tone to the Middle East crisis and the oil crisis that emanated from it. Energy prices rocketed. Sustainable development and the sufficiency of natural resources started to be discussed. On the basis of the Geneva negotiations treaty negotiations were later organised in the ECE concerning environmental protection and limiting air pollution caused by long-distance haulage. Environmental protection became a focal point for Finland and the Nordic countries in preparations for the Vienna follow-up conference.

By 21 June 1974 work on Basket II was reaching its conclusion. Following a two-week period of plain sailing significant progress in the work could be registered.

But the preamble to basket II was sorely incomplete. The stumbling block was the demand by Romania, Turkey and Malta for a statement on strengthening the position of Europe's developing countries. The issue of migrant labour, considered important from the FRG and Swiss standpoint, remained unresolved. Countries supplying migrant labour stuck to the original aim of including in Basket II regulations facilities for the unification of families in the context of human contacts.

By June 1975 the remaining unresolved items of Basket II were threatening for the first time to slow down the rest of the conference's work. The Western delegations decided, because of this, to take part in the talks at head of delegation level. Reciprocity was now discussed on a fully equal basis, which the delegations of the socialist countries in Geneva were hitherto not at all used to.

Broader cultural exchange under cover of UNESCO

From the outset, the socialist countries' activities highlighted cultural cooperation as a form of CSCE humanitarian cooperation. It would be between governments and would minister to Europe's multiculturalism. This was pretty much the contribution of the socialist countries to the regional UNESCO EUROCULT conference held in Helsinki in June 1972. Finland's Minister of Culture Pentti Holappa chaired the conference. It was one of several such regional events following from the first world conference on cultural policy, held in Venice in 1970. It had 30 participants. Of the European countries, Malta and Albania did not take part, and the US and Canada attended as observers.

The conference resulted in written recommendations that included ideas on a broader conception of culture and for principles of cooperation. Cooperation should be "in the spirit of international law and the ideals of the UN, respecting national rights of self-determination and sovereignty, the principle of equality and non-interference and the promotion of the interests of both sides." Cultural cooperation was seen as emphasising activities between governments and their representative institutions. Bilateral cultural agreements and other reciprocal arrangements had prime place in the array of types of cooperation.

Attention was paid in separate recommendations to the fact that the course of economic development was leading to imbalance that was consequently reflected in the essence of civilisation. In some societies production and consumption were ends in themselves, while in others they were just means among others. Such was the outcome of the joint deliberations of ministerial officials, professionals in the field of cultural policy and artists.

The introductory words of the conference conclusions stated that a broader notion of culture would include the obligation on governments to fully implement their cultural policy. The possibility for individuals to monitor the development of their society could be mentioned separately as an objective. Instead of individuals being under the guidance of society, the new cultural policy would make individuals the subjects of their environments and give them the opportunity to express themselves freely, communicate and take part in creative activity. According to cultural counsellor Margareta Mickwitz, the expansive dialogue that started then continues today within another generation.

The socialist countries' proposals for the final recommendations of the Dipoli consultations referred to the EUROCULT conference. This was not without problems, as Unesco was a worldwide specialised agency under the UN. Not all CSCE participants were involved in the work of the UN, or of Unesco. Switzerland strongly opposed references to EUROCULT's work at the Geneva talks. The Swiss saw the matter as a precedent whereby non-participating Mediterranean countries could appeal to increase participation in the work of the negotiations. They would be granted the opportunity to present their positions in the form of oral interventions. Unesco representatives would be given the opportunity to speak to the sub-committee on culture and education.

The Swiss representatives were also concerned about the possibility that the recommendation produced at the EUROCULT conference on communications would steer the work of the CSCE Geneva talks. One of the proposals stated that the mass media had not exploited all opportunities for opening the eyes of citizens to see the world as a whole. Instead of being active agents, people had become the passive objects of audiovisual technology.

Opening up military secrets

The CSCE made history on the matter of military security, even though the first steps taken were characterised as small and initially modest. Under the CSCE framework tests were started on military openness in the form of confidence-building measures. It was natural in the conditions of détente, and sometimes a challenge, to open up the main issues of military security. On the other hand, there was an assumption that if the development of détente were to be credible, questions of military security and the exchange of information had to be aspects of the European security process.

The big powers already had the national technical means, through existing intelligence channels, to obtain information on military manoeuvres. The prospect now was that the use of such prior notification would become an obligatory and permanent part of military information exchange among all the parties involved. The objective was to nurture a reciprocal confidence databank. The threshold issue from the start would be the level to which the obligations of notification would be compulsory: would they be legally, politically or morally binding decisions by the participating states?

Initially the Soviet Union was prepared to give five days' prior notification of manoeuvres involving military forces that were held within 50 kilometres from the frontier zone of its Western border. The West wanted the prior notification period to be 60 days and troop numbers of 10,000 to be within the sphere of notification.

The neutral and non-aligned countries took a special interest in this. They put their own confidence-building proposal to the conference in February 1974. The intention was for it to be a constructive mid-way position between the very different starting points in the proposals of the military alliances. It proposed a 50-day prior notification period for manoeuvres or deployments involving divisions of about 18,000 troops on the territories of all participating states. The proposal also said that notification of all other military activity should be given voluntarily as a gesture of good faith.

The issue now was not of revealing major military secrets. It was rather that the participating states' readiness to give notice of military manoeuvres, according to mutually agreed parameters, was being tested. Military observers would be able to follow such manoeuvres on site.

The extent of military manoeuvres within the sphere of prior notification, the time of prior notification and the areas in Europe to be included in the sphere of such notification remained the main negotiating issues for the duration of the Geneva stage of the talks. A particular problem was the Soviet Union's extremely cagey attitude to lifting the veil on military secrecy to the outside world. The extent of the Soviet Union's European regions and the specification of Turkey's eastern regions formed the biggest problems in the search for geographical balance.

The Soviet Union and socialist countries tried by tough negotiating tactics to balance a situation in which the countries of North America, the US and Canada, would be excluded from the notification obligations.

Achieving a balance of dissimilar interests was impeded in part because the role of the military in decision-making and its influence in defining national security varied greatly from country to country. In those days it was not possible to start a debate on the 'democratic supervision of the armed forces', which is nowadays a key subject.

When Gromyko and Kissinger held talks in Washington on the CSCE situation, on 20 September 1974, confidence building measures were central. Gromyko suggested right at the start that discussion of troop deployments should be put off as a subject for further analysis. The Soviet Union was prepared to discuss the role of observers voluntarily present at manoeuvres.

In October, discussions in Moscow revealed that confidence-building measures were one of four key issues that were still unresolved. In Kissinger's view there was room for compromise. A decision should be made on the area of application, between 50 and 100 kilometres, and the size of forces under prior notification, between 20,000 and 40,000 men. Because the US was also a CSCE participant, Brezhnev expected that the Americans would provide prior notification of all naval activity and, with Canada, troop movements on the North American continent as far as California. Brezhnev's idea of inviting observers was immediately changed into a demand to open up the whole Soviet area as far as the Urals. "I let the genie out of the bottle."

Soviet representatives had told State Secretary Tuovinen already in April that the West's proposals could not be the basis for the final negotiations because they were "absurd". They did not take into account certain "national feelings", of national pride, that could not be encroached upon. The operative unit in military manoeuvres was not a division but "an army". Concerning the invitation of observers, the Russians had proposed the principle of voluntariness.

The outcome was as follows: 250 kilometres from the Soviet Union's western border, manoeuvres of 25,000 men, a prior notification period of 25 days and an invitation to send CSCE observers on a voluntary basis. If the notification norms differed from the aforementioned, an invitation to follow the manoeuvres would be given only to neighbouring countries, not to all participating states.

Since the start of the 1973 autumn session, the Finnish delegation had debated the possibility of introducing the idea of the Nordic nuclear weapons-free zone at the Geneva negotiations. Iloniemi said at an internal meeting on 8 November 1973 that the notion of the nuclear weapons-free zone had become current – unless the issue was raised emphatically, it would not carry much weight later on.

The unassuming opening of the final document framed important military cooperation. Once agreed there would be no turning back. The discussion at the latest Madrid follow-up meeting indicated that there were abundant possibilities to develop further confidence-building measures.

Mediterranean: OK, Middle East: no way!

From the opening moments of the CSCE Malta was the Mediterranean 'superpower' driving cooperation in the region. Thanks to its skilful negotiators and diplomats it was frequently able to keep a high profile in the conference right to the closing stages. It was conspicuous for the first time in connection with the first Helsinki conference of foreign ministers, in 1973. Malta's Prime Minister Dom Mintoff, who also held the post of Foreign Minister, only took part in person in this first foreign minister's conference. The conference's more dramatic points included Malta's demand that the Middle East question and the participation of Arab countries be included in the CSCE's work.

Malta would not have accepted the inclusion of Israel. At a meeting of the informal working group led by Ambassador Mendelevich, Gromyko thundered and threatened that if Malta prevented consensus it could be excluded from the whole conference by a decision of 34 countries.

The Helsinki recommendations agreed at the Dipoli discussions did not yet contain a separate section on cooperation in the Mediterranean. The preliminary references to cooperation in the European and Mediterranean regions were contained in the section on principles and in the preamble to the section on commercial cooperation. Dom Mintoff brought up the issue of the Middle East at his meeting with Foreign Minister Karjalainen on 4 July 1973. Mintoff was of the opinion that Arab countries must be assured that the superpowers would not force a Middle East settlement on their shoulders. "Because the Middle East affects European security, all the countries of Europe must be included in creating this atmosphere." Karjalainen said that he hoped the CSCE would not be burdened with problems that were not geographically European. In Karjalainen's view the Middle Eastern crisis was at that moment "the most difficult and dangerous in the world".

Mintoff's pronouncements stemmed from the assumption that the CSCE framework could test the readiness of the European states to get involved in the interests of Middle Eastern countries in a new way. These countries would not be CSCE participating states. The dispute was to what extent they would have the opportunity to launch initiatives in relation to the discussion on the Mediterranean and to be involved in that discussion. On several occasions during the Geneva negotiations Ambassador Iloniemi expressed his admiration for the Maltese delegation's diplomats and their work. They must have had a personal conception that original instructions from Valetta were completely impossible to follow.

In his memoirs published in 2007, Evarist Saliba, a veteran CSCE diplomat and later Malta's Foreign Minister, clearly refers to this remark by Iloniemi. Prime Minister Mintoff's general instruction to the negotiators was that they "must particularly detest the policies of the two superpowers".

On 12 September 1974 in Geveva, Malta formally proposed that the CSCE, Mediterranean Arab countries, Iran and the countries of the Persian Gulf should establish a "European-Arabic union". Parallel with the "development of this new sovereign union, the United States and the Soviet Union would commit themselves to withdrawing their forces from the region," It was clear that this sort of ambitious proposal concerning a global political flash-point could not be a serious topic of discussion in the CSCE.

Cooperation in the Mediterranean region was finally limited by the Geneva negotiations to techno-economic and environmental matters. The security aspect was clearly left out of the debate. What was important for the participating states was that nearby crises would not be placed on the CSCE agenda. The same applied to the ongoing oil crisis. They were the business of other forums.

The non-participating Mediterranean states had the right to have a role in relation to the CSCE. They were given the opportunity to contribute addresses of a general nature to the opening phase of discussions concerning a variety of subjects, but not to the committee work proper. In addresses of a general nature, too, it was possible to present concrete initiatives. North Mediterranean coastal states of the CSCE endeavoured, through their own actions, to promote these initiatives to various degrees.

Follow-up continuity pledged in a new manner

There was an interesting debate during the negotiations on the continuity of the CSCE process. Would the CSCE compete with the UN Security Council by having a permanent secretariat or political consultation mechanism? The initiators of the discussion were Czechoslovakia from the socialist countries, neutral Finland, non-aligned Yugoslavia, and Denmark from the EEC.

Czechoslovakia proposed that there be only political follow-up, multilateral political consultations. Yugoslavia suggested political follow-up, but considered it important for the conference's decisions to be implemented. Denmark proposed only the implementation of decisions, and the transfer of political follow-up of decisions to the future.

On 13 December 1973 the Finnish delegation spoke of emphasising the importance of the continuity of the process. The CSCE could not, given the realities of the moment, be a one-off event. It could not solve all problems at once. "The follow-up of implementation and the possibility for making new decisions as positive development in the international atmosphere proceeds would open up new areas of consensus," said Iloniemi in his address.

It was in Finland's interest to maintain multilateral consultation mechanisms among the participating states. Consultations were taking place beyond the alliances and on the basis of the consensus principle. The political significance of follow-up meetings was not touched on at this stage. It was known that some EEC countries and the US were suspicious of follow-up. The French justified their caution towards follow-up because, they felt, it could grow into a Soviet-driven European body similar to the UN Security Council.

The French also had their own reservations about the continuation of the CSCE. The creation of a pan-European negotiating body could complicate the development of the EEC's internal integration. "If pan-European consultations were to start, the EEC would have to significantly increase its common foreign policy collaboration in order to be a credible negotiating partner with both the Soviet Union and the United States."

Iloniemi calmed the sceptics by saying that there was no such danger. A 35-country body working on the basis of consensus had not been a troubleshooter, or a tribunal. According to the Finnish proposal, it would always be junior civil servants who would prepare in advance agreements related to matters under consideration and timetables. In April 1974 the Finnish delegation confirmed a proposal, based on its instructions, according to which the coordination of the follow-up to the conference would be handled by a steering committee.

Reference to a negotiating body led to the prevailing assumption that not all the matters at hand could be resolved in the Geneva talks. The negotiations would therefore have to continue in some form within a CSCE follow-up framework.

Denmark presented a proposal on behalf of the EEC for the follow-up to the conference. This envisaged that the number of unresolved issues left after the Geneva talks would be considerable. For this reason the idea of a separate Basket IV was not in Denmark's view justified. The Danes and the EEC endeavoured to dissolve the CSCE's comprehensive political component and thus lessen its future dynamic political energy by putting the emphasis on the future role of expert conferences and meetings. In this sense the Danish proposal reflected political prejudices about the continuation of the process and its organisational form.

Secretary of State Kissinger was on 3 November 1974 still clearly for the continuation of the process. He told his Romanian counterpart in Bucharest that he would not consider the foreign minister to have failed in his task if the CSCE conference did not continue.

The February 1975 draft budget of the British government reflected the assumption that the decisions achieved in the CSCE must take practical effect and from this basis "ensure that the multilateral dialogue started in the framework of the conference must continue".

The work of the Finnish delegation could well incorporate the narrative of a British delegate's personal experience. Those who would fare best in the discussion and outcome concerning the follow-up were those who knew what they wanted, remained patient to the end, remained awake during all stages of the negotiations, wrote down precise ideas clearly in all phases and were outspoken when necessary and entertaining when circumstances allowed.

Finland's official and comprehensive proposal on follow-up was presented in Geneva on 7 June 1974. It was tabled at a point in the negotiations when it was expected that the content of the final document would be near completion. President Kekkonen confirmed the making of a separate follow-up proposal.

Article 53 of the Dipoli recommendations concerning follow-up set the requirement that progress had to be achieved in the process. The main ingredients of the Finnish proposal therefore referred to progress made. To accomplish its aims the conference must strengthen efforts for continuity and thereby promote the development of European security and cooperation. The participating states decided to put the decisions into effect unilaterally, bilaterally, when activities so required, and multilaterally when urging existing international organizations to make conclusions concerning the conference's decisions.

In addition to these solutions concerning the implementation of decisions, Finland proposed that the CSCE establish an active follow-up committee on consensus decisions. This would give consistent administrative support for organising conferences in joint understanding, creating the necessary arrangement of coordination with existing international organizations and in other respects coordinate all multilateral activity. The follow-up committee would arrange special conferences when needed at high civil servant level to assess the implementation of decisions, deliberate on ways of improving European security and cooperation and decide, on this basis, other multilateral measures and new conferences. The timing of the last-mentioned and their frequency were not specified in the original proposal. Neither was it proposed that the follow-up committee should have a permanent secretariat.

Denmark presented a revamped version of its proposal on 11 June 1974. Under this, the continuation of the conference would be prepared, but not until 1977, in conjunction with the first follow-up meeting. Continuity could not yet be confirmed. It was only possible to begin discussing continuity on the basis of implementation and adherence to decisions.

There were intense discussions on the nature of this continuity until the final days of the Geneva talks. The Finnish position was that continuity would be brought about by consensus as a characteristic of the CSCE process. It could only be broken off by consensus decision. The EEC's and Denmark's stance was that after 1977 continuity would require a new consensus decision. The differences over the issue were based on principles.

As for the Soviet Union, Iloniemi reported to the Finnish delegation, following talks with deputy minister Kovalev; that the Soviet Union "has now been Finlandized by the follow-up question!"

When proposing that the CSCE follow-up conferences be periodic, the Finnish proposal had been aiming at the continuity of the process. Each conference would agree on its successor before finishing its business. When the Romanians, among others, voiced fairly strong criticism of this point, Iloniemi said that unless the mechanism of the process was extended, all would be driven into the situation that prevailed before the start of the Dipoli consultations.

The organisation of periodic follow-up events was achieved by consensus only as a result of the Belgrade preparatory meeting, in summer 1977.

The Italian CSCE Ambassador Luigi Ferraris wrote in his book on the CSCE (1979) that for countries like Finland and Yugoslavia the CSCE multilateral political negotiating forum meant stability and security in a concrete form. It was due to this that their interest in the continuation and follow-up of the process was not merely procedural but was politically motivated.

Finnish activity rewarded

At a meeting of the Parliamentary foreign affairs committee in May 1975, Iloniemi elucidated on Finland's activity on key matters and excellent timing in light of the conference's outcome. Finland had frequently joined in common initiatives with the neutral and non-aligned group.

Iloniemi explained that Finland's industriousness focused variously on investigating with the main parties, in the manner of a scout, the possibilities for compromise proposals. It was only when it was thought that a proposal could contribute to the desired direction of the negotiations that it was made. The Finnish aim during the Geneva negotiations was to bring the talks to a swift and successful conclusion. It was clear that the final stage constituted an important political event in expressing the détente process. It would also contribute to the public image of the event. Because of this it was important that "what Finland must do, as the host, is firstly to become closely familiar with the expectations of others".

In February 1975, Iloniemi collated his ideas to assess the schedule of the final stage of the CSCE. At the time there was still much work left to do. The only credible yardstick in estimating the use of time was to look at what would be the remaining insuperable obstacles.

There were still two principles incomplete and untreated, namely cooperation among states (9) and the fulfilment of international obligations in good faith (10). There would have to be a second reading, and it wouldn't be a matter of proof reading. There were still many real issues to be negotiated.

Some sorts of concession were expected from the Warsaw Treaty countries on military matters. Even minor concessions could ease the situation. There were no longer any major trade policy compromises by the East and West concerning commercial issues expected from Geneva. Decisions on trade policy problems had to be made at a very general level. Basket II issues did not delay the final stage.

The situation was different concerning Basket III. The aim was to register both lofty goals and 'insignificant' details. By 25 July Iloniemi no longer believed that these questions would prolong the ending of the second stage. The same applied to questions of cooperation in the field of culture. France still stuck to its own sweeping proposal.

Concerning the follow-up of the conference, the Western countries still refrained from revealing their final position. As many issues as possible had to be decided in Geneva and not held back for follow-up consideration. The design of the follow-up did not need to take up extra time. The concepts were clear, as were the limits of compromise.

Parallel with these questions of substance, the hosting of the third stage had to ensure that all matters linked to the final stage could be agreed in good time in Geneva. By February 1975 it was evident that the final stage would be held at the highest political level. Because of this Messrs Brezhnev and Ford had to know in good time when the final stage would be held. Participation in the Helsinki summit meeting would take up at least four or five days. Iloniemi thought it important to reach an agreement before Easter whether or not the then 'ghost schedule' was correct, i.e. that the final stage was to be held in Helsinki at the beginning of July. In case this was impossible, the next date would not be until the beginning of September.

On 19 February, the coordinating committee decided to start preparations for the third stage. It appeared that there were still differences of opinion in the Western alliance about the level of participation. In a joint communiqué issued when they met in Geneva, Gromyko and Kissinger spoke of the summit level of the third stage as a done deal. Italy and the FRG had misgivings about this. The coordinating committee's decision to set up the preparations of the neutral countries' working group was seen as a joint 35-country decision and a countermove to the attempted diktat policy of the two super powers.

Most informal work, both oral and written in the form of working papers, was in English. In May, when the last open questions on compromises were addressed, again in English, the secretariat was able to report that in the preliminarily agreed texts over 400 different translation problems had already been identified. The main problems concerned making the English and Russian language texts match.

Assessing the outcome

The principles guiding the relations between states were characterised in a report submitted to the 29 May 1975 meeting of the Parliamentary foreign affairs committee as the most sensitive core area of the negotiations. The matters of contention had not always been politically clustered East-West problems. They were often a matter of national interest. One example mentioned was Romania, which even in the finest points emphasised the importance of national rights of self-determination. Romania's and the Soviet Union's opposing positions had become glaringly evident in the Geneva talks. The same kind of attitude typified Yugoslavia's behaviour too, sometimes with more restraint.

Harmonisation of the principles agreed in the CSCE with the UN Charter constituted a joint problem: Switzerland and four other CSCE participating states were not yet UN members (Liechtenstein, Monaco, San Marino and the Vatican).

On 23 May 1975 the Finnish delegation tabled its own proposal for the preamble to the passage on principles. It was hoped that Finland's proposal would speed up finalisation of the text. Iloniemi had frequently emphasised to Helsinki that this was not a matter of "a manuscript composed by jurists or poets". The formulations might have appeared abstruse. Their only justification was that they might then be acceptable to all the main parties.

At the beginning of March 1975, France launched an appeal in the CSCE capitals in the context of the final negotiations. It proposed that the post-war responsibilities of the allies vis-à-vis Berlin and Germany be registered as a separate clause in the preamble to the 10 principles. France announced that there had been no opportunity to negotiate the text and that it had to be accepted as it stood. This sort of proposal and the way in which it was offered had a fairly discordant reception. Non-aligned delegations in particular saw in it a danger that all the stipulations that had been agreed might be watered down on account of it. The proposal was not accepted.

The finalization of the section on confidence-building measures was furthered by a compromise proposal by the neutral and non-aligned countries. It was agreed that the method of prior notification of military manoeuvres would be applied on a voluntary basis. The last contentious matters were the definition of the territorial dimensions of military manoeuvres, particularly eastwards from the Soviet Union's western border, and the notification threshold of the number of troops taking part in manoeuvres. Compromises concerning the size of military manoeuvres had to be sought from between the Soviet Union's suggested 100-kilometre parameter and the West's proposal of a 500-kilometre parameter, and from the West's 15,000 men and the East's 35,000 men. Finland and the other neutral and non-aligned countries proposed a minimum of 18,000 men and a 30-day notification period.

The focus on confidence-building measures produced a rare arrangement whereby the neutral and non-aligned countries had the most far-reaching original aims. Sweden and Yugoslavia took the lead on this issue. Because of the MBFR negotiations under way in Vienna, the decisions reached in Geneva were naturally important to the alliances' delegations. The general impression in Geneva was that unless the confidence-building measures led to concrete results, the rationale of the sceptics would become stronger. There would otherwise be no essentially new results to be expected from Geneva. This scenario worked as an element of pressure on the neutral and non-aligned group.

The most difficult matters in the section on commercial cooperation that remained were most favoured nation status and reciprocity. Only the conference's follow-up clarification could determine the decisions concerning future arrangements. On the issues of reciprocity and safeguards Finland took account of the experiences of other market economy countries in the sphere of earlier KEVSOS free trade agreements.

Agreement on the subject matter of Basket III was a fundamental condition for the West's involvement in the CSCE negotiation process. Discussions on human contacts and information exchange were new matters in multilateral diplomacy. Commitments and degrees of concreteness set new kinds of challenge for the differing administrative cultures. An open question throughout was whether the participating states would commit themselves only on a theoretical level to develop travel and tourism, or would they state their intention to extend citizens' opportunities for travel in a definite way.

On the exchange of information the benchmark was whether the enhanced exchange of and access to information as such would serve to boost détente and understanding between peoples. Or was the desire only to promote the kind of exchange of and access to information that would serve the principles of peace and the coexistence of peoples?

Differences of view over cooperation in culture and education were familiar in the emphasis of the socialist countries on agreements establishing cultural exchange between states and the primary importance of this. The West argued in favour of removing obstacles from the road to more extensive and liberated cultural exchange.

On the subject of follow-up, Finland and the other neutrals made a definite proposal in May 1975 with the intention of strengthening the implementation of agreed decisions, unilaterally, bilaterally and multilaterally by the work of international organisations, continuing multilateral cooperation at the level of conferences of officials and by organising such conferences with multilateral preparation.

In explaining the content and character of the Finnish proposal, Iloniemi said that no such proposal had been brought about by consensus by which the CSCE could immediately set up an international organization. Some form of permanent secretariat would be the first distinctive feature of an organization. Although the Geneva talks had proceeded for almost two years, they had not had an international secretariat. The extent of a secretariat's services, conference venues, the number of conferences and frequency of sessions were agreed on the basis of separate unofficial consultations and preparatory work by the neutral countries. On occasion, further work could only be agreed for a few weeks at a time.

In his address of 29 May 1975 to the Parliamentary foreign affairs committee Ambassador Iloniemi stressed that the two years since the first Helsinki ministerial conference had seen substantial changes in many of the participating states, even systemic ones in Greece and Portugal. The starting point generally adopted at the beginning of negotiations was the acknowledgement of prevailing realities. Iloniemi thought that the detailed handling of exceptional issues did not only require ascertaining the prevailing situation, rather the aim "was to change it, at least in the long run." Iloniemi's opinion was that all the participants were of the view that the purpose of Basket III, in particular, was to change the prevailing state of affairs and not just to ascertain what it was.

In a statement broadcast on Finnish television on 7 August 1975 President Kekkonen said, "Finland can be proud that the CSCE participating states have chosen the neutral soil of Finland as the venue for the historic conference. The progress of the conference, both in spirit and external circumstances, correspond to our boldest expectations." Kekkonen concluded with the words, "I owe a debt of gratitude to all the Finnish people, who, by giving their unwavering support to our foreign policy, have made this achievement possible."

The statement encapsulated, from Finland's perspective, the different stages of the more than six-year CSCE initiative. This impressive political event in post-Second World War European history irreversibly sealed Finland and its capital to the CSCE process. Ambassador Iloniemi said in a speech at Dipoli in October 1975 that due to the CSCE process Finland had come to be taken seriously as a discussion partner. "It became known that Finns could be relied upon in positions of trust in international politics."

The Helsinki spirit

The 1975 Helsinki summit

The decision to hold the summit meeting in Helsinki was not confirmed until 21 July 1975. The summit would start in the Finnish capital on 30 July, last for two and a half days and at its end, on 1 August, there would be a signing ceremony.

Altogether 550 delegation members of the CSCE participating states attended the summit. About 3,000 secretariat and security personnel were responsible for the practical arrangements. The security measures for the conference were put into effect on 28 July: 400 soldiers and 150 police officers guarded the airport. Security at Finlandia Hall was exceptionally tight. Helsinki's residents could keep track of the event from the lines of black limousines moving along the streets and close to Finlandia Hall. The Hall earned the epithet 'Kekkonen's katiska', a katiska being a fish trap used in Finnish lakes. There were 1,110 journalists accredited from abroad and 300 from Finland.

President Kekkonen was the undisputed host of the summit conference. He provided the Liinamaa caretaker government with a clear objective, to ensure that the CSCE summit conference would end successfully. Foreign Minister Mattila took on the job conscientiously. He ordered that all contacts with the President would go via him.

At the same time, the composition of the delegation forged the CSCE into one of the central pillars of Finland's foreign policy consensus.

Highest level

To entitle the Helsinki conference a 'summit conference' meant many things. When explaining the Finnish proposal to the Parliamentary foreign affairs committee, Iloniemi explained how the summit conference participants should be defined in mutual understanding. Finland worked from the assumption that the participants represented the "highest political level". This meant different things in different countries. At some point the idea was that the representative level of the participating delegations would simply be "highest level". This term, however, met with a practical reservation from the representative of the Holy See: "Unfortunately our Highest Representative cannot be here in person."

In the case of countries that were monarchies, it was natural that their representatives would be prime ministers. In some countries, where a party leader held the highest power in political decision-making, it would mean that the party leader would attend. The host country expected that in addition to the highest holders of political power the foreign ministers would also be present. In order to indicate in a tangible way the solidarity between this European process and a larger international community, Finland proposed that the UN Secretary General should also be invited. The Secretary General had attended the conference of foreign ministers in Helsinki in summer 1973.

The opening session of the summit conference began on 30 July at 12.00 with a speech by President Kekkonen. This was followed by a message of greeting by UN Secretary General Kurt Waldheim. Prime Minister Liinamaa then hosted a lunch in honour of Waldheim. At the same time bilateral meetings got under way, including one between General Secretary Brezhnev and President Ford. The Federal German Chancellor Helmut Schmidt and Poland's General Secretary Gierek met one another for the first time. It was announced that as an outcome of their discussions 120,000 ethnic Germans in Poland would be able to move to Germany.

At the first working session the first official speech began in Finlandia Hall at 14:30. The chair of the session was the representative of the Holy See, Secretary of State Agostino Casaroli. The first speaker was the UK's Prime Minister Harold Wilson.

President Kekkonen hosted a dinner on the opening day of the summit at the presidential residence. Four representatives were invited from each delega-

President Urho Kekkonen opens the CSCE summit meeting in Finlandia Hall, 30 July 1975, to a packed auditorium and press gallery.
(Photograph: Atte Matilainen)

The Finnish national delegation during a break in the Summit. From the right: the Chairman of the Communist Party of Finland Aarne Saarinen, Prime Minister Keijo Liinamaa, Ahti Karjalainen, President Urho Kekkonen, Foreign Minister Olavi J. Mattila, the Chairman of the National Coalition Party Harri Holkeri, the Chairman of the Swedish Peoples' Party C.-O. Tallgren and Ambassador Jaakko Iloniemi. (Photograph: Atte Matilainen)

tion. Among the guests was UN Secretary General Kurt Waldheim, who, in addition to the President, delivered a short address to the gathering.

General Secretary Brezhnev left the occasion for an hour and then, while the other guests continued with dinner, for another hour. The incident reinforced rumours that had spread around for years from different quarters that the General Secretary suffered from a serious illness. The table of the Soviet Delegation in Finlandia Hall drew the attention of other participants, who had noticed that Brezhnev had in front of him a glass containing a coloured liquid.

Brezhnev's authority grew weaker due to his worsening health and diminishing working capacity. His close colleagues were positively surprised that he performed at the Helsinki summit so well without longer breaks.

Questions had been asked earlier about what the main reasons were for the Soviet Union's and then General Secretary Brezhnev's haste in convening the CSCE summit. One key factor was the 25th congress of the CPSU, set for summer 1976. In preparing for it Brezhnev decided to increase the number of Politburo members from 11 to 14. A numerous group of his supporters and sympathisers had become members or deputy members of the Central Committee. The reality was that his reformist and pragmatic leadership started to suffer at the end of the 1970s from his increasing long-term absences. Confidence in the victory of détente was not as clear cut as had been believed at the start of the decade.

The crown of the host

The Helsinki summit conference is generally considered to have been the climax of President Kekkonen's foreign policy. Six years had passed since the Finnish CSCE initiative. Preparations for bringing about the summit had been under way practically without a break since November 1972, since the start of the Dipoli consultations. The Finnish national delegation at Finlandia Hall demonstrated that the CSCE represented a broad-based consensus in Finland's policy of neutrality. The delegation comprised representatives of all the parliamentary parties.

As President Mauno Koivisto later remarked in an interview, President Kekkonen's role as the pilot of the process leading to the closing summit conference was crucial. "If the tractive responsibility had been with the prime minister, it would, in accordance with Finnish political practice in those days, have changed hands every year." These were Kekkonen's times.

Finland's tractive function concerning the CSCE remained at a high political level and in the same hands. The more the process took a credible and viable form, the more specifically the Finnish political leadership was able to benefit it.

At the same time there is reason to look again at the operative ability of the Finnish negotiating delegation: it was extensive and flexible. The nation's capital did not interfere in matters of detail, except in exceptional cases. The credibility and fitness for purpose of Iloniemi's delegation was established in Geneva. The whole of Finland's Foreign Service network was harnessed for the negotiation process. It continually sought to keep abreast of events. Due to the organisational responsibility entailed by the summit conference, Finland's missions abroad cancelled all summer leave. The flow of information had to be prompt and seamless. Though the hosting could be classed as a practical and technical matter, its credible handling required a comprehensive and up to date understanding of all the main parties' expectations and opinions.

Kekkonen summed up Finland's policy of neutrality and CSCE activity in a speech delivered on 31 July 1975 as follows:

"Six years ago, in 1969, Finland wanted to launch an initiative to find new ways to create a security and cooperation project across Europe's internal borders. By endeavouring to be a positive contribution to a joint effort the initiative reinforced Finland's own security. In accordance with its policy of neutrality, Finland was glad to see that disagreements between groupings of states had been reduced and that "tense" as a description of Europe's situation was a term of the past. Only in such a Europe can people develop their individual lives without hindrance and fulfil themselves enlivened by the goals and values that they embrace."

Finland made a significant contribution to the process both in terms of human resources and particularly in connection with the 1975 summit conference in a new way that involved the security and comfort of the guests. Ambassador Joel Pekuri's secretariat went into operational mode on May Day 1975. Each visiting delegation had at its disposal both a military attaché and the Finnish ambassador accredited to their country.

The practical arrangements proceeded without any major problems. The traffic regulations were exceptional due partly to the fact that many heads of state were accommodated at their own ambassador's residence in Helsinki.

Speeches were delivered and signatures put to the final document during the closing session, at 17.00 on 1 August. President Kekkonen chaired the session. The French alphabetical order was used, beginning with the FRG and ending with Yugoslavia. Archbishop Makarios was the only signatory who was

Ambassador Joel Pekuri receives the original copy of the CSCE Final Act from his Swiss counterpart Alfred Rappard in Geneva.
(Photograph: Archive of the Finnish Foreign Ministry)

not happy with the pen and ink provided by the organizers and opted to sign with his own pen, using red ink. After champagne and strawberries from Suonenjoki, the soft fruit centre of Finland, the delegations left Finlandia Hall for their journeys home.

The CSCE summit reached a successful conclusion. It was seen to have provided Finland not only with a good reputation but also with important backing for its foreign policy in a wider sense. All political capital and substantial financial investment were put into hosting the summit. When, in November 1975, the accounts of the conference were finalized, they showed that overall costs were approximately 14.8 million Finnish marks. For operations, the benefit of which remained permanently with the host country, Finland announced that it had paid 2.5 million marks above the 12.3 million marks or 2% share of the joint costs originally budgeted.

The Helsinki summit conference and President Kekkonen's gala dinner. At the main table from the left: US President Gerald Ford, GDR Party Leader Eric Honecker, FRG Chancellor Helmut Schmidt, UN General Secretary Kurt Waldheim, Yugoslavia's President Josip Broz Tito, the Soviet Union's General Secretary Leonid Brezhnev, Turkey's President Süleyman Demirel and Czechoslovakia's President Gustáv Husák. (Photograph: Atte Matilainen)

High level compliments

President Kekkonen had a historic opportunity to receive the political leaders of 34 European states, the US and Canada in Helsinki. It was the first time this had ever happened in Europe's history and it was indisputably the most important political event to have taken place in Finland following the Second

World War. It was compared by public assessment to two very different events that had previously put Helsinki and Finland on the world map, namely the 1939-40 Winter War and the 1952 Olympics.

In addition to the official programme at Finlandia Hall, President Kekkonen held bilateral meetings with the guests. These were held at the presidential residence on North Esplanade, in downtown Helsinki, and in the annexe to Finlandia Hall, as the programme allowed. The meetings were clearly courtesy calls. The time reserved for them was rarely more than half an hour. The visitors' retinues were proportionately small. The head of state was accompanied by a foreign minister and personal assistant, as well as the country's ambassador to Helsinki.

The common denominator of all the meetings was appreciation of President Kekkonen's personal and long-term input, which meant that the Conference on Security and Cooperation in Europe was started and that the final stage was held in Helsinki. The Prime Minister of Denmark, Anker Jörgensen, said that the conference had been "a complete success for President Kekkonen, Finland, the Nordic countries and all the participants". President Ford said that Finland had created an exemplary picture of itself in the United States ever since the repayment of debt after the Second World War. "A country and people such as this continues to be highly regarded in the United States." The FRG's Chancellor Helmut Schmidt said that he had always admired "the excellent way in which President Kekkonen had guided his country's policy over the last 20 years."

General Secretary Brezhnev said that he greatly appreciated Finland's and President Kekkonen's personal part in bringing about the conference. "The Soviet Union is deeply grateful for this great contribution. There was a moment of confusion at the start of the meeting when the esteemed guest asked, "Where is comrade Gierek?" Due to his health, remarks made about General Secretary Brezhnev's comments at the summit were therefore diplomatic politeness.

The First Secretary of the GDR Unity Party, Erich Honecker, expressed his appreciation particularly of President Kekkonen's part in bringing about the security conference and the good work it had done. "It is a great joy and honour for the GDR delegation to be a guest in Finland and Helsinki."

The Czechoslovakian President and party leader Gustáv Husák stressed that the deep appreciation of Finland and President Kekkonen's work were

The courtesy visit by Soviet leaders to President Kekkonen: General Secretary Leonid Brezhnev, Ambassador Vladimir Stepanov, Foreign Minister Andrei Gromyko and Finnish Foreign Minister Olavi J. Mattila.

not merely compliments. Kekkonen replied that he was pleasantly surprised at this remark. "The conference was indisputably historic. Now the basis has been created, though it may be still a little unsure, from which each must proceed to implement the agreed decisions. When so much ground has been covered and a favourable atmosphere created, it is hard to imagine that we might still turn the clock back. The world had grown smaller and we all needed one another." President Husák endorsed General Secretary Brezhnev's assessment that the final document represented "as a whole, a wisely drawn up and negotiated compromise."

Several of the top guests, among them FRG Chancellor Helmut Schmidt, came to the summit conference in their own cars. (Photograph: Atte Matilainen)

Kekkonen admitted in several speeches that in the course of the journey there had been many great difficulties but they had been overcome. Hungary's party leader János Kádár said he was proud that the CSCE process had started and ended in his kindred country. It combined the active endeavours of Finland and President Kekkonen. "The CSCE was a new and better beginning, and not the conclusion of a development." Kekkonen agreed with this viewpoint. Exceptionally, he said in his discussion with Kadar that in the West there had been some press criticism of the process. This had not however posed any political difficulties. The only sensible option was to con-

Security arrangements at the Helsinki Summit. © Estate of Kari Suomalainen

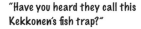
"Have you heard they call this Kekkonen's fish trap?"

tinue with the work, a matter on which he had been optimistic throughout the process.

In his discussion with Poland's party leader Edvard Gierek on 30 July, Kekkonen made the observation that also "in Finland there had been disparaging assessments of the CSCE process". He had, due to them, asked for concrete alternatives to be given but had not received any sensible answers. Gierek had asserted, "The Helsinki spirit must be preserved." The most important aim had been accomplished: the establishment of trust. The work would not end today but rather would require continuous effort by all parties. Poland was ready to give each part of the final document its appropriate weight. "The concrete issues must be brought to the fore."

There are very few clear references in the President's diary to those who along the way had openly disparaged the importance of the CSCE process and Finland's role. We can perhaps logically conclude that they belonged to that school of thought in Finland that maintained that Finland's involvement in the process had been dictated purely by adherence to its neighbourly solidarity policy and readiness to listen to wishes expressed by the Soviet Union. The question could be asked that if Finland's self-made 'added value' was not wanted or could not be recognised, why show any recognition at all? The newspaper Suomenmaa wrote on 22 July 1975 that Finland's role should not be exaggerated. There was reason to be content with a modest role.

During the discussion between Kekkonen and Giscard d'Estaing the presidents surprisingly went into the prospects for continuation of the CSCE. According to the French president, now was the time to consider how, when it came to disarmament, the middle-sized and small states would not be at the mercy of the big powers. "A level has to be found that guarantees everyone's security." Kekkonen admitted that the arms race had caused problems for small and medium-sized countries. In the view of the French president the two superpowers were all too easily invested with too much responsibility for everything. "Something should be done within the European framework. The autocracy of the two superpowers should be reduced – you couldn't get rid of it altogether."

The arrival of Portugal's new President, Costa Gomes, was one of the most dramatic. It had for some time been uncertain whether he would be able to travel to the Helsinki summit. He told President Kekkonen candidly at their meeting in Finlandia hall on 1 August that the country's domestic situation was difficult and complicated. The formation of the new government was at that moment still unfinished: "I hope we get some information about it tomorrow."

President Gomes said that the background to the problems was 48 years of dictatorship. The aim now was to change to socialism and to develop Portugal, taking into account its special conditions. "There was no precedent for the transition."

President Kekkonen commented on what his Portuguese counterpart told him and tried to console him. "Finland was in a slightly similar situation in 1944. It took unlimited patience to survive it." Finland sought to express solidarity with Portugal's new leaders by saying that "Finland did not sympathise with or have a neutral attitude to Portugal's earlier colonial policy. Now, of course, we are following what is happening in Portugal with sympathy. After the Second World War Finland had time to level the road to social justice." Kekkonen believed that "the situation in Portugal has a similar purpose."

US President Gerald Ford announced at the bilateral meeting held on 29 July in the presidential residence that Finland's outstanding post-Second World War debt could be used for continuing and expanding scholarship exchanges. Kekkonen thanked him for raising the ASLA scholarship issue in the context of the CSCE. "This sort of bilateral meeting is highly refreshing alongside a large conference."

"Christmas has gone but the presents remain"

The Helsinki Final Act was characterised in many speeches as a historical document. Many considered it to be in practice a substitute for a Second World War peace treaty. The document was not made under international law, neither was it binding on national parliaments nor did it require their ratification. Because it was signed at summit level its symbolic value and political authority was as great as it could be. The European Economic Community adopted it via Aldo Moro, the Prime Minister of Italy, the EEC Presidency country. He signed the final document among the formal group of signatories. In this way, the socialist countries finally had to recognise the Community's authority in the CSCE process and, thus, more broadly as a party to European security.

Bearing in mind the historical background of the CSCE process, it was clear that General Secretary Brezhnev's speech would be closely followed. He said that in the view of millions of people there were expectations and hopes linked with the CSCE that had not been awakened by any other collective measure since the Second World War. He gave an assurance in his speech, and in other comments, that the Soviet Union would put all the decisions of the final document into practice.

The big power leaders of the West were, together with President Ford, pleasantly surprised by Brezhnev's speech. They appreciated the fact that the Soviet Union did not try to take the credit for the materialisation of the summit conference. Brezhnev was instead satisfied with saying that in such a situation there were neither winners nor losers.

The spectrum and diversity of speeches delivered at the summit conference confirmed the view that there were as many interpretations of the final document as there were participants. Expectations for realizing the action programme of the final document varied greatly. The main differences were over whether what was then agreed was an affirmation of Europe's current status quo, or whether the final document signified a new kind of cooperation among states, paving the way for a new dynamic in international relations. The difference between public activity and government activity was considerable, depending on the system. Nevertheless the information technology already developed would in part have the effect that national borders and barriers between countries would gradually recede.

The British delegation led by Prime Minister Harold Wilson arrives for the summit conference. Second from the left is the UK ambassador to Helsinki Anthony Elliot. (Photograph: Atte Matilainen)

President Kekkonen drew attention in his speech to the international appreciation and recognition of Finland's foreign policy, for which he thanked the Finnish people for their broad support. "Value your own situation and value that of others", "Security and cooperation are not about putting up fences but opening doors". Such statements, in addition to factual analyses of the final document, have remained as permanent expressions of Finland's, the host country's, interpretation of its position in the CSCE.

Had Finland's position and room for manoeuvre over the pervious six years altered or perhaps expanded? External assessments of how Finland acted in the

A Finnish export-minded break from the official programme of the summit conference: US President Gerald Ford inspects an icebreaker. Secretary of State Henry Kissinger is third from right.
(Photograph: Atte Matilainen)

CSCE had changed considerably from the opening at Dipoli in 1972 up to the Helsinki summit in 1975. A widespread observation was that the attitude of the socialist camp's representatives was very favourable. The impression given was that the progress of the CSCE, from their point of view, generally supported the goals of the socialist camp.

When we compare the report of the British Ambassador, Anthony Elliott, on the first conference of foreign ministers in June 1973 with his report at the end of the summit conference in August 1975 the difference is remarkable. The 1973 report reflects strong suspicion of the motives for the Finnish endeavours and the closeness of Soviet and Finnish bilateral relations. As further justification for this, Elliott stated at the time of the Dipoli talks that because of its duties as host Finland did not blend with the group of European neutral countries.

In August 1975 the tone of Ambassador Elliott's report was totally different. He wrote that he understood the motives underlying Finland's foreign policy, notably the pursuit of a clearly Finnish policy of neutrality in the Europe of the CSCE period. He appreciated the way in which Finland had acted in Geneva as a delegation and Finland's management of the practical arrangements for the Helsinki summit conference.

The French Ambassador Gérard André met with President Kekkonen on the former's departure from Helsinki on 15 October 1975. He had not agreed with those Western assessments that had belittled the significance of the CSCE. He voiced his astonishment at the behaviour of the Soviet Union, which had gone remarkably further in making concessions than he had expected. Finland had, in André's opinion, performed a great service within the CSCE.

In an interview with the 8 November 1975 issue of the magazine Eteenpäin President Kekkonen said that the CSCE had become the permanent meaning of Finland's position in the world.

Councillor of State Harri Holkeri was involved in Finnish policy during the entire period under review, from the beginning of the 1970s to his period as Prime Minister and the holding of the Vienna follow-up conference. From the start of that period he worked for a long time in the political opposition – in the National Coalition Party – and in the final stage as Prime Minister. During conversations with him in summer 2006 he recalled the CSCE's activities as part of the construction of Finland's foreign policy consensus. The National Coalition Party, too, whose other views placed it permanently out in the cold, gave almost unqualified support to the national CSCE project. When asked what the significance of the CSCE was for Finland after the 1975 summit conference, Holkeri, without a moment's hesitation, replied: "Christmas had gone but the presents remained."

Finland inspects CSCE practices

With the arrival of autumn came the shift from being host of the summit conference to the everyday reality of the CSCE. The change was considerable. In place of speeches it was time to have a closer look at the possible impact of the decisions taken on Finland's administrative behaviour domestically, bilaterally with the CSCE countries and multilaterally with the organisations mentioned in the final document, such as the UN, the ECE and UNESCO. Because the recommendations of the final document were not juridically binding, the assessment of administrative behaviour could be carried out fairly flexibly and with broad-minded political appraisal.

The government presented a report to Parliament on the CSCE. It was delivered by Foreign Minister Olavi J. Mattila on 27 November 1975. At the same time as the report was prepared the CSCE final document was printed in separate Finnish and Swedish editions – 65,000 copies in Finnish and 5,000 in Swedish. A few newspapers also published the text of the final document in full.

In presenting the CSCE report to Parliament, Foreign Minister Mattila went over the whole historical background of the European security conference, from the time of the 5 May 1969 memorandum.

Matttila said that the 10 principles corresponded well to Finland's national interests. These emphasised the sovereignty of states and the prohibition of violating values and interests that were important to Finland. Finland had no special interests to be defended.

From the outset Finland supported attempts to reduce military confrontation and to promote disarmament in Europe. The final document stated the complementary nature of security from political and military perspectives. The cooperation between Finland and the other neutral and non-aligned countries had had a clear influence on the outcome of this passage of the final document.

The field of commercial cooperation was a strongly familiar area in Finland at the time of the negotiations. According to the Foreign Minister, the EEC countries comprised a representative core of market economy countries in the negotiating process. The Finnish reference group consisted of the Nordic and the neutral countries. When trying to promote compromises, the neutral countries naturally considered the interests of the market economy countries as the point of departure.

Mattila said that from the Finnish stance it was particularly useful to follow comprehensive talks in which East-West commercial questions were dealt with in the current stage of integration.

Regulations were set down on business contacts and facilities, information exchange and marketing, which served organisations, enterprises, businesses and personnel operations in all respects. The preamble to the section on industrial cooperation was mostly prepared on the basis of discussions led by the Finns. The section covered the process of industrial cooperation, from first contacts to final implementation. The section also contained a separate clause on cooperation projects. Separate sections on standardization and arbitration were drawn up for Basket II. Active joint work by Finland, Austria, and Switzerland had brought about definite results on the harmonization of standards. The subsection on scientific and technological research listed 14 areas for cooperation in which activity was already under way at either bilateral or multilateral level.

The 1972 UN conference on the environment, held in Stockholm, acted as a catalyst for putting environmental issues on the CSCE agenda. The experience of the Stockholm conference was that activity was dispersed. The hope was to centralise it. At the Geneva talks the main principles and forms and methods of cooperation on the environment were registered for the final document. Concerning the forms and methods of cooperation, much was used in the form presented by Finland, including numerous references to the special position of the ECE in connection with follow-up.

Basket III, broadly speaking bilateral and multilateral cooperation in humanitarian and other fields, represented compromises, according to Mattila. The original proposals differed greatly from one another. Despite the prevailing differences in systems, there was now cooperation "to reach a new stage linked closely to the final document's creation of a different entity."

New terrain was covered in the area of human contacts and information exchange. Although there were no automatic solutions provided for the manifest problems in relation to these issues, the participating states had decided to improve the general frameworks for resolving humanitarian issues. Basket III supplemented the dimensions of the CSCE at the individual level. The concepts of peace and security were given more active content – it was no longer merely the absence of war but also increasing the construction of relations among people.

In the area of information exchange, a new subject was the improvement in opportunities for journalists to work in other CSCE countries. Increase in the exchangeability of information did not delve into questions of the content of material. The general aim was to diversify information.

At the end of March 1977 Finland's Consulate General in Leningrad was able to confirm information based on Soviet Estonian sources, according to which Soviet citizens had been offered the possibility to order certain foreign newspapers. The only Finnish newspaper in the permitted list was the communist *Tiedonantaja*.

The development of cooperation in the areas of culture and education continued from the point which UNESCO's work on the 1972 EUROCULT conference had reached. The recommendations then contained politically charged issues, such as the establishment of reading rooms and cultural centres. A key question arose in connection with increasing cooperation on the matter of cultural minorities and small languages.

Détente – atmosphere, method and substance

In defining détente and the internal relations of the CSCE it was important to be precise and to clearly differentiate one from the other. They were not a hundred percent commensurate with one another. It is a trap you do not want to fall into, wrote the British Ambassador to Washington in a report. The implementation of agreed decisions was important. But it should not be built up into a threshold issue and a conditional criterion that could lead to the discontinuation of the détente process at the next follow-up conference, in Belgrade in 1977.

It then seemed that the Soviet government decided to classify publicly those who doubted the sincerity of Soviet policy as 'enemies of détente'. The Americans stressed that the CSCE did not entirely cover the operational field of détente. For Washington, and particularly Kissinger, the Vienna MBFR negotiations were of greater symbolic importance than the CSCE.

In the preparations for the 1975 summit conference and President Kekkonen's speech, Ambassador Iloniemi drew up a draft in which he explained line by line the phrasing and the message of the speech. This was the occasion when Iloniemi set out for the first time what was understood in Finland by détente.

A positive aspect of détente was that it facilitated contacts between peoples and enriched the lives of individuals. The claim that détente acted only in favour of nations at the expense of individuals was, in Iloniemi's view, a tendentious allegation. Fences were lowered as tensions eased. Iloniemi did not state directly that the interpretation of many Western countries corresponded to Finland's interpretation of the relationship between détente and the commitments in the final document. The lowering of fences with the advance of détente was the traditional precondition of the Soviet Union and the socialist countries for further and increased cooperation.

When presenting the government report on the CSCE to Parliament in November 1975, Foreign Minister Mattila ended by saying that the attempts in Finnish foreign policy to improve the preconditions for cooperation between East and West and the solution of problems were the contribution of the CSCE to longlasting political confrontation. The CSCE was seen in Finland "as a fruitful method by which we can further the policy of easing tensions realistically and step by step". The relaxation of tension was the overall objective of the conference. The same aim would, according to Mattila, govern the follow-up process, which was started in Helsinki following the summit conference. Against this background the form and content of relations were often described as examples of the productive development of détente between two different social systems.

The Soviet Union wanted to further "the materialization of détente" by extending it to the military arena thus publicly conveying the impression that the Soviet Union was no longer a danger or, on the other hand, that opposition to all Soviet policy was pointless.

The FRG's Foreign Minister Hans Dietrich Genscher visited Moscow in November 1975 and there discussed the essence of détente with Foreign Minister Gromyko. Genscher's assumption was that the aim of détente was to be a universal concept of peacekeeping. The creation in Europe of Gesamtkonzept der Friedenssicherung.

Genscher did not forget to refer to the FRG's hopes for the peaceful unification of Germany. He also made this point in his speech on 8 October 1976 to the UN General Assembly. He emphasised that due to the CSCE the participating states had expressed their readiness to compete in the area of ideas and opinions. "It did not mean that as a consequence of détente the different social systems would meld together. Gromyko responded that the aim of the Soviet Union was that détente would be made irrevocable.

During the period after the Helsinki summit conference and the preparations for the Belgrade follow-up conference the EEC countries' security policy analysts were required to arrive at a common view of détente. The working group on the CSCE reached a common understanding on 2 November 1976 on the definition of détente. According to the draft of this "the countries of the West understood détente as a policy that respects the different political concepts/ideas in East-West relations." According to this interpretation, the definition by the Soviet Union and its allies of "peaceful coexistence" also contained new political and ideological areas. This therefore meant seeking immutable objectives with new methods. The concept of the détente process was burdened by a fundamental lack of definition. There had been an effort to streamline it so that it would be more understandable: "Some want peace without victories, others want victories without war."

Secretary of State Henry Kissinger attended, for the last time, the NATO council of ministers conference, which was held in Brussels on 9 December 1976. Kissinger now recognised that the policy of détente had been shown to be the only correct and possible policy of the Western alliance. The participants at the conference must have listened to this with some surprise. Kissinger's reasons were the following:

- No single NATO member country could claim on the basis of its domestic policy not to be working for peaceful aims.
- The attempt to dispel the causes of disputes were irrefutable and worthwhile.
- The policy of détente set incentives for the Soviet Union to behave with restraint.

To those critics of détente who assumed that the process stripped the Western alliance of its moral arms and that the strong military alliance was unable to create good relations with its eastern neighbours, Kissinger replied that from now on Western governments should show a greater understanding towards the policy of détente. The prevailing difficulties were not due to "us but them". According to Kissinger, the Soviet Union had in these conditions to struggle with massive problems. It had only achieved success when it had used military force. In other respects the socialist countries that had been in power for the last 30 years still appeared to be suffering from a crisis of legitimacy in Eastern Europe.

The original objective of the readiness and ability of the Soviet Union and the other socialist countries to "control" the terms of the development of détente in the end remained a fantasy. The final document's recommendations on humanitarian matters and information exchange were increasingly starting to take on a life of their own. The implications were long-term and inestimable.

When Jimmy Carter was elected US President in November 1976, the significance and functional use of détente in US policy changed decisively. During his election campaign, Carter had openly stated that US involvement in the CSCE should be reconsidered. The US must take a stricter stance on the Soviet Union's détente policy. He called for a more aggressive policy.

In his report on the international situation, delivered to the Parliamentary foreign affairs committee on 16 November 1976, Foreign Minister Keijo Korhonen assumed that the US involvement in the Belgrade follow-up conference would be more active than previously and, particularly on the Basket III issues, tougher. The Carter administration expected a more conspicuous détente and a more integrated international system than its predecessor. The ideological struggle was intensifying and tension increasing. Moral issues were given more emphasis in Carter's policy programme.

The basic point about détente was to bring the Cold War to an end, Ambassador Dubinin said in an interview in Moscow in June 2007. The ten principles of the Helsinki final document meant for the Soviet Union a practical guide for peaceful coexistence. In this respect the Helsinki summit conference was a big step forward in a process that had begun with the death of Stalin. It was understood as signifying the gradual opening up of Soviet society to the rest of the world, step by step. Before the adoption of the CSCE decisions, foreign travel and particularly travel to the Western world had been tightly controlled and was generally only the privilege of the Soviet elite.

On 22 June 1977 the Soviet Union and France issued a declaration, signed by Brezhnev on his visit to France, which aimed to strengthen the irrevocability of détente. The declaration contained the first joint East-West comprehensive interpretation of the development of détente at government level. As the veteran Soviet Ambassador to the CSCE, Yuri Dubinin, states in his memoirs (2001/2002) this was the first time that the main ingredients and characteristics of détente were written down in full:

- Détente was by its nature universal; it was an international political objective.
- Political détente must be supplemented by military détente, particularly by taking preventive measures in the area of disarmament.
- Détente cannot be merely limited to being a matter between the military alliances.
- The document also referred to respect for human rights and freedom of expression.
- In order to eliminate disputes and the threat of war, states must coordinate their activities.
- States and civil society must demonstrate greater solidarity before the threats that hang over them.
- In this spirit, all the principles of the Helsinki final document were to be put into effect.

Dubinin described the declaration as having "a stimulating effect on international relations." The same autumn, the UN General Assembly adopted a corresponding resolution on the stabilisation of international détente. This came at the right time, as the Belgrade follow-up conference was heading for a new type of crisis. The speeches in Belgrade emphasising the vitality of détente had left practical matters in the background.

In 1980 Klaus Törnudd analysed the perspective of Finland's security policy in a work dealing with the future visions of détente in relation to the CSCE process. He wrote that the concept of détente was a new one. The UN Charter was not acquainted with it. In day-to-day language it was used as a synonym for 'peace' and 'peaceful coexistence'. These were too one-dimensional and ideologically charged. With détente there was a desire to eliminate tension, mistrust and the Cold War atmosphere. In this respect, the Helsinki final document offered as yet unused opportunities, regardless of the fact that there was no clear dynamic built into it. In order that the expectations directed towards it could be preserved there would have to be more done for its implementation than had otherwise been the case. A new characteristic of the final document's programme for détente was the continual series of negotiations between the participating states.

The third Parliamentary committee on defence issued a report in March 1981 stating that the détente process had, since the end of the 1960s, been able to reduce the risk of a major confrontation between the superpowers in Europe. Now that the international situation and atmosphere had become strained, the report continued, conceptions of the meaning of détente had evidently been different since the start of the process. In the view of the committee, the goals of détente were a ban on the use of force, the deepening of commercial, scientific and technological cooperation, cooperation on matters of security and the maintenance of military armament at a low level. Not all of this had so far materialised. Military armament, in particular, appeared to be continuing strongly.

In examining visions of European security the report found that détente had offered the neutral and non-aligned countries improved possibilities to influence matters concerning European security. "The CSCE process made possible a more active dialogue between the military alliances and across borders." Détente and the CSCE had not been able, however, to carry out what was necessary for a real breakthrough in the area of disarmament. The European military equation continued to rely on parity between the two leading powers of the military alliances, the Soviet Union and the USA.

The CSCE changes shape

A national report into the possible impact of the Helsinki final document on Finnish administrative practices was commissioned in autumn 1975. A general observation, that became a virtual mantra, was that the Helsinki final document did not necessitate any new administrative or legislative decisions in Finland. In particular, in the relations between Finland and the socialist countries, and in discussions among those countries themselves, it was emphasized that in many fields interaction surpassed the stipulations of the CSCE final document. In these statements it was acknowledged by both sides that the impacts of the CSCE would be followed up in interaction with the socialist countries in particular. Finland had not succumbed in its conference speeches to dealing with country-specific problems. It had adhered to the Dipoli recommendations, the *Blue Book*, in examining matters on a subject-specific basis.

In January 1976 Foreign Minister Kalevi Sorsa held talks with Foreign Minister Gromyko, in which Mr Sorsa stressed that the relations between their countries developed extremely favourably on the basis of the treaty of friendship, cooperation and mutual assistance. The treaty was still up-to-date in all its parts and as a whole. It was also fully in harmony with the CSCE final document. The CSCE reinforced Finland's national security and supported Finland in exercising its peaceful policy of neutrality in the same spirit as the treaty.

One reason why Sorsa stressed the importance of the treaty with the Soviet Union may have been the response of the Soviet Embassy in Helsinki to the Finnish government report. Sorsa had organised a farewell lunch for Hungary's outgoing Ambassador to Helsinki, Rudolf Ronai, on 8 December 1975. The

Soviet Ambassador Vladimir Stepanov was there too, and he criticised the report on the CSCE by the foreign minister of the previous government, Olavi J. Mattila: "There was not one word of reference to the treaty." The Embassy's number two, Mikhail Streltsov, had also expressed his surprise at this when he invited State Secretary Matti Tuovinen for a sauna on 10 December. The Finnish report had strongly emphasised neutrality – both the right to neutrality and the general roles of the neutral countries in the CSCE. Streltsov had asked why the treaty had been forgotten.

As examples of the implementation of the final document, Sorsa mentioned multiple visas and the improvement in the Soviet Union of the working conditions of press correspondents from abroad, including Finland. The final document was both a declaration of principles and an action programme, on the results of which it was too early to draw conclusions. Implementation had also started in some international organizations, for example the ECE and Unesco. That there was positive progress was indisputable. The final document had been made widely known and the intention was to include it in school curricula, according to the principle of permeation, as had been done with peace education. Sorsa believed that public opinion in Finland was in favour of the CSCE. The overall aim was to move the development of détente realistically forward step by step.

Sorsa gave his assurance that the close contacts between foreign ministries on the CSCE would continue. He also announced that the Nordic foreign ministers had decided to include the CSCE on the agenda of their half-yearly meetings. The case was the same with contacts among the foreign ministers of the neutral countries, which had been established in the days of the Geneva negotiations. The aim now was to keep an eye on preparations for the Belgrade follow-up. Sorsa affirmed that Finland would continue to be active in taking the CSCE process forward.

The neutral countries' cooperation and preparations for the Belgrade follow-up were from this point on a particular source of interest, both in Moscow and the Soviet Embassy in Helsinki. The heads of the political departments of the foreign ministries of the neutrals met on 29 April 1976 in Helsinki, at the invitation of Iloniemi. It was to be their first meeting since the summit conference. The agenda included the preparations for the Belgrade follow-up conference.

The first CSCE country with which Finland raised the issue of human contacts was Romania. On 31 May 1976 the chargé d'affaires at the Romanian Embassy in Helsinki was sent a note requesting that certain open issues concerning Finnish-Romanian marriages be favourably resolved.

On the issue of the voluntary prior notification of military manoeuvres and the inviting of observers to attend them, senior officials of the Foreign Ministry decided on 5 April to monitor existing experiences and practices before Finland itself would decide on notification.

Dissidents and Finland

The organisation of the Soviet secret service was changed in 1954 when Nikita Khrushchev became leader of the Soviet communist party, CPSU. The institution was renamed. Instead of the secret service it became the committee for state security, or KGB. It was made into an institution to work more closely with the party leadership and it was stripped of certain powers, such as the right to hold trials. It retained the right to arrest people, investigate their activities and prepare cases for trial.

Khrushchev's earlier criticism of Stalin gave rise to the idea that citizens could differ in opinion with the authorities to a certain extent. Dissidents became more actively fearless. Article 70 of the penal code was adopted in 1956. It defined as punishable political activity that involved anti-Soviet agitation and propaganda. The preparation, dissemination and collection of anti-Soviet literature were punishable offences. The law was supplemented in 1966 by Article 190, which was of a more general nature. Labelled as criminal was activity "which disseminated false information and which was offensive to the Soviet states and the socialist system". Samizdat publishing, the clandestine copying and distribution of banned or dissident literature, flourished.

The status and esteem of the KGB grew. Its operational capacity improved so that it became the main monitoring authority concerning all forms of opposition, whether by dissidents, other sources of opposition or Jewish activity.

In 1968 the Chronicle of Current Events began to be published in Paris. The aim of the publication was to provide information on actual events in the context of Article 19 of the UN Declaration of Human Rights: "Everyone has the right to freedom of opinion and expression; this right includes freedom to hold opinions without interference and to seek, receive and impart information and ideas through any media and regardless of frontiers."

Although the group of dissidents in the Soviet Union comprised just a few hundred activists, it was conspicuous in the media in the West. As Richard Lourie says in his biography of Andrei Saharov (2002), "At that time there was perhaps no public opinion. But that did not mean that people had no opinions."

On 13 June 1968 the KGB leader Yuri Andropov sent his first observations concerning academician Andrei Saharov to the Central Committee of the CPSU. He recommended that a Central Committee member have "an appropriate discussion with the academician in order to remove the possibility for anti-social elements to exploit the academician's politically harmful activities." The appeal by Saharov to stop censorship led to a lively debate and feedback, some from Czechoslovakia, the socialist country that from January 1968 had been governed by Alexander Dubček. 1968 happened also to be the year of the UN Declaration of Human Rights. Saharov was asked to write on the subject.

The article he wrote, in May 1968, was "Ideas for promoting coexistence and intellectual freedom." The New York Times published the article in full on 22 July 1968. Andrei Amalrik's work Will the Soviet Union last until 1984? had conveyed the article to Western journalists. The nuclear physicist further developed as a social critic and finally became a Nobel Peace Prize winner in 1975.

Alexander Solzhenitsyn was awarded the Nobel Prize for Literature on 8 October 1970. The response of the Soviet authorities was initially calm, by Soviet standards. They clearly did not want a repetition of the mistakes made with Boris Pasternak. The human rights committee was established in 1970.

At New Year 1971 Saharov wrote a letter to Brezhnev in which he continued with his reflections and announced the establishment of the human rights committee. "We hope that we are of use to society, and we hope for a dialogue with our country's leaders." The Soviet Union, he wrote, must not be the first to use atomic weapons.

Solzhenitsyn was arrested on 12 February 1974. In response an appeal was launched in Moscow demanding his release and an investigation of the crimes recounted in the Gulag Archipelago. The Politburo decided to expel him from the country, and allowed his family to accompany him to Zurich and then to the FRG.

Saharov began his first hunger strike at the time of President Nixon's state visit to Moscow, 27 June 1974, "to draw attention to the situation of political prisoners and psychiatric prisoners in the Soviet Union and the right to emigrate."

In conversation in Helsinki with Sweden's Prime Minister Olof Palme, Kalevi Sorsa referred to his meeting with Andropov during a visit by a Finnish Social Democratic Party delegation to Moscow. "Andropov made a dynamic and unusually open impression." The main changes in Soviet policy would perhaps be expected in commercial policy, not foreign policy.

President Kekkonen wrote in his diary on 20 August 1973 remarks made by Saharov to Western journalists at a press conference in Moscow: The reduction of tension without the democratisation of the Soviet Union would take the form of a dangerous easing of tension, because the West would then be accepting the Soviet Union's ground rules. This would solve none of the world's problems. Saharov urged the West to be cautious if closer relations with the Soviet Union did not lead to the democratisation of the country and an end to its isolation, in other words to the freer movement of people and freedom of communication.

As for Solzhenitsyn, the news of autumn 1974 was the debate on the publication in Finland of the Gulag Archipelago. One Day in the Life of Ivan Denisovich had appeared in Finnish in 1964. Now, all the major publishers rejected the Gulag Archipelago and the Swedish-owned publishing house Wahlström-Widstrand published it.

The inter-governmental committee on human rights and international migration put a question to the Finns in June 1976, on whether the Finnish authorities were prepared to work with the organization, which collected statistics and information on the movement of people in Europe. The enquiry was made via the Finnish Embassy in Geneva and received an answer from the Foreign Ministry only in October. A confidential working memo stressed that the problems related to the issue were "extremely few" in Finland and that the examination of open questions by the state authorities involved was already under way: "It was best to take care of them on a bilateral basis."

Director general Klaus Törnudd and head of section Arto Mansala from the Foreign Ministry wrote a thorough analysis of détente from the Soviet stance. Centre place in the 25-page report was given to the position and treatment of dissidents. According to the report, the group of dissidents was extremely heterogeneous. It represented a variety of views. They were scattered around, working in Moscow and some other large cities. The number of intellectuals who were active comprised, according to cautious Western estimates, "a group of a few thousand". The Soviet authorities appeared to have reached some sort of modus vivendi in dealing with them. There was a clampdown on public speech but the attitude to the emigration of dissidents was more flexible.

In autumn 1976, Andropov had given a speech to Soviet leaders in which he said that the activity of dissidents had become possible only because "socialism's opponents had been able to forge networks with the Western press, diplomats and intelligence and other services". On the other hand he admitted that it was no wonder if among the 250 million-strong population there was one person who thought differently from the majority. The Foreign Ministry report concluded that the possibilities for dissidents to act had recently decreased rather than grown.

In June 2006, State Secretary Matti Tuovinen said that the Soviet dissidents and Estonian emigrants were a subject that official Finland wanted to keep separate. "Their stated public Finnish opinions did not help their cause in the slightest, but only disrupted the bilateral relations between our countries."

As Eric Hobsbawm says, the dissident infection spread to other socialist countries. There was everywhere a desire to test the tolerance of the authorities and the boundaries of artistic activity and free expression. The East German cabaret singer Wolf Biermann received the startling news on 17 November 1976 while on a concert tour of the FRG that he had been stripped of his GDR citizenship and was banned from returning home. The reasons for the decision were given by the SED Politburo the next day. Biermann was accused of "gravely violating his responsibilities as a GDR citizen and of hostile actions against the GDR".

The legacy of the ideological war

Ideological matters were not clearly approached when the principles of the Helsinki final document were confirmed. There was an attempt to avoid confrontation in formulating the texts. The relationship between many principles could be read in such a way that the requirements of honest competition between different ideologies and economic systems preserved some sort of balance. There was a movement from many quarters to "an intense mental struggle" in which the fronts were multifaceted, methods were both open and concealed and sights were usually set well beyond traditional frontlines.

The change in the language used in the socialist camp from Cold War vocabulary to the parlance of cooperation and détente could be seen during the first CSCE conference of foreign ministers and in the adoption of the mandate of the negotiations. The consistent work of the forces of peace had achieved a turnaround, which paved the way for the European security conference that had long been sought by the socialist camp. Its main objective had been to strengthen peace, prevent the start of a Third World War, expose the aims of the imperialist forces and above all confirm the post-war situation of Europe. Prime place in this was the inviolability of borders and recognition of the GDR. To Poland, international confirmation of its western border was important.

The statements of the Warsaw Treaty countries faithfully repeated the peace programme of the CPSU's 24th congress and also acknowledged it as a key objective of the CSCE. At a world congress of communist parties in Moscow on 26 October 1973, General Secretary Brezhnev touched on current challenges facing détente. He said that in the context of the policy of peaceful coexistence it was often asked whether this policy was compatible with a revolutionary world view. Brezhnev affirmed that no forces could prevent societal reform. Massive political movements were a concrete indication of this.

The Soviet government did not market revolution as an export commodity, but it felt solidarity towards all class comrades. Peaceful coexistence was a struggle on behalf of millions of people for justice and freedom from the destruction of war.

Shortly after the Helsinki summit conference, on 7 October 1975, the Soviet Union and the GDR concluded a new treaty of friendship and cooperation. During talks in Bonn on 7 July 1976, the FRG's Foreign Minister Hans Dietrich Genscher drew the attention of his Romanian counterpart to the fact that there was a thesis written into the treaty according to which the principles of the CSCE final document covered "the relations of groups of states with other groups of states". Even after the signing of the final document, there was a wish for relations between Moscow and East Berlin to affirm the topicality and validity of the Brezhnev doctrine.

Romania's Foreign Minister Macovescu, admitted that already at the time of the Geneva negotiations of 1973-75 such ideas had been put forward by the Soviet Union. "They were against the Romanian standpoint." On the other hand, according to the Romanians, there had been a satisfactory outcome at the conference of European communist and workers parties held in East Berlin in June 1976, following two years of tough party-level negotiations. Each party could independently confirm its own domestic and foreign policy and in doing so "keep an eye on defending its own national interests." Macovescu stressed that within the communist movement there were forces gathering strength that wanted to break away from the central leadership. "The Berlin conference turned into a conference of compromise."

Discussions on the CSCE's information exchange often considered the working principles and activities of Radio Liberty and Radio Free Europe, and the same was true of the BBC's and the Voice of America's programmes directed at Eastern Europe. The first of these operated from West German soil and had been transmitting since troops from the victorious Western powers had been installed there. At the time of the Geneva negotiations their activities had not yet led to any insuperable disputes.

It is likely that the Soviet representatives worked from the assumption that because the ideological struggle was, in principle, continuing, it was impossible for the Soviet Union to require the radio stations to cease operations, even though that had often been suggested in discussions. On the other hand, Western analysts could appeal to sections of the final document, recently approved, based on which access to foreign information should be unhindered, without the issue of content being used as a filter from the stance of the recipients.

At talks in Bonn on 11 June 1976 between German Chancellor Helmut Schmidt and Poland's communist party General Secretary Edward Gierek, Chancellor Schmidt openly admitted that the operation of Radio Free Europe and Radio Liberty from German territory was a violation of the FRG's right to self-determination and of its sovereignty. He said that the federal government had extremely limited possibilities to intervene in the matter. He had complained about this to his American colleagues President Gerald Ford and Secretary of State Henry Kissinger. Kissinger had personally agreed that the radio stations' operations should rightly be stopped. He understood that in many ways they strained the FRG's bilateral relations with Eastern Europe. According to Kissinger, however, some in the US Congress considered that the continuation of the radio stations was particularly important.

Detente ecstacy abates

The Parliamentary foreign affairs committee in Finland submitted a report on 3 June 1976. It dealt with the situation in Europe mainly in terms of the perspective and spirit of the CSCE. The easing of superpower tension was described as a characteristic factor in the European situation. "European security remains based on military balance." Concerning northern Europe, it finds that the application of confidence and security building measures, approved by the CSCE, could diminish mistrust among countries belonging to the different military alliances.

A few weeks after this report was published, the US Arms Control and Disarmament Association submitted a report of its own to President Ford, on 29 July. The Soviet Union's armed forces had started to deploy new SS-20 medium-range missiles. The range of the multiple warhead missiles was less than 5,500 kilometres. The range of the missiles with a single nuclear warhead and otherwise lighter payload was, however, as far as 9,500 kilometres. The report estimated that due to these weapons the nuclear threat in Europe had grown considerably, both quantitatively and qualitatively.

The Soviet press had drawn its readers' attention in autumn 1976 to the fact that the NATO countries had, a year after signing the Helsinki Final Act, held massive military manoeuvres in the border region of the Warsaw Treaty countries. The Soviet press accused the operation of "warmongering and being a campaign of intimidation," the aim of which was to stir up fear in the Soviet Union and its allies.

The Helsinki final document's confidence-building measures left the signatories much room for manoeuvre in observing them. Invitations to inspectors were voluntary. And based on this the Soviet Union, for example, would invite only representatives from its closest neighbouring countries. In autumn 1976 the 'Shield 76' exercise was held in Poland, to which inspectors were invited only from Finland, Sweden, Austria and Denmark. The Warsaw Treaty's representatives, conversely, were banned from attending the Teamwork exercise in Norway, even though Poland and the Soviet Union had military attachés in Oslo. This "psychological warfare, ideological confrontation" continued between the alliances. Before the Belgrade follow-up, the CSCE's modest confidence-building measures had not had time to influence countries' routine behaviour.

Western specialists and the neutral and non-aligned countries started close preparatory work together in good time before the Belgrade follow-up meeting. This work combined the interests of both the EEC and NATO. The EEC's expert CSCE working group had intended first to sketch out the general parameters of the EEC's confidence-building measures. This was necessary if, for instance, France was to be included in the joint deliberations. More detailed proposals could then be discussed among NATO experts, such as those from the US and Canada.

The assumption of the EEC and NATO experts was that the Belgrade conference must deal with both qualitative and quantitative confidence-building measures. Up to that point the actual confidence-awakening function of the measures had remained minimal. There had been noticeably fewer notifications given than the number of exercises conducted by the socialist countries above the notification threshold. The fact that the Soviet Union's notification obligation was limited only to a 250-kilometre zone along its western border gave a distorted picture of its actual manoeuvres.

Western military specialists and politicians were constantly aware that the mental battle continued at other levels. "To maintain a credible defensive capability in Western Europe, it was necessary to take into consideration the Soviet Union's superiority in Central Europe."

The Soviet Union's diplomacy for comprehensive collective security included a proposal at the UN for a worldwide ban on the use of force. Foreign Minister Gromyko made the proposal to the General Assembly in autumn 1976. This had already been supplemented by General Secretary Brezhnev at the CPSU congress in February 1976 when he presented his initiative on ending the arms race.

The NATO council of ministers, meeting on 5 November 1976, posited that the Soviet Union's disarmament activity and propaganda were clearly contradictory to its arms build-up on land and at sea. Disarmament was naturally directed at the West, at the same time as the Soviet Union sought to present a sense of duty and responsibility as a global power, particularly towards the third world.

This sort of challenge had to be answered from the Western side. The Soviet Union's readiness to promote détente had to be tested in as many zones of activity as possible. "While the CSCE recommendations cannot by themselves decisively change the Soviet system, they must influence it, so that the Soviet Union pays more attention to respecting human rights."

On the other hand, the weak economic condition of Eastern Europe and indebtedness to the West meant that the Americans, for one, regarded Eastern Europe as an area of potential instability. "The countries of Eastern Europe were sovereign states and had to be treated as independent units, so that room to manoeuvre could be created for them in their relations with the Soviet Union."

Nature of CSCE alters

Following the Helsinki summit conference, it was decided to hold the first follow-up meeting in Belgrade. The preparatory meeting for this started on 15 June and the follow-up meeting proper on 4 October 1977. The meeting was organised at record speed in the newly built SAVA conference centre. There was plenty of space. The conference centre was located away from the city centre and other built-up areas.

At the same time as the preparations were carried out, there was once again an appraisal of what precisely had been decided in Helsinki. In addition, the Council of NATO had stated unanimously at its conference in Brussels on 5 November 1976 that the adoption of the Helsinki Final Act had marked the climax of détente. "The vitality of the détente process has since weakened." But at the same time it had to be continually borne in mind that détente was a long-term process that required patience and trust, because "the ideological goal of détente is undisputedly more difficult to bring about." In its own work the West had to stress that détente was indivisible and global.

The Helsinki Final Act was a politically binding international document. There were no time frames or deadlines set for putting the tangible decisions into effect. It was unrealistic to expect that only two years after the Helsinki summit the majority of decisions would have been realized. In the implementation discussion the general state of bilateral relations became decisive. The weaker and more insubstantial relations were, the tougher the criticism expected.

Finland's stance in the preparations for the discussion on implementation had been that it preferred to talk about its own actions rather than criticise others. Finland was also prepared to put the Basket III stipulations into effect without reservation or selectivity. Nor were any additional conditions on them expected at the Belgrade meeting. It was seen that decisions concerning national matters of the participating states in part contributed to the enlargement of the concept of security, by, for example, increasing the credibility of détente and improving its prerequisites. Increasing access to information and interaction were improving mutual trust among peoples.

In a memo of 15 March 1977, Markku Reimaa says that appeals to authority and the use of just certain parts of the Final Act as means of exerting pressure would not promote the general preconditions for the future of détente and fix the development of the CSCE's ground rules. Instead, such practices were often dictated by short-range objectives. Long-term ones were important so that the Final Act would retain its dynamism. For this reason Finland intended to stress continuity in the discussion on human rights in Belgrade.

Various follow-up groups were established in the West to examine developments. The US Congress set up a CSCE commission in autumn 1976. Its first chairperson was the democrat Dante Fascell of Florida. The long-term general secretary of the commission was Spencer Oliver, who later worked as head of the CSCE and OSCE's parliamentary office in Copenhagen.

In autumn 1976 the US Congressional CSCE commission went on an extensive introductory tour of Europe. The original aim was to include visits to the socialist countries and ascertain how the CSCE's decisions had been implemented. However, the members of the commission were refused visas. Kissinger could have called the Soviet Ambassador in Washington, Anatoly Dobrynin, and asked for the visas not to be granted as in Kissinger's view the NGO level had no role in matters of this kind. The conclusions drawn in various parts of the West were that the socialist countries were not ready to openly discuss implementation. Fascell's commission, for its part, received abundant publicity and a sounding board in Congress.

Reports from the Finnish Embassy in Washington in autumn 1976 and spring 1977 confirm that the CSCE commission was established against President Ford's and Dr Kissinger's wishes. They thought that the work of the commission would denote interference with executive matters.

The Embassy cited a *New York Times* article, which stated that the US delegation must take a "firm stand" on human rights issues. The preparations of the Soviet Union to participate in the debate on this were good. Yuli Vorontsov, the long-time number two at the Soviet Embassy in Washington, had been appointed leader of the delegation in Belgrade.

When Fascell's delegation announced its readiness to pay a visit to Finland, a programme was prepared for the commission that, according to Iloniemi, resembled a state visit. Fascell met President Kekkonen in Helsinki on 15 November 1976. Kekkonen wrote in his diary: "Fascell was optimistic that the spirit of Helsinki would spread."

Finland made careful preparations for the Belgrade meeting. In the space of a year Finland held over 60 rounds of talks with representatives of many CSCE countries. These talks included assessments at a general level of the outcome of the Helsinki summit, the development of détente and the initial preparations for the follow-up meeting. When in 1977 Iloniemi made closer contacts with the CSCE capitals, his message was: "Belgrade should be a contribution to détente, not a test of it."

Détente was the prevailing circumstance and nurturing it required concrete measures. At the same time, avoiding a Belgrade "test" was a signal from the Finns that a tribunal-like first follow-up meeting was not thought desirable.

The Russians had various problems concerning Belgrade. In the West, various NGOs had clearly become active on the basis of the CSCE Final Act. President Carter had made human rights one of his political priorities. Emphasis on these priorities was counter to the oft-repeated stance of the socialist countries that the Final Act should be viewed as a whole and that individual details could not be detached from it for separate implementation.

When Iloniemi visited Moscow in February 1977 to meet Ambassador Lev Mendelevich, the latter stressed that a "constructive political conception" should be agreed upon in advance for the Belgrade meeting. The main aim would be to show that it was a working meeting. It could not compete with Helsinki. Mendelevich thought it important that Finland continued with its sustainable policy, which aimed at the success of détente and the realization of the Soviet Union's and Finland's common goals.

Preparatory meeting gives no early warning of collision

Iloniemi, as Undersecretary of State, attended the preparatory meeting in Belgrade in June 1977. He thought the situation encouraging. The US delegation had instructions to focus on the meeting proper and to avoid disputes and issues of a delicate political nature. The bilateral talks between the heads of the US and Soviet delegations, Ambassadors Sherer and Vorontsov, had dealt with matters broadly, candidly and in a friendly spirit.

The US delegation's instructions were that human rights questions must be handled with restraint, refraining from criticism of governments by name. This corresponded with the line agreed at the meeting of EEC foreign ministers in London on 18 April. According to a British representative at the meeting, consensus prevailed that human rights would be raised in Belgrade in a way that did "not provoke" and stayed closely within the framework of the Helsinki Final Act.

Ambassador Sherer said, however, that by the autumn the situation might change, because it was "expected that Senate and Congressional representatives would be in Belgrade". This gave the prior impression of unexpected and perhaps serious risk factors for reasons of domestic policy. There had been no prior discussions concerning the visit of the senators and congressmen. From the standpoint of the State Department the situation was new. Dante Fascell's CSCE commission might visit Belgrade *in corpore*.

US State Department officials had a closer dialogue with Czechoslovakia's representatives during the Belgrade meeting than with the Soviet Union. They did not, however, get to meet dissidents and Václav Havel, one of the founders of Charter 77. The Congressional CSCE commission were then gradually granted visas to Poland, Hungary and Yugoslavia. But it was not until the Gorbachev era that they were granted visas to the Soviet Union.

At the preparatory meeting both West and East made comprehensive proposals for arrangements at the follow-up meeting. The differences between them were traditional. The West thought that the work at the Belgrade meeting should be divided into two parts, namely detailed examination of the implementation of decisions and the future development of cooperation and détente. The Soviet Union thought that the issues should be examined as a whole. Neither side made any reference to a sequel to the Belgrade meeting or a new conference.

The neutral and non-aligned countries made a supplementary proposal at the preparatory meeting, where, in addition to the implementation of the Final Act and an analysis of the European situation, matters of cooperation after Belgrade were discussed in detail with emphasis on the importance of continuity. Iloniemi's visit was put to further good use in the sense that the Finnish approach in particular to the working procedures of the follow-up meeting was outlined to the heads of the US and Soviet delegations. There would be a discussion on the implementation of each of the principles of the Final Act and an assessment of current and future measures. This procedure was similarly applied to the three sub-committees.

On leaving Belgrade Iloniemi could say that the Finnish delegation's working procedures with both superpower delegations was trustworthy and close.

At the closure of the preparatory meeting in early August, Esko Rajakoski had to state that the wind was against the active agents of détente. Relations between Moscow and Washington were strained and the SALT talks were at a standstill. President Carter's strong emphasis on human rights was colouring the CSCE discussions. The Middle East situation, the Vienna MBFR negotiations – all were regressing due to the current atmosphere. Despite all this, in Belgrade some exact working procedures for the follow-up meeting had been agreed upon regardless of differing points of departure.

The West's overall attitude to the CSCE forum had changed for the better, while that of the socialist countries had become cautious. Soviet Ambassador Vorontsov had said that the work at Belgrade was not based on the experience of Geneva or the Helsinki model. A new basis had now been agreed, which meant the start of a new era.

Finland's involvement continues – alone and with the other neutrals

Part of the continuity of the CSCE was established by Finland in Geneva through a separate policy unit of the permanent mission, headed by Ambassador Esko Rajakoski, following the 1975 summit. Its task was to monitor both the CSCE and the disarmament negotiations. The Geneva unit was centrally involved in the preparations for Belgrade.

Ilomiemi took the initiative in November 1975 to find out whether the three other neutral countries were prepared to continue with the work among the neutrals started in Geneva with talks among the heads of the political departments. Early 1976 was suggested as the date for a meeting in Helsinki. In reports compiled for Bern, Stockholm and Vienna it was stated that the aim would be to clarify how joint activities could be continued in the preparations for the Belgrade follow-up meeting "informally and without predetermined procedures."

The matter was initially tested in connection with events such as the visit by the Finnish President to Sweden. Interest in it was forthcoming. The intention was to focus on the handling of each current issue. Because what was involved was the preparations for Belgrade, there had to be separate agreement on how Yugoslavia, as the host country, could be included. In Helsinki's view this would be justified.

Switzerland and Sweden approached the inclusion of Yugoslavia in very different ways. Sweden considered it to be practically a precondition. Switzerland thought that in the initial stages the negotiations should be limited to just the four neutral countries.

A meeting of the heads of foreign ministry political departments of the neutral countries was held at Königstedt, a mansion near Helsinki, in April 1976. At Finland's initiative there began a neutrals' contact processin which the organising country was rotational. There was interest in this activity beyond the four neutral countries. Their discussions were followed and there was a desire to be in touch with them.

The Soviet Union's Ambasador to the CSCE, Lev Mendelevich visited Helsinki in March 1976 for talks with Iloniemi, a month before the first meeting of the neutrals. Mendelevich gave a report on his talks with Iloniemi to the Helsinki embassies of the socialist countries.

In this he stated that he and Iloniemi had agreed that there was no alternative to détente. Apparently referring in part to the lack of or slow progress on the implementation of the commitments of Basket III, Mendelevich said diplomatically "in this connection there were differences of nuance, though the general development was regarded by both sides as positive." Iloniemi had said that in some countries the reunification of families had been dealt with in a very leisurely manner. He did not, however, mention any countries by name. With regard to follow-up, Mendelevich urged his comrades to be in contact with Ambassador Rajakoski in Geneva. He was a good contact and specialist on the follow-up process.

Mendelevich said that Finland appeared to want to keep the CSCE process to some extent in its own hands. It wanted to continue with its position of responsibility in Europe, regardless of Yugoslavia's hosting work. Finland had good qualifications for this, in Mendelevich's view. "Yugoslavia did not have these political qualifications, because this non-aligned movement's socialist state was, by European standards, relatively isolated. " It did not enjoy the same degree of trust among all the participants as Finland did. In this context the Soviet diplomat came very close to recognising Finland's policy of neutrality on the premises approved by the Finns themselves – not in public, for sure, but among colleagues.

Mendelevich said to his ideological comrades that the Soviet Union was not interested in the close grouping of the neutrals. Nor did it want to disturb their activities. Finland's interest in this activity was clearly bipartite, and so the Soviet attitude to it was lenient, said Mendelevich.

"Finland's role could be positive, provided that in future it consults closely with representatives of the socialist countries. The Soviet Union tries to do its utmost so that Finland would become close to them. For this reason, in many matters we must in future extend positive courtesies (towards the Finns)."

There was visible and palpable tension in Finnish-Austrian relations at different phases of the CSCE, at the political level and at the working level in the conference corridors. In many situations Chancellor Bruno Kreisky was deeply cynical, uncaring and disparaging towards the CSCE. There may have been, between the lines, a certain envy of Finland's CSCE profile. This reflected the disappointment Kreisky felt at the decision of the superpowers to divide the venues for the political CSCE process and the military MBFR negotiations between Helsinki and Vienna. There had been no progress in the Vienna talks for years, and yet the host country had to bear all their costs.

In an interview with *Le Monde* on 29 June 1976, Kreisky proposed the creation of a kind of "political OECD" so that the Western powers could prepare for the Belgrade meeting better than they had for Helsinki. It would, said Kreisky, be appropriate for such a meeting to be arranged in Strasbourg in conjunction with the inauguration of the Council of Europe's new building there. This would naturally have sidelined Finland, which was not yet a full member of the Council of Europe. When Kreisky put these ideas to his West German counterpart, Chancellor Helmut Schmidt, in Vienna on 8 July 1976, Schmidt did not warm to them. They would only have meant highlighting the East-West posture and confrontation during the preparations for Belgrade.

Switzerland's profile at different stages of the CSCE mainly encompassed two points. First was the placement in the CSCE framework of Switzerland's long-time project on the peaceful settlement of disputes, in which the head of the Swiss delegation during the Geneva talks, Professor Rudolf Bindschedler, had played a key role.

Second, for Switzerland the CSCE offered an exceptional forum for multi-lateral diplomacy, as the country was not yet a member of the UN. Switzerland held fast to its political and internationally validated neutrality. While Finland's neutrality was coloured by being a neighbour of the Soviet Union, Switzerland wanted to stress its close relations with the US. It emphasised that its neutrality hinged on having a strong defence: armed neutrality. Switzerland's State Secretary Albert Weitnauer straightforwardly told his West German counterpart during talks in Bonn that Switzerland's and Austria's position as neighbours did not blur this situation. "On the contrary, Switzerland wanted to distance itself from Austrian policy."

The Swiss had an attitude very similar to Finland's in the preparations for the Belgrade meeting. There was no reason for the meeting to alter the Helsinki decisions or to try for some new stipulations over and above the Final Act. While in Bonn, Weitnauer commented on Chancellor Kreisky's ideas on the role of the Council of Europe; Switzerland did not want to be involved in the creation of a "Western council of war".

Soviet relations hit a cold spell

There was an essentially different conception in Finland of the repercussions of détente from that of the CSCE delegations at the time of active negotiations. At the conference site the main aim was to develop and maintain the preparedness of the neutral and non-aligned group so that it could contribute to constructive results and compromises. The working community was a forum of representatives of 35 participating states with various relations towards each other. Personal relations were built up over many years, and they had an appreciable significance regardless of official instructions and national policy. The CSCE was a conference of people.

In September 1976 the Russian original edition of a book published under the pseudonyms Bartenjev and Komissarov appeared. It dealt with current

Finnish-Soviet relations and their interpretation by the Soviet Union. The first impression the book gave was worrying: military vantage points were given centre stage in the interpretation of the Finnish-Soviet treaty. Moreover, a deep sense of suspicion towards Finnish policy pervaded the book. Finland's relations with third countries were considered suspect and limiting to Finland's freedom of action. Soviet Embassy representatives told State Secretary Tuovinen directly that they were concerned about Finland's numerous visits to and other contacts with the West. In reply, Tuovinen appealed to the CSCE and Finland's role in it: a multiplicity of contacts was unavoidable.

The speech to the Paasikivi Society delivered by the new Foreign Minister Keijo Korhonen in Oulu in November 1976 reflected the new formation. A competing party challenged the Centre Party's key position as an assistant to the President. Korhonen stated that at all stages of the CSCE both the Finnish and Soviet sides had emphasised in their bilateral meetings that "however Europe had changed, the Finnish-Soviet relationship, which was based on the Treaty of Friendship, Cooperation and Mutual Assistance, had not changed."

The message of the Bartenjev-Komissarov book was that the development of the CSCE process from 1972 to1975 had not at all influenced the Soviet Union's Finland policy. Trust in the policy of neutrality practised by Finland had not grown. Traditional suspicions remained.

Leading civil servants from the Foreign Ministry and Ministry of Defence continued to deliberate over the current situation at the Königstedt meeting on 21 December 1976. They stated that the Finnish-Soviet treaty was not an active factor in the military situation. Contrary to the Bartenjev-Komissarov interpretations, it was still in Finland's interest to emphasize, the content of all the articles and the treaty in its entirety. The Soviet Union was clearly trying to extract more from the treaty than before.

The discussion came to the conclusion that "The change to stricter and narrower Soviet interpretations since 1969 was due apparently in part to Finland's CSCE initiative, the package proposal on Germany and activeness over SALT".

The promotion of détente was an effort to raise the threshold of the use of force. This was also Foreign Minister Korhonen's message to his Swedish counterpart. The CSCE was important from the viewpoint of détente because it raised the price of using force. In this process it was important that the neutrals were conspicuous as a group of their own.

The mood in Belgrade grows tense — in Finland the CSCE consensus dwindles

The two-day meeting in Königstedt following the September 1977 Belgrade preparatory meeting went through Finland's objectives concerning the follow-up meeting.

There was relative satisfaction with the results of the preparatory meeting, bearing in mind that the political situation internationally was in poor shape, overshadowed because the SALT and Vienna MBFR talks were bogged down, the arms race continued and the Carter administration's policy emphatically focused on human rights and arms control. It remained to be seen whether the UN General Assembly would steer Carter's human rights policy into a more global framework, so that a fractious East-West dialogue in Belgrade could be avoided.

The decision of the preparatory meeting that during the general discussion there must be a "thorough exchange of views" on the basis of the Helsinki Final Act did not rule out the possibility that the follow-up conference would turn into a tribunal. Finland's main goal was for political détente to continue.

On the matter of the principles it was decided to emphasise the neutrality clauses contained in the principle of sovereignty, the Swiss stand on the peaceful settlement of disputes and the ninth principle on cooperation among states, which to a great extent were in accordance with Finland's proposals in the Geneva talks. The CSCE principles as a whole well depicted Finland's own situation and reinforced its policy line.

Ambitions concerning confidence-building measures were modest. The N + N group had to make an active impression and Finland had consequently to be an active rank-and-file member of the group. Disarmament had to be stressed but not over and above the CBM talks.

Détente in the area of commercial cooperation had not reached a proper pace. A problem left over from Geneva concerned making the clauses on favoured nation status clearer. Despite this, Finland decided to make a strong appeal for the resolution of East-West trade policy problems. It presented its own comprehensive trade policy proposal, though it was not an example for others. "Finland's aim was to bring about the kind of atmosphere that could promote the elimination of difficulties."

A lively debate on the humanitarian basket was expected. The neutral countries would have an important role in efforts to ensure a businesslike and constructive discussion. With this in mind, Finland aimed for "balanced activeness" in Basket III matters.

It was also most important for Finland to ensure the continuation of the process in Belgrade. If a substantive overall text could not be produced, it would be necessary instead to make sure that at least three to six different expert events were organised before the next follow-up meeting. If this materialised, the speedy organisation of the next follow-up would not be a priority issue.

Madrid had declared its wish to be the next host for the CSCE. Vienna was a less noticeable candidate, because it knew that on principle France would oppose the presence of the MBFR talks and the CSCE in the same place. Finland had no problems with either candidate.

In a report to the Parliamentary foreign affairs committee on 15 November 1977, Foreign Minister Paavo Väyrynen said that based on the decisions of the preparatory meeting actual work on the follow-up meeting had got off to a positive and constructive start. Contrary to reports in Finnish and other media, the meeting had not yet at least been on the "verge of crisis" or at the point where delegations had intended to leave Belgrade. The meeting had a nature and dynamic of its own. It had been possible to apply decisions of the preparatory meeting flexibly. The discussion on implementation had been businesslike and there had been plenty of new suggestions.

Väyrynen assured the members of the foreign affairs committee that Finland's interest in the CSCE follow-up had not started to wilt. The follow-up was still a central part of the general process of easing tension, which from Finland's standpoint was "the only sensible option ".

As if anticipating criticism, Väyrynen added that in future Finland's role could not be as conspicuous as previously. There was also no desire to maintain a visible profile artificially. Finland worked in close cooperation with other delegations, the Nordic countries and the neutrals. "In addition, Finland's activity in measures that required implementation placed us in the position of a sort of forerunner in matters concerning trade and culture." Väyrynen believed that the meeting could be completed in a constructive spirit. "The delegations have the talks well under control."

The mood towards the Belgrade meeting had varied and there had been a number of clashes, including disputes over human rights issues. When the work had shifted from examining implementation to dealing with future activities it had proceeded in a businesslike spirit.

Väyrynen assured the committee that Finland had prepared carefully for the meeting. The government foreign affairs committee had given instructions to the delegation and thus the work was "on track". Finland had not been polemical. If there were a need for a more visible input in order to bring about a final result, the matter would be considered separately.

Undersecretary of State Keijo Korhonen had just returned from Belgrade and reported on his simultaneous meetings with the US and Soviet representatives. Korhonen acknowledged that the policy of the Carter administration pursued in Belgrade was different compared with earlier times. Korhonen noted that there were reasons of domestic policy for this. The chief US representative, Ambassador Arthur Goldberg, was a well known human rights activist. Now, a still unanswered question was whether it was sufficient that matters had been raised for discussion and would their presentation affect the content of the final act.

Director General Klaus Törnudd said that the discussion on human rights had gained symmetry at the Belgrade meeting. The Soviet and Czechoslovakian representatives had aimed detailed criticism at the deficiencies and imperfections of the West. Human rights issues had acquired a more established place in discourse.

When the matter of Finland's activeness was raised again, Undersecretary of State Korhonen said that Finland had had no special problems in Belgrade that "needed to be strongly aired". When, on the basis of a proposal, the work changed to drawing up a joint document, there was an effort to identify unifying issues. He refuted the claim that Finland had been inactive. "It was a matter of working appropriately."

The N + N group showed its activeness in Belgrade in questions of procedure and substance. Finland's resources were sufficient for both, as was the case in the CSCE earlier, said Törnudd.

Neutrals face crucial test – as does Finland

In human rights issues or Basket III challenges concerning freer contacts among people, and information exchange, the neutral countries did not represent 'neutral' policy. As President Kekkonen had said in a speech on 24 October 1962 during his visit to France; "Finland is, in accordance with its culture, traditions, politics and economic system, a Western republic. It was a part of Western civilization."

In Belgrade there was the matter of how issues were examined. When there was talk of détente it was always a reference to something general and positive.

The atmosphere during the Belgrade follow-up was continually tense due to the possibility of human rights trials being organised in Moscow, and the situation in Prague. The Czech writer Václav Havel had established the Charter 77 group, which criticised his government's policy and became the target of tough government measures. Western speeches at the follow-up meeting's session on Basket III contained quotes from fresh news reports on the pressure imposed by the authorities on Charter 77.

Following a thorough exchange of views the delegates looked ahead to "further efforts", for which they made concrete proposals. This was the 'dynamic element' that had been sought. In contrast, the representatives of the socialist countries had general instructions not to accept any new recommendations for action that either went beyond or complemented the commitments of the Helsinki Final Act. The socialist countries' proposals were therefore mainly matters of form and balance.

The US tabled a concrete human rights-related proposal on 25 November. Its aim was to get all the participating states to put into effect all the stipulations of the Final Act that applied to human rights. This was a consequence of President Carter's foreign policy emphasis on human rights.

FRG Foreign Minister Genscher wrote in his memoirs that in this respect the basic attitudes of the Americans and the Europeans to the CSCE process diverged. In Europe the character of the Final Act was regarded as being comprehensive. Emphasizing individual parts and separating them was artificial in light of the negotiating process. The achievement of consensus on this political stance was impossible in advance. As Genscher had said on several occasions, "The dynamic of the process was best promoted in a way that allowed everyone, including the socialist countries, to benefit from it."

Ambassador Goldberg also presented the proposal to the group of neutral and non-aligned countries. He emphasised that without a text of this kind the US would not accept any substantive outcome in Belgrade. He officially requested that the N + N group support the proposal and be its co-sponsor.

It was known in the Finnish delegation that not only were not all of the NATO countries but also not all of the EEC ones were delighted by the proposal. Ambassador Rajakoski took the view that the N + N countries should not specifically endorse it. It was too simplistic and the situation too aggravated. It was targeted against the Soviet Union and other socialist countries in criticism of their human rights policy. No constructive compromise could be expected on the basis of the proposal.

At the same time the rumours in Moscow of the start of human rights trials were gathering strength. If they were to take place during the Belgrade follow-up, the Western response could be expected to be "strong". The trials were seen as sharply in conflict with the stipulations of the Final Act and with the information to be given on its content.

It was clear that simply the fact that US Ambassador Goldberg had had the opportunity to present the American proposal to the N + N countries aroused suspicions within the Soviet and other socialist countries' delegations. It was on this basis that Ambassador Vorontsov sent critical observations to Moscow concerning Ambassador Rajakoski's actions. Rajakoski's salvation was that the Americans too had complained about his activities. Goldberg was also clearly dissatisfied, but for different reasons.

Before the Christmas break in the Belgrade follow-up the N + N countries drew up a draft of the general part of the concluding document. On 2 December, France had made a proposal of its own concerning the general structure of the concluding document. From the ensuing discussion it was clear that these documents contained so many factual, contradictory and divergent aims that it would not be possible to proceed from such a basis to the drafting of the concluding document.

When the meeting resumed work in mid-January 1978, the message from the Russians was clear and blunt: preparations on a substantial concluding document could stop. There were no preconditions for it. The meeting had to brought to an end by the preliminary deadline of mid-March 1978. With this in mind, the Soviet Union presented a short draft for the Belgrade conclud- ing document. Prime place in it was given to the commitment in principle of the participating states to the continuation, strengthening and expansion of détente. Specific measures were only proposed in the area of military security — there was a need to reduce military confrontation and to begin work to promote arms limitation and disarmament. In the sphere of commercial cooperation, the Soviet Union proposed that three special meetings be convened, on envi- ronment, energy and transport.

Both the Western delegations and the N + N group worked from the as- sumption that during the Christmas break the Soviet Union's fairly radical change of attitude on the work of the follow-up challenged the participants to make new efforts.

Thus, at the end of January the N + N delegations hurriedly drew up a number of reports that tried to take account, in as balanced a way as possible, of the points of view expressed in the discussions after Christmas. Based on them it would be possible for the work to be transferred to unofficial contact groups, chaired by N + N representatives. Undersecretary of State Korhonen and department head Andreani of the French Foreign Ministry were still of the same view on 27 January, at their talks in Helsinki, that no artificial deadlines should be placed on the work of the follow-up meeting. According to Andreani, the US "human rights crusade" had introduced a clear element of danger. "Conceptions of the relationship between the individual and the state in the East and West differ from one another." On the other hand, the trials taking place in the Soviet Union affected public opinion in France, as elsewhere. "The French delegation in Belgrade had to respond to the trials."

Insurmountable stumbling blocks were again found concerning Basket III human contacts and information exchange, as well as matters of domestic policy. With accusations continuing to fly in the plenary speeches not even the informal work was able to make progress. In mid-February, the Soviet Union announced that that there were not the necessary conditions for a substantial concluding document.

Spain and Denmark started work on a brief document, in which the main aim of the neutral and Western delegations was to ensure the continuation of the process. Initially Madrid and Vienna competed for hosting the next follow-up. Denmark presented a draft document in its role as EEC presidency country, on 2 March. A week later, on 9 March, the Belgrade follow-up came to an end. The closing speeches of the participating delegations were made in exceptional haste. All of the speakers wanted to avoid characterising the follow-up meeting as a failure.

Madrid was chosen as the host city of the next follow-up meeting, to start on 9 September 1980.

The results of Belgrade ensured the continuation of the CSCE process. This was a significant achievement, according to many assessments, including those made in Finland. It had to be said, however, that détente had met with new challenges.

The idea of further development of a Nordic nuclear weapons-free zone now shaped Finland's very individual profile and became a favourite topic amidst the strained international situation in the Nordic area. At the same time as Finland's first CSCE concertmaster, Undersecretary of State Jaakko Iloniemi, was posted as Ambassador to Washington, in November 1977, tensions started to mount within the civil service. In the new situation, Undersecretary of State Keijo Korhonen found himself under the conflicting pressures of active CSCE policy and the traditional relationship with the Soviet Union.

Following the Belgrade meeting, France became active in discussions on disarmament. "France broke its silence", as the French Ambassador to Helsinki Jacques Chazelle remarked candidly during talks with Korhonen on 21 February 1978. In an interview on 9 February 1978, President Giscard d'Estaing had, with his prestige, opened a dialogue in which France would fulfil a key role over the next decade. In the French view there was a contradiction between the general development of détente and the prevailing superpower relationship. Moreover, France did not want the disarmament commission in Geneva, led by the superpowers, to have the leading role in disarmament issues. "Discussions among the CSCE member states would offer a fresh opportunity." Disarmament should be dealt with more as a regional issue and more attention should be given to reductions in conventional armaments. Nuclear weapons-free zones should not be ruled out.

A speech was drawn up for President Kekkonen by the Foreign Ministry, principally by Undersecretary of State Korhonen, which was delivered in Stockholm on 8 May 1978. This linked current challenges with the original 1963 initiative on the NWFZ.

Initiative and activeness in matters of arms control were conspicuous. As Keijo Korhonen said on many occasions, we had to run fast in order to remain on the spot. Finland had to demonstrate activeness in the name of its own interests and at the same time try to steer the Nordic countries' debate in a way that would ease tension and make possible concrete measures based on Finnish initiatives. Having an initiative of one's own made it easier to adopt an attitude to the proposals of others. A lively Nordic dialogue was one intermediate goal.

Détente under duress

The Belgrade follow-up meeting showed that the Spirit of Helsinki had not travelled to the Balkans. The creative phase of the CSCE, from Dipoli in 1972 to the summit in 1975, had not continued. The yardstick of the principles and definite measures of the Final Act were now being tested. The principle of non-interference in internal affairs and the way it was interpreted led to the biggest arguments. A definition was sought on the extent to which obligations concerning the implementation of various principles were common property and when they could be primarily subordinated to prevailing national customs and stipulations at any given time. Consensus decisions indicated that they were fixed in time and place. They were products of the moment. In addition to the confirmation and approval of written texts, there was a lot more agreed that had to be read between the lines. There were several ways of reading.

The architect and executor of superpower relations during the Nixon and Ford terms was Henry Kissinger. His policy on Moscow did not place emphasis on the commitments and impacts of the CSCE. On the contrary; Kissinger started from the premise that the Soviet Union deserved to be treated correctly and not bullied in public about its human rights policy.

The Carter administration changed these presuppositions in many respects. When Prime Minister Kalevi Sorsa paid an official visit to the US in November 1978 he was told that the worsening turn in US-Soviet relations had in fact started during President Ford's term. Following the election of Carter these relations had been uneven due to human rights policy and differences over what was happening in Africa. Secretary of State Cyrus Vance's advisor Marshall D. Shulman told Sorsa openly that a return to the sort of détente of 1972 was unrealistic. The Soviets too had admitted as much to the Americans. In place of declarations, the focus should now be on individual issues, such as the SALT negotiations and the Middle East question. There was reason to lower aims and expectations.

Shulman said that from the West's standpoint it was important to reach a closer understanding on what could be accomplished in relations with the Soviet Union in general. The experience of Belgrade was that very different views on this issue persisted in NATO and EEC circles. Shulman admitted that human rights questions and their objectives required realism and selectivity. Everyone knew that the Soviet Union acted within very limited bounds. "If human rights policy became a priority theme, it could backfire." Shulman said that the US was only now learning where the limits of these means of leverage ran, between actions that were useful and those that were harmful to oneself. There had to be a channel left for one's opponent to act without coercion. "The Americans did not master that skill (in Belgrade)."

The same day, 2 November, Sorsa met with Carter's National Security Advisor Zbigniew Brzezinski who said that arms control was proceeding with more detailed objectives than with the preliminary Vladivostok agreement. The biggest challenge was to control the fast pace of weapons technology, particularly when dealing with new cruise missiles and laser weapons. The second strategic challenge was the general nuclear weapon situation in Europe. Brzezinski said that the Soviet Union had already shown understanding over American worries concerning Africa. In the sphere of human rights the situation was different. The Soviet aim seemed still to be some sort of world revolution – not perhaps as a precondition but an end. "It was the Soviet Union's own internal problem if after 60 years of existence it didn't feel that its position was secure." Human rights required a long-term process of adjustment. "Nothing was ever heard of Saharov under Stalin. Support and encouragement from the United Sates were now important."

Brzezinski said that the previous Republican administration had been pre-pared to accept maintaining the Soviet-US status quo as a partnership, because "their thinking was tinged with historical pessimism on the role of the United States." The Carter administration was a lot more optimistic. "It saw that the Soviet Union did not have much to offer to the modern world. The Soviet Union's worry was that it was not taken seriously. The Soviet Union was histori-cally irrelevant except in purely military terms."

A change in Europe's strategic situation?

Finnish-Soviet discussions during spring 1978 had been dominated by the 30th anniversary of the treaty between the two countries. In September, Foreign Minister Paavo Väyrynen held talks with deputy foreign minister Igor Zemskov in Moscow. Zemskov stressed that the time was right to deepen détente and prevent an arms race. Although American policy appeared to Moscow to be zigzagging, Zemskov believed that détente could not be nullified. At most, it could be slowed down.

An interview with Undersecretary of State Korhonen published in the Finnish newspaper Kaleva, on 17 September, was entitled 'Détente looks for its limits'. Korhonen took the view that détente meant maintaining the possibility of dialogue in superpower relations. Without mentioning ideological struggle explicitly, Korhonen considered that in the climate of détente the "competitive element" in international politics could be eliminated to a large extent. It was wrong to say that détente had one foot in the grave.

There was a competition in Finland for the role of disarmament sector top dog. Korhonen had been a key mover when President Kekkonen visited Stockholm on 8 May 1978 to speak on the Nordic nuclear weapons-free zone. A nuclear-free North would be extended to cover a larger arms control system. The Nordic NWFZ was now the Nordic Disarmament Arrangement.

Kalevi Sorsa had just been made chair of the Socialist International's working group on disarmament.

At talks in Finland between US Vice President Walter Mondale and Presi-dent Kekkonen, on 20 April 1979, it was suggested to the Americans that rep-resentatives of the US, the Soviet Union and the Nordic countries hold a joint meeting on the issue of the Nordic NWFZ. The chargé d'affaires at the US

Embassy in Helsinki had delivered the US official position to the Foreign Ministry on 9 May 1979: "The United States does not consider that the proposal would have enough of a relevant and promising basis for negotiations."

At a meeting in Moscow with the Secretary of the Central Committee of the CPSU, Boris Ponomaryov, Sorsa explained the idea of the Nordic Disarmament Organization. Sorsa also had to explain that President Kekkonen's 8 May 1978 speech in Stockholm had not produced the desired effect.

General Secretary Brezhnev delivered a highly publicised speech on disarmament on 6 October 1979, on the 30th anniversary of the foundation of the GDR. In it he sketched out broad principles of Soviet thinking on a peace programme.

On 31 October 1979, President Kekkonen gave a statement on disarmament issues to the Soviet news agency APN. In the statement Kekkonen said that the arms control and disarmament talks concerning Europe should be planned comprehensively, all types of weapons should be dealt with and all parties must be able to take part in the discussions. Kekkonen linked the Finnish initiative for a European disarmament programme to the preparations for the CSCE Madrid follow-up meeting. "These are already in a hurry." The background to the President's statement was the address by Undersecretary of State Korhonen at the UN General Assembly, on 19 October, in which he gave a more detailed account of Finland's latest initiative.

When France's Ambassador Jacques Chazelle met with Foreign Minister Paavo Väyrynen on 30 October he expressed astonishment. "The enthusiastic statements on President Brezhnev's speech have given a strange image of the Finnish response in the world. The speech seemed to have been accepted as it was, without more detailed examination." Chazelle asked what was Finland's official position. Chazelle was a popular figure in Helsinki and as a CSCE specialist well acquainted with Finnish policy. Väyrynen said that in some ways Undersecretary of State Korhonen had been responding to Brezhnev's speech. The Finnish initiative for a European disarmament programme had, Väyrynen stressed, come about well before the Soviet leader's speech, and Finland's official position on the speech had been presented two weeks after it.

Finland considered Brezhnev's offer to withdraw troops and equipment from Europe to be positive. Brezhnev pledged in his speech that the Soviet Union would unilaterally withdraw 20,000 men and 1,000 tanks from the GDR.

In remarks to the press repeated in Finland Western military specialists rated the offer as peanuts.

Väyrynen said that in the West Soviet aims were often seen only as an effort to prevent NATO from modernising its nuclear weaponry in Europe. "As there was a threat of a new spiral in the arms race, Finland could hardly have given a negative response to the Soviet initiative."

In December 1979 NATO agreed finally at its meeting in Brussels to deploy 572 Pershing II and ground-launched cruise missiles in five West European countries: the FRG, Belgium, the Netherlands, Great Britain and Italy. The Western alliance's decision was seen as a necessary countermeasure to the Soviet Union's deployment of SS-20 missiles in its Western area. The actions taken by the alliances prompted much public debate. Citizens' movements became active both to prevent a new round of the arms race and to freeze the current levels of armaments.

The European disarmament programme

It was in this spirit that Finland aimed to modernise its own standing proposal. It was decided to distribute the first confidential working paper on the European Disarmament programme on 22 January 1980. The aim of the programme would be to strengthen the CSCE's military dimension and continue the development of confidence building measures agreed in the Helsinki Final Act. The purpose of the programme was not to replace or interfere with other negotiations. The working paper recognised the importance of the Vienna negotiations between the alliances, and the negotiations concerning nuclear arms located in Europe and targeted at Europe.

There were other initiatives and proposals, too, concerning Europe. The Finnish working paper now offered the CSCE countries a new approach and dynamic. The idea for a European disarmament programme was first presented to the First Committee of the UN General Assembly, on 19 October 1979. The purpose of the programme was now described in more detail under the following headings:

- Defining and outlining concepts
- Access to information on bilateral and multilateral negotiations under way

- Coordination of negotiations and tabled proposals
- Registering the objectives of the negotiating parties
- Codifying existing commitments
- Registering the indirect effects of valid and current negotiations from the standpoint of participants and outsiders, and
- Adapting the European Disarmament Programme to a universal framework.

The initial comments on the Finnish working paper by representatives of the Western alliance were in principle positive. Comments from London and Brussels urged the Finns to specify their objectives and give more concrete examples of what they sought. The Western comments referred frequently to the Warsaw Treaty's disarmament declarations, which had no clear intention of actually taking disarmament forward. The same sort of concern was now directed at the Finnish proposal.

Department head Klaus Törnudd said that, based on discussions in London and Brussels, the European Disarmament Programme required as soon as possible new specification to which concrete questions could be attached for the main parties. The maintenance of CSCE contacts was considered valuable in itself. There was also a wish to wait and see how discussion of the matter would proceed at the Madrid follow-up.

The first response by the Soviet Union indicated that the Finnish paper was considered highly important. Department head Farafonov did not, however, comment on it in more detail. The comments of other Warsaw Treaty countries were in principle positive, but non-committal.

The only exception was Sweden's Foreign Minister Ola Ullsten. Cabinet Secretary Leif Leifland's positive and supportive comments on the Finnish initiative were endorsed in Ullsten's address to the Geneva-based UN Conference on Disarmament on 5 February. There was no comment at all from the Swiss. Instead the Swiss representative Anton Hegner focused on the prospects for the Madrid follow-up.

In Finland, it was initially thought that there would be a natural connection between the CSCE process and the European Disarmament Programme. At a meeting on 22 January 1980 Keijo Korhonen and Esko Rajakoski agreed that Finland's European Disarmament Programme idea should be linked to the concluding document of the Madrid follow-up. A separate mandate would have to be made at working group level. This would be Finland's maximal objective. Finland was also ready to consider other forums.

Korhonen was aware that there were risks associated with the European Disarmament Programme idea. Leading representatives of the superpowers and the alliances might have felt that it was too intrusive to probe them and request information about the negotiations. It was an advantage of the CSCE follow-up forum that everyone was present at them on an equal basis. In contrast, the UN Special Session on Disarmament in 1978 offered suitable basic material for the Finnish project. Because of this, Korhonen considered the idea of a centralised inventory, the registration of negotiating processes and proposals, to be a minimum objective. The European Disarmament Programme would be a clearinghouse. "In this way President Kekkonen's initiative for an arms control system in the North could be brought in for discussion."

A new English language version of the working paper was drawn up and distributed for information purposes to all the CSCE countries in autumn 1980. Since January, the comments of the main parties had been heard in the bilateral discussions that had been in principle positive but non-committal.

Despite setbacks in the international situation, the turn of the year 1979 -1980 was seen as being even more of a reason to continue to develop the initiative. Finland aimed for the creation of a disarmament negotiations "umbrella" to cover proposals already made and possible new proposals and ongoing negotiating processes. The word "programme" meant that a comprehensive approach would be involved, seeking to create a reference framework for the main guidelines and a clearinghouse for European disarmament issues. Consensus decisions would have to be reached on the concrete content of the programme.A structured discussion on this could be started at the Madrid follow-up. The aim would be to give a push to the discussions on an "unprejudiced and comprehensive basis".

A main issue and problem was to adapt the disarmament programme to the Madrid working programme. Confidence building measures belonged naturally on the agenda of the Madrid follow-up meeting. The main protagonists prepared for the meeting with an impressive arsenal of heavyweight experts, both nationally and within their respective alliances. Very rarely did new and spontaneous initiatives then get any living space.

Ambassador Rajakoski visited Paris for bilateral talks on the new working paper, on 7 October 1980. The preparatory meeting for the Madrid follow-up meeting had already started, and all the participants knew of France's proposal on applying confidence and security building measures from the Atlantic to the Urals. In a military working group at the follow-up meeting proper one of the chief negotiators Benoit d'Àboville told Rajakoski that the timeframes of the French and Finnish proposals were very different.

France's assumption was that it was now time to concentrate on confidence building measures that were as concrete as possible and could achieve results as quickly as possible. d'Àboville considered that items in the Finnish working paper such as "adapting European disarmament efforts to a universal framework" and "agreement on the applicability to all disarmament negotiations of acceptable key principles" would require extensive and prolonged negotiations.

The third target of d'Àboville's criticism was Finland's proposal for the creation of an information retrieval system for ongoing multilateral and bilateral superpower negotiations. It would be unrealistic because the superpowers would provide information on their negotiations when they wanted to.

Rajakoski returned to the issue of the transitional stage of confidence building measures for disarmament. d'Àboville answered that it would help the process if the measures were given greater importance militarily, as had been agreed in the Final Act.

Ambassador Jacques Martin, who took part in the discussion, wound up the conversation with the encouraging comment that perhaps France, together with Finland and Sweden, could sound out the possibility of speeding up the talks on military security before the Christmas break in Madrid.

The Madrid follow-up
meeting, 1980—1983

In the shadow of Afghanistan and Poland's solidarity movement

The preparatory session for the Madrid follow-up meeting began on 9 September 1980 at the Palacio de Congressos. The prognoses for the meeting were unfavourable. In December the previous year, the Soviet Union had occupied Afghanistan. Although Afghanistan was not part of Europe the actions of a CSCE participating state naturally led to immediate criticism in the meeting and weighed heavily on the general atmosphere.

In Poland, the Solidarity movement had assumed the role of the political opposition. This created tension not only within the country. Developments in Poland were being followed non-stop in its neighbouring countries. Would the Solidarity virus threaten to spread to the rest of the socialist community?

Polish-born Karol Woytila was chosen to become Pope John-Paul II in 1978. The ramifications of the choice extended well beyond religious communities.

Poland's internal crisis intensified in December 1981 with the declaration of martial law. All the Madrid documents thereafter carried a subtextual reference to martial law and Solidarity. The crisis in Poland nevertheless did not sever the negotiating ties in Madrid. FRG Foreign Minister Hans Dietrich Genscher reiterated on many occasions that it was precisely in such a situation that follow-up dialogues and forums were needed. Although the meeting had a nine-month adjournment from the beginning of 1982, the process remained alive and there was strong hope for a positive outcome.

The head of the Hungarian delegation, Ambassador Janos Petran, even estimated that the CSCE would benefit from the fact that the Soviet Union had occupied Afghanistan. The Soviet Union had neither the practical possibilities nor the resources to consider the use of force against Poland. This idea was also put about at the time by Ambassador John Kornbloom in West Berlin, who was later the US OSCE Ambassador. He confirmed in a discussion in Berlin on 12 June 2007 that, according to American intelligence, at no time during the period of martial law in Poland did the Soviet Union increase its intelligence operations or any other military preparations above normal.

Washington could therefore be confident that nothing dramatic was expected from Moscow apart from booming rhetoric. This had an impact on the possibilities for manoeuvre of the US delegation in Madrid. It would be possible to avoid florid dramatics and to solve emerging problems through negotiation.

Preparatory meeting hits dead-end

The Finnish delegation to the preparatory meeting was directed from Helsinki by department head Klaus Törnudd. The deputy heads of delegation were the Finnish Ambassador to Madrid Joel Pekuri, and Ambassador Richard Müller, assigned to the CSCE from Dar es Salaam. Secretary of legation Jaakko Laajava joined the delegation from the Madrid Embassy and legation counsellor Markku Reimaa came from the Embassy in London. This group dealt with the preparatory meeting.

As with the Finnish Embassy in London, the Embassy in Paris had to contribute a civil servant to the Madrid delegation. He was assistant Kari Veijalainen. Work on Basket II was strengthened by counsellor Seppo Kauppila, whilst secretary of division Alpo Rusi, was to assist Müller in the coordinating work on the CSCE principles. Major Kimmo Lehtosuo was the delegation's military specialist.

The forecast for the preparatory meeting was not good. When the Western alliance proposed that the model of the Belgrade meeting be applied in Madrid, too, the Warsaw Treaty countries, particularly the Soviet Union, found grounds to accuse the West of outright sabotage. Does the West want once again to lead the meeting, both its working method and final outcome, to a dead-end? Was the intention again to let constructive discussion and cooperation descend into a tribunal?

Fruitless polemics continued from one week to another. The neutral countries tried to bring about reconciliation. It was not easy to calm the atmosphere in such a situation. The polemics could last for as long as the time booked for the preparatory meeting. Neither of the main parties would give in. Finally the situation reached the point where the starting date of the follow-up meeting proper threatened to slip past altogether. It would then have to be said that the Madrid follow-up never got going. The process would come to a halt for the time being. Its resuscitation would have required a new consensus decision.

At that point the Spanish government intervened. It invited, in its own name, all the delegations to send high representatives, preferably foreign ministers, to Madrid to deliver speeches normal for the opening stage of the follow-up meeting. It was also expected that the presence of political level representatives in the capital would loosen the stalemate so that the follow-up meeting could begin normally.

The Madrid follow-up meeting lasted exactly three years, from September 1980 to September 1983. The Finnish delegation at the opening stage of the meeting was led by Ambassador Richard Müller. Pictured from the right are Ambassador Joel Pekuri, Legation Councillor Jaakko Laajava, Ambassador Müller and the author.

A mood of tension and nervousness also dominated the N + N circle of countries. It was hard to find any intercessory proposal between the aggravated stands of the East and West. During the Geneva stage the neutral countries had already proposed the most binding possible decisions for the follow-up. Within the N + N group this was also the threshold issue for the starting phase of the Madrid meeting.

When Foreign Minister Väyrynen arrived in Madrid he was a general object of interest. Various groups were curious to hear what was the Finnish Foreign Minister's solution for the problem. Väyrynen said that during talks in Moscow it had been evident that Finland's and the Soviet Union's views of the role of the follow-up clearly differed from one another. This was a reality that had to be accepted, but was undoubtedly news to many CSCE colleagues.

Work in Madrid gets under way

Spain's Prime Minister Adolfo Suarez's contribution to the preparatory meeting resulted eventually in a consensus on the arrangement of the work of the follow-up meeting.

The US delegation, led by Ambassador Max Kampelman, had come well prepared. When the opening address of Sweden's delegation contained a mention of the Raoul Wallenberg case, and the need to investigate the case openly with the Soviet Union, Kampelman was happy. It was not solely at his initiative that the general addresses at the CSCE Madrid meeting raised the matter of individual human rights violations. The general discussion at the meeting took on a different tone.

US presidential elections were held towards the start of the Madrid meeting, in November 1980. The Carter term ended and the new president was the Governor of California and former movie star Ronald Reagan. He was known to be a plain speaker. Reagan's election did not affect the work or composition of the US delegation in Madrid. Reagan and Kampelman were old acquaintances, and so the President's confidence in the delegation and its headman was solid.

The work of the preparatory meeting had shown that this would be no run of the mill follow-up. It was clear from the level of participants that the socialist countries assumed the position of underdogs at the follow-up meeting.

At the opening stage they were represented by deputy ministers. The presence of Romania's foreign minister was an exception. In contrast, numerous foreign ministers representing the Western countries plus the N + N countries descended on Madrid.

The opening address of the US was given by Senator Griffin B. Bell instead of Ambassador Max Kampelman. He used his speech to focus on peoples' rights to self-determination and on stressing human rights on the basis of the Final Act. Bell said that the Final Act had developed into a "dynamic and positive process", because

- slowly but surely it was breaking down the barriers of the Cold War
- it was bringing together people across the East-West divide, and
- it was facilitating the exchange of ideas and information and commercial contacts.

According to Bell, the first follow-up meeting in Belgrade had shown that a common examination of the implementation of commitments strengthened the continuity of the process. Without repeated opportunities for scrutiny the Helsinki process would have ground to a halt. Bell disputed the interpretation according to which human rights should be examined by varying criteria depending on the system. "This sort of interpretation would be harmful from the stance of the spirit of the process. People have human rights as people and not as members of some social system."

Bell said that the Soviet occupation of Afghanistan cast a shadow of gloom over East-West relations. The number of emigration permits granted to Soviet Jews had dropped sharply. Members of the Moscow-Helsinki group, established in 1976, had been victimised. Bell reiterated academician Andrei Saharov's appeal to avert a nuclear war.

Kampelman's speeches at plenary sessions became a custom to which the Soviet Union and other socialist countries did not have an opportunity to react effectively. The head of the Soviet delegation was deputy minister Leonid Ilyichov. He had been the head of propaganda under Khrushchev and had negotiated on bilateral relations with China for decades. Ilyichov was fairly advanced in age and the world had changed irrevocably since his most active years, thus his arrival in Madrid did not essentially alter anything.

Deputy minister Kovalev and the Soviet Ambassador to Madrid Juri Dubinin represented their country's CSCE heritage. The figure of influence in the Soviet delegation and the broker on delicate matters was still General Sergei Kondrachov. Kampelman and Kondrashov respected one another. Both had direct links with the highest political level back home.

Ilyichov stated bluntly in his opening address that certain forces wanted to turn the Madrid meeting into a propaganda forum, a rhetorical bullfight. The Soviet "delegation sensed an icy gale blowing against détente". The US opening address was a clear example of interference in the internal affairs of another participating state. The attempts to raise the matter of Afghanistan at Madrid were based on no agreed mandate. "It is pointless to interfere in Afghanistan's internal affairs in Madrid!" The Soviet delegation had come to Madrid so that the mandate of the meeting could be fulfilled with a positive outcome. "This approach is based on the Soviet Union's peaceful foreign policy constructed 60 years ago." The speech referred to the Soviet Union's latest disarmament initiatives and to the disarmament proposals reiterated by Foreign Minister Gromyko at the UN General Assembly. "Political détente must be complemented by détente in the military arena."

The Warsaw Treaty countries had launched a joint initiative for convening a disarmament conference. The convening of such a conference would be possible provided "that all sorts of marginal conditions were not placed on it." "Economic sanctions" limited the opportunities for economic cooperation with the socialist countries. A new form of cooperation was needed in the areas of energy and the environment.

Ilyichov said that the Soviet Union consistently and resolutely respected human rights and fundamental freedoms. "The new constitution guarantees for Soviet citizens the broadest possible rights and freedoms; the right to a peaceful life, to work and to social security."

The Soviet Union was ready to advance all matters under examination: family reunification, international marriages and an increase in cooperation in the spheres of exchange of information, culture and education. "Actions such as these can succeed only if the laws of each country are fully respected and interference in the internal affairs of others is avoided."

The FRG's Foreign Minister Hans Dietrich Genscher conceded in his address that the Madrid meeting was taking place at a time imbued with difficult international disputes. The prognoses for the future of the CSCE varied greatly.

Genscher was one of the few Western alliance members who directed his attention in the early stage of the meeting to the N + N countries "They have an irreplaceable role in the deliberations for peace and cooperation in Europe."

Foreign Minister Väyrynen repeated the traditional Finnish CSCE line. Referring to the recent occupation of Afghanistan, he said that the implementation of the Final Act could not be divorced from events outside Europe. Väyrynen considered that the international situation was worse than at the time of the Belgrade follow-up. Expectations were modest. Väyrynen considered that the principle of human rights required clearer internal changes within the participating states than the other principles, including changes in their attitudes to one another. Respect for human rights required continual and explicit action in all the participating states.

Väyrynen's reference at the opening of the Madrid meeting to the need for change was a significant innovation in Finland's CSCE policy and strategy towards principles. It was a step forward from the unambiguous statement concerning the implementation of the 1975 Final Act that Finland did not want to publicly interfere in the affairs of other participants. It had concentrated on dealing with any Basket III matters by discreet bilateral diplomacy. Although the call for change was not specifically directed at anyone in particular, it was a new policy line. And it was used to support future work.

Väyrynen confirmed that Finland would, together with the N + N countries, present proposals on how to further develop confidence-building measures. Finland was interested in continuing discussions on the basis of various initiatives for bringing about a European disarmament conference.

In the context of cooperation on Basket III, Väyrynen said that Finland's experiences of recent years had been positive, if sometimes few in quantity. There were few international journalists in Finland. The usual problem was an inability to speak Finnish. The postion of a small culture and a small language continued to be one of Finland's focal points at the Madrid meeting. Finland, together with other Nordic countries, had translated the Final Act into the Saami language spoken by some 50,000 indigenous people in the far north of Europe.

At the end of his address Väyrynen emphasised Finland's perennial interest in the continuation of the CSCE. "This process must continue without interruption."

The speeches of the neutrals' foreign ministers reflected clear differences of emphasis. Austria's Foreign Minister Willibald Pahr reiterated Chancellor Kreisky's opinion, expressed at the Helsinki summit that it was "unfortunate there was no ideology of peaceful coexistence". Pahr regarded the occupation of Afghanistan as a clear violation of the global indivisibility of détente. "Austria was prepared for an ideological struggle."

According to Sweden's Foreign Minister Ola Ullsten, the occupation of Afghanistan was the watershed between détente and distrust. In Sweden's view the arms build-up between the superpowers required that nuclear weapons be included in the work of a European disarmament conference. Actual negotiations could take place between the key participants. On human rights, Ullsten called for more effective implementation of the Final Act. There was a need for countermeasures concerning those subjected to pressure, whether it was a case of Raoul Wallenberg, Andrei Saharov or Vaclav Havel.

Switzerland's Secretary of State Edouard Brunner said that the Soviet Union's occupation of Afghanistan was a serious source of concern because détente was indivisible. Switzerland was still in favour of balanced progress; issues concerning a disarmament conference could not be allowed to push aside other subjects. The example of the preparatory meeting and the sluggish pace of its work had significantly increased doubts about the CSCE. Despite this, Brunner gave assurance of Switzerland's faith in the CSCE process and the power of dialogue. "Genuine dialogue could not be replaced by polemical or self-satisfied disputation."

France leads the way to the Urals

The superpower disarmament negotiations formed a significant yardstick and barometer of developments in the international situation. France's activeness during the final stage of the Belgrade meeting, in March 1978, formed the 'European' dimension of that discourse. France proposed the start of disarmament talks within the CSCE framework.

At the Madrid meeting, France honed its proposal so that the area of application of confidence and security-building measures would be expanded to cover all of Europe. CBMs would acquire a more emphatic military significance, and they would be appropriately monitored and verified. A precise mandate would have to be drawn up as an outcome of the Madrid meeting for the start of a negotiating process within the CSCE.

France tabled an official proposal on 10 December 1980. In addition to the aforementioned aims, France considered that the promotion of disarmament and a lessening of military confrontation must be realized without isolating a single party. A credible new system would be a guarantee of effectiveness. The French proposal worked from the assumption that the new conference could start work as early as 1981.

Ambassador Max Kampelman confirmed on 19 December 1980, before the Christmas break, that he would continue as head of the US delegation under a new US President. The delegation's instructions remained the same: it would focus on respect for human rights and basic freedoms, open up a genuine dialogue on these issues, and seek practical measures to improve human contacts, the reunification of families and the freer exchange of information. At the same time, Kampelman predicted that the United States would be prepared to investigate strengthening and expanding the area of application of confidence building measures that were militarily significant and verifiable.

When the follow-up meeting resumed after the Christmas break, in February 1981, Kampelman conveyed the greetings of the new US President, Ronald Reagan. The Reagan administration had thoroughly examined France's proposal concerning the disarmament process. In the opinion of the Americans, there were in the proposal many new and, from the outcome at Madrid, decisive matters. These included new confidence-building measures of "credible military significance", and the effective verification of measures to be agreed – a demand that the US had made a key focus in all disarmament negotiations since the end of the Second World War. In place of voluntary actions, actions to be agreed now would have to be carried out under " strong political obligations".

France suggested that confidence-building measures would be further developed by convening a conference after Madrid. In this conference there should be closer scrutiny of how the participants would gain more information through measures that increase confidence, how actions could increase European stability and how inspection and monitoring measures together could be developed in a new way. France now proposed that the area of application be from the Atlantic to the Urals. Further measures would be examined only after it had been possible to assess the results of the negotiations on the use of confidence building measures and to assess development in other aspects of arms control.

Ambassador Kampelman announced in his speech of 16 February 1981 that on this basis President Reagan, and therefore the US Madrid delegation, fully supported France's disarmament proposal. This announcement was important news in Madrid. It immediately raised expectations and boosted faith in an intensification of the work of the follow-up meeting. Skilled negotiator that he was, Kampelman did not rule out the possibility that the Americans might make additional proposals of their own. "The main criteria set by France for bringing about a new conference comprise the minimum requirements for the US for a security conference after the Madrid meeting."

Kampelman also pointed out that the success of the follow-up meeting could not be measured purely in terms of decisions on military security. "The subtlety of the Final Act was that in it genuine security also requires progress in the areas of human rights and economic cooperation."

Soviet General Secretary Brezhnev made an offer on 23 February 1981 under which Moscow would be prepared to expand the area of application of confidence and security-building measures to cover the whole of the European part of the Soviet Union, provided that the West agreed to a similar corresponding concession. Brezhnev made the proposal in a speech to the 26th congress of the CPSU, in which he dealt comprehensively with the international political situation. He announced that the Soviet Union was prepared to continue with bilateral arms control talks with the US on strategic weapons, the banning of new submarines and the development of missiles for them – cruise missiles – and the deployment of medium-range missiles in Europe by NATO and the Soviet Union.

Prior to Brezhnev's speech, Ambassador Kampelman had held talks with Richard Müller in which he emphasized that notwithstanding the pledges of his proposal, the US would endeavour to ensure that the work of the Madrid follow-up could be concluded as quickly as possible, even without substantive results. "Some kind of follow-up could perhaps be agreed." It was most important to end in a conciliatory atmosphere so that it would not be labelled a failure.

Müller nevertheless estimated that the US would perhaps have to reconsider its strategy in Madrid on the basis of the new opening given in General

Secretary Brezhnev's speech. "A conclusion without results no longer appeared as inevitable as earlier. And what was more important was that NATO's European member countries might me more interested in a result than they were earlier. Moreover, the prospects of development in the bilateral relations of the superpowers now came into the picture."

Deputy minister Ilyichov presented the Soviet Union's new offers in his address on 3 March 1981. He stressed that Europe was both a geographical and strategic concept. The US and Canada were signatories of the Helsinki Final Act. They should therefore also be involved on an equal footing in military détente and disarmament in Europe. The Soviet Union reiterated the suggestion made by General Secretary Brezhnev in October 1979 that naval and air force exercises and major troop movements should definitely be included in the new confidence building measures. The enlargement of the area of applicability to cover the whole of the European part of the Soviet Union raised the issue that the Western powers should correspondingly expand their area of applicability.

Ilyichov rejected the notion that the Soviet Union and the Warsaw pact countries would plan for this sort of conference to be held outside the CSCE process. The foreign ministers of the Warsaw Treaty had openly rejected this in a declaration at their Warsaw conference in October. "The conference would be an essential part of the development of the pan-European conference started in Helsinki."

Neutrals' beauty contest

The neutrality of the four neutral countries varied significantly in content and character. This divergence was present in practical matters and in the use of language in CSCE affairs. The importance of the CSCE in their foreign policy differed greatly. It was dictated not only by their different geographical locations and their neighbours, but also by the role of their national foreign policies and their experience in the daily work of their governments.

In Belgrade, the joint role of the neutral countries remained modest. This perhaps was partly why the preparations for Madrid were made very purposefully. The meetings of state secretaries and heads of political departments compared general expectations and the opportunities to act. The neutrals were both in principle and practice prepared to offer their services in the coordination of working groups. This procedure was agreed when the working programme was decided upon. Finland and Ambassador Richard Müller were put in charge of Committee I, which dealt with principles. Sweden and Ambassador Karl Johan von Rappe headed the committee on military security and Austria and Ambassador Franz Ceska took charge of economic cooperation. The Swiss Ambassador Edouard Brunner handled the work of head of delegation mainly from Bern, while Counsellor Peter Troendle acted as coordinator on matters related to follow-up work.

These duties obliged each coordinator and his delegation to be active and to closely follow the situation within their own sector. This required being well up to date with the work of the meeting and possible changes of direction. In Madrid, too, the representatives of the neutral countries comprised a sort of data bank for the whole conference. They had to know as precisely as possible at all times about the intentions and wishes of the other participants. In addition to matters of content, the timing of presentations and options for decision-making was of great consequence. Each neutral delegation also wanted to reinforce its own position and national influence.

In general, the assumption was that Switzerland and Ambassador Brunner, in accordance with Switzerland's neutrality heritage, were very close in their work to the US line, particularly on human rights issues. Ambassador Matti Kahiluoto reported an observation to this effect to Helsinki during the intense negotiations of summer 1983. Austria and Switzerland did not shy away from agreeing with the West even in contentious issues.

Yugoslavia and Cyprus often reflected the arguments of the socialist countries. Liechtenstein was usually in close cooperation with the Vatican's representatives, as matters of freedom of religion in the socialist countries were close to its heart. Austria and Sweden's activities varied from one meeting to the next. As a Swedish representative remarked at a conference in February 2007, Sweden had no specific national objectives when its delegation left for Dipoli in autumn 1972. The general instruction was solely not to forget the document on friendly relations concluded within the UN framework and to remember that the CSCE should not become a forum primarily for disarmament issues.

Sweden's general attitude towards the CSCE was to be in principle understanding and supportive of what Finland did. But there were those in Stockholm who were at first deeply sceptical about the likelihood of definite results coming from the CSCE process. Interest in the CSCE grew over time. During the Madrid meeting, Sweden made a significant contribution to the CSCE for the first time. Now the issue was the mandate for a conference on the CSCE's confidence and security-building measures. Sweden wanted the conference for Stockholm.

Finland was considered to be a neighbour of the Soviet Union, by nature, in the East-West line-up, a factor that was too often interpreted as meaning understanding and acceptance of Moscow's strategies. Hans-Jörg Renk, a member of the Swiss delegation in Dipoli and then Geneva, said in his 1996 book on Switzerland's involvement in the CSCE that suspicion of Finland was rife at the Dipoli and Geneva talks. He thought that this was partly due to the fact that few of the delegates attending the Dipoli discussions had ever visited Helsinki before or knew anything about Finland's history. Because of this they had formed their impressions of Finland and its politics on the basis of superficial information in the mass media. Over the long-term such misconceptions were convincingly dispelled in the work of the CSCE.

If Finland had not had this image as the Soviet Union's neighbour, the interest shown in the work of the Finnish delegation could have been notably weaker. The Soviet Union undisputedly and unreservedly recognized Finland as a part of the CSCE neutral group. The Geneva stage of the negotiations and the hosting work in Dipoli, as well as the hosting of the 1973 and 1975 conferences, had strengthened Finland's role as a credible partner. This view was reinforced in Madrid, Stockholm and Vienna.

On the basis of CSCE consensus decisions it had become clear over time to all that the only way to obtain favourable decisions was to make compromises. The knowledge that a representative of the Finnish delegation was prepared to listen to the hopes of a Soviet colleague made it clear to the Soviet representatives that their wishes could not be advanced in their present form. The Finnish delegation assessed the potential for moulding a Soviet hope into a compromise acceptable to all.

In a discussion on Finland's role in the CSCE with Ambassador Yuri Derjabin in Moscow, in June 2007, reference could be made to several Soviet statements connectd with the cooperative and coordinating work of the N + N countries. The Nordic reference group received the unreserved recognition of the Soviet Union in relation to UN policy, regardless that the group includ-ed three NATO countries. "Denmark, Norway and Iceland were completely harmless in this respect," said Deryabin.

The scope and efficiency of channels of information were indispensable in the daily work in Madrid. The work was dialogue -based on the principle of reciprocity, both in negotiations and social contacts. The neutral coun-tries and the non-aligned delegations, at each stage of the meeting, formed a conception of what the outcome of the Madrid follow-up meeting would be. They drew up a full draft for a concluding document based on the proposals made and the discussions held. This helped to see details as well as entireties. It made it possible to concentrate on those subjects that continued to be the most contentious issues in the East-West configuration from the viewpoint of a final outcome.

Discussions between Poland's Solidarity movement and the government in Warsaw now raised, for the first time in the CSCE, the role of the trade union movement and NGO activity. The West's proposal compared trade union rights to those of cultural and sports organizations, whose role was separately recog-nized in the Final Act. In contrast, the socialist countries tried to exclude this new element by stating that issues concerning trade union rights were already dealt with in the International Labour Organization. But just as at the Geneva stage, when it had been important to keep disputes between the Germanies out of the conference halls, it was now in everyone's interest in Madrid to avoid official discussion on the internal situation in a given country.

The reports and consultations that had continued throughout spring 1981 on bringing about a N + N countries' draft concluding document did not lead to mutual understanding within the group. There were many cross currents. The main problems were to do with the perennial N + N issue of the role of the decision on the continuation of the CSCE, and its validity as a part of the concluding document.

In the neutral and non-aligned draft, the commitment to continuation was divided into several subjects: the follow-up, the regular holding of follow-up meetings as hoped, the decision on the time and place of the next meeting, the preparatory work required for it, possible expert meetings following the Madrid meeting, and the idea that had already been presented for holding a CSCE 10th anniversary conference in Helsinki in 1985.

In the absence of confirmation on a substantive final outcome, the Western delegations estimated that an improvement in the international situation would take years. Because of this, the next follow-up would come about only several years after Madrid. The assumption of the N + N countries was that a two to three year interval would be sufficient. Judged by its general comments, the Soviet Union concurred with the West.

A second major dispute concerned striking a balance in the concluding document between humanitarian questions and military security. The priority aim for the Soviet Union in Madrid was to bring about a disarmament conference dealing with military détente. Because the Soviet Union wanted to extend the regional parameters even beyond the continent of Europe, some Western delegates suspected that its aim was to include China and Japan in the process.

At the plenary session on 17 March, the Soviet Ambassador Juri Dubinin reiterated the offers made by Brezhnev: to extend area of application of confidence building measures from the 250 kilometre zone agreed in the Helsinki Final Act, to the Urals, 2,500 kilometres away. "This was a great step forward," said Dubinin. He claimed that the Soviet Union would take a tolerant attitude to the achievement of a new balance as a consequence of Madrid. "Why bother wasting time blaming both sides. What is needed now is political will – time is not decisive, the success of the Madrid meeting is."

At the meeting of N + N countries, on the same day, Ambassador Richard Müller calculated that the Madrid meeting could go on for a long time unless something exceptional happened. It did not seem likely in this situation that the neutral and non-aligned group would come up with a solution to the impasse.

There were three weeks to Easter. Easter was considered as a target deadline for winding up the conference. The Western group distributed its main proposal on Basket III, known as a composite paper, which in the view of the Soviets did nothing to help the negotiating situation. It could not, with its maximalistic demands, form a substantial base for negotiations. This position also forced the socialist countries to oppose it along the same lines. The impasse would only worsen, making it more difficult to continue a constructive discussion.

In the neutral and non-aligned group, the Swiss delegate Peter Troendle, responsible for the follow-up to the conference and the timetable of the Madrid proceedings, had already proposed a draft for the official conclusion of the meeting before Easter. Troendle made the proposal by discussing it with representatives of both the Western group and the Soviet Union. The concluding document, which is what it would be, was to be adopted on 8 April 1981. Then the closing speeches would be held and the meeting would end on 10 April, before Easter.

Malta and Finland had differing views of their own. They were not ready to be dictated to by the blocs. Ambassador Müller still adhered to the view that the main goal of the Madrid follow-up meeting was to bring about a substantive final result. The Maltese delegate did not accept that the meeting should end at this stage. The representative of Yugoslavia, Ambassador Ignaz Golob, wanted the concluding document to be adopted in conjunction with confirmation of the time and place of the next follow-up. The Austrian Ambassador, Franz Ceska, was not prepared to submit to a reckless all-or-nothing game. He was convinced that the West was prepared to end the Madrid meeting without a commitment to the next follow-up.

Intense unofficial consultations continued in the weeks before Easter. In the absence of a credible readiness to compromise on matters of substance, the N + N countries continued with their unofficial compilation of a concluding document on 31 March 1981, under the pressure of time. It included the preliminary ingredients of consensus noted down previously, proposals that were ripening and hopefully soon to be adopted, and also the original proposals of the main participants. The composition was therefore not solely a joint N + N view of a possible outcome. It was clearly unripe.

Thus the response to the proposal before Easter was contradictory. The Soviet Union was able, in principle, to adopt a positive attitude because the US stance was cool. Many other Western delegations expressed disappointment that not all of their proposals were written into the text. The Netherlands crystallized Western thinking by saying that the proposal could not be "a basis for negotiations but a starting point". In the Dutch view more meat was needed on the bones before the proposal could form the basis for the final talks.

At the meeting of the Nordic countries, on 7 April, the Norwegians and Danes expressed noticeably more encouraging comments on the N + N effort. In Oslo the attitude to the paper had been "favourable". In the view of Ambassador Leif Mevik the balance of substance was well presented, the mandate for the disarmament conference was clear, the Basket III principles could be regarded favourably, the follow-up was ensured and Basket II had taken up the Nordic proposals. The Norwegians stated candidly that not all the requirements for alterations and complements put by the NATO countries would be essential. The Danes concurred. Ambassador Thomas Rechnagel said that the 10 EEC countries were prepared to construct a compromise on the basis of proposals made, some of which concerned human rights and the implementation of principles.

"Your cookies are great"

The first substantial proposal drawn up by the N + N countries opened discussion on the materialisation of the disarmament conference. There was such strong criticism, and the main delegations' willingness to compromise was so meagre that the faith among several of the N + N delegations for a substantive outcome in Madrid began to fade. The summer break intervened. When the delegations returned to Madrid in September, the Finnish delegation decided to try once again.

Superpower relations remained bogged down during 1981. The superpowers leaders did not meet regularly at summit level. They had last done so in 1979 in connection with the signing of the SALT II treaty. President Reagan's first year in office meant a new situation to get used to. Basic principles were demanding and anti-communist rhetoric was high profile. When President Koivisto went on his first state visit to Moscow in June 1983, the head of the Scandinavian department at the Soviet Foreign Ministry, Georgi Farafonov suggested in the communiqué negotiations wording for the declaration that would condemn those "who maintain political confrontation because it could lead to the destruction of civilization in Europe."

Bilateral discussions with the main delegations were held once again in autumn 1981 under the direction of Ambassador Müller. While earlier the N + N countries' substantive proposal had been a preliminary compromise between the Eastern and Western viewpoints, Müller's own estimate was that the inclusion of the US and the main EEC countries would now necessitate a bolder compromise. There was pressure to register more from the West's viewpoint. At the same time, the proposal should adhere as closely as possible to the phrasing and aims of the Final Act.

The bilateral discussions with the US delegation and the group led by Ambassador Kampelman in October 1981 proved both encouraging and decisive. At the end of an expert-level discussion Kampelman passed a note across the table to Müller with a defining message: "Your cookies are great!" Kampelman's point was that the Finnish approach and viewpoint contained the ingredients for further work.

After this it was easier for Müller to approach the other neutrals as the messenger for the beauty contest finals. The neutrals still had one opportunity to provide their good offices for the Madrid follow-up, on condition that it followed the adjustments and specifications tested in the preparatory work of the Finnish delegation in place of the earlier neutral and non-aligned proposal.

In November and December 1981, as a result of intense consultations, the N + N countries presented a new draft for a concluding document to the Madrid follow-up meeting on 11 December 1981. On Sunday 13 December Poland declared martial law, and so rose the curtain on the Madrid follow-up's next dramatic act. The meeting adjourned for Christmas and returned at ministerial level in February 1982 to discuss the CSCE's situation in the shadow of Poland's martial law.

The foreign ministers of the neutral countries and their senior officials held numerous joint meetings during the Madrid follow-up. Their aim was two-fold: to assess the possibilities of the neutral countries to further assist the follow-up meeting to reach a substantive outcome; and to maintain an active public profile in current international discussions. Thanks to the CSCE the four neutral countries had the opportunity to take part comprehensively in issues affecting and concerning continental Europe.

The neutrals wanted the CSCE to show the way towards the development of a pragmatic, more secure Europe, as well as towards increasing cooperation and contacts among citizens regardless of the prevailing state of relations between the superpowers and the blocs. Solidarity within alliances still had, in the 1970s and 1980s, an indubitable importance and role in the CSCE.

The CSCE principles on the equality of the 35 participating states, – members of alliances and those outside them – meant, in reality, work for the benefit of the small and neutral countries.

Martial law in Poland and the CSCE's pause for reflection

Poland's state of martial law caused a suspension in the work of the Madrid follow-up of almost a year – from February to November 1982. Civil liberties were curtailed under martial law, the Solidarity movement was banned and the obedience of journalists and teachers towards the emergency government was monitored. As a result some two thousand journalists and teachers lost their jobs. The economy suffered from the state of emergency. The authorities tried to keep coalmines running under military supervision. The work of government was carried out by the "Military Council of National Salvation", whose members were 15 generals and other officers. Martial law was in force until 22 February 1983, but an effort was made to gradually ease its effects from late summer 1981. The Soviet Union, too, imposed restrictions on citizens' dealings with the West.

The first session of 1982 took Poland as its theme. The Western delegations attended at foreign minister level. Poland's delegation took this as a political challenge against which it was able, as chair of the plenary session, to use all possible opportunities for CSCE consensus decision-making.

Poland's deputy minister, later ambassador to Helsinki, Josef Wiejasc, did all he could with his group of assistants, and particularly the new head of delegation Ambassador Konarski, so that the Western foreign ministers could not prepare their presentations in peace. The French foreign minister, who had arrived in Madrid, was prevented by procedural methods from speaking at the opening session. This was of course unheard of and an insult to the French delegation.

In December 2007, Ambassador Konarski explained that the presence of delegations from Poland and the other socialist countries in Madrid in February 1982 for the resumption of work had hung seriously in the balance. The attitude of the military government was that the Polish question should not become an international issue through the Madrid meeting. Poland first had to be able to resolve its internal problems, and then its delegation could take part in the work of the Madrid follow-up. This stance was supported by certain other hard-line socialist countries. The GDR and the Soviet Union expressed their readiness to show solidarity with Poland by being prepared to stay away from Madrid. In Konarski's opinion the opting out of the work in Madrid by Poland and the other socialist countries could have meant an end to the whole

CSCE process. Konarski appealed to General Wojciech Jaruzelski, arguing that if the Polish delegation were not to take part in the work of the Madrid follow-up meeting in February 1982, it would turn out to be extremely costly to Poland and a clearly disastrous decision for the continuation of the CSCE. At the end of their discussion Jaruzelski agreed that Konarski and his delegation would return to Madrid, but on strict conditions. If there were direct attacks on Poland, the Polish delegation would walk out in protest. Poland's socialist country counterparts could then follow Poland's example. Poland would not be left isolated.

Konarski's behaviour as chairman of the plenary session eventually led to a dispute over procedure. France's Foreign Minister Cheysson had not been given a turn to speak.

In his messages to Warsaw Konarski stressed that it had been possible to prevent the internationalisation of the Polish issue. It had been possible to transform discussion into procedural dispute. Despite his embarrassing position, Konarski survived unscathed. The head of the Polish delegation at Madrid, deputy minister Marian Dobrosielski openly expressed his opposition to the declaration of martial law. Jaruzelski dismissed him from his post as deputy minister on 30 December 1981. In May 1982 Konarski was appointed as the new head of the Polish delegation and as Poland's Ambassador to the Madrid follow-up meeting.

Finland was represented at the session on Poland by State Secretary Matti Tuovinen, first deputy of the Finnish foreign minister. His address to the session on 12 February 1982 was restrained, reflecting in an exceptional manner concern over the international situation and the role of the CSCE. Tuovinen said that the work of the follow-up meeting had been branded by deep mistrust between the alliances. He asked whether this was just a momentary lack of mutual trust or a fundamental difference of opinion on the content and significance of the CSCE. Finland wanted to see a continual expansion of the concept of security through the CSCE, so that it would take account of the distinctive features of relations among the 35 states and the qualitative and structural change of European security.

Finland emphasised the necessity of the continuation of the CSCE process. The work of the Madrid follow-up must not be allowed to founder on the events in just one participating state, Poland. The CSCE process would retain its credibility only when each participant conscientiously and continually endeavoured to respect the commitments that had been made. "If we accepted gradual progress, we also accepted that that progress was assessed and examined critically." The scrutiny of implementation must not become an end in itself.

The implementation of the stipulations of the Final Act must be carried out in practice by unilateral, bilateral and multilateral measures. The Final Act was not intended as a mechanism for resolving individual crises, as was the case with the UN Security Council. The Madrid meeting was able to complete its task, as long as it is accepted that the original objectives were long-term ones that required gradual progress. At the end of his speech, Tuovinen referred to the December 1981 proposal of the N + N countries for a concluding document. This RM-39 proposal could still offer the basis for a substantive outcome in Madrid.

Soviet deputy foreign minister Iljitchev said that there were no grounds for dealing with the Polish issue in Madrid. "It would be contrary to the principles agreed in the Helsinki Final Act. The United States must cease interfering with Poland's internal affairs and undermining Poland's economic situation."

The Soviet Union could not of course observe the fate of socialist Poland from the sidelines. "The Soviet Union faithfully carries out its promises and remains prepared to provide all possible assistance to the Polish people. This was the best way in which to observe the principles of the Helsinki Final Act."

Iljichov confirmed the Soviet Union's support for continuing the work of the follow-up meeting on the basis of the N + N group's 16 December draft concluding document. This presented the possibilities and limitations of the Madrid meeting in a concrete form.

FRG Foreign Minister Genscher said that since August 1980 the Soviet Union had presented demands to Poland that clearly breached the principle of non-interference in internal affairs. The Soviet Union had adhered to military measures openly reminiscent of the events of 1956 and 1968. It threatened to use military force.

US Secretary of State Alexander Haig, in his speech of 9 February, said directly that the continuation of work in Madrid "as business as usual" would give the wrong signal and validate the breaches of Helsinki decisions that had taken place in Poland. The deliberations must focus on the integrity of the Final

Act and the challenges of the CSCE process, so that, as soon as circumstances permitted, negotiations could begin "on the basis of the N + N countries' constructive overall proposal."

When the follow-up meeting reopened in Madrid in February 1982 it faced a complex problem. How could the N + N proposal be dealt with in a businesslike way? Amidst the atmosphere that prevailed in February and March it was not possible to hold a pragmatic discussion of this kind. The alternatives were either to tear open the neutral and non-aligned proposal so that it was no longer a basis for serious negotiations, or to concentrate on the examination of the international situation in the general addresses, and return to substantial negotiations later.

Prior to his transfer from head of the delegation at Madrid to the post of a head of department in Helsinki, the Director General of the Political Department, Ambassador Müller, wrote a report on the overall state of the Madrid meeting. He had to admit that the declaration of martial law in Poland made it impossible for the West to accept any agreement that the Soviet Union was party to concerning the follow-up to the CSCE. Suspicion and mistrust ran deep. Müller concluded that martial law in Poland even constituted an insurmountable challenge for action of a consequential and logical nature. An example was the demand by some Western countries in December that the Christmas break be cut short. Did they expect events in Poland to change rapidly?

Müller said that in such an atmosphere the speeches by the Poles and representatives of other socialist countries rejecting interference in the internal affairs of other countries rang hollow. One could ask why the Polish military authorities had temporarily ceased to implement some of the decisions of the Final Act.

Müller reiterated one of the notions given of the Madrid follow-up meeting. According to the West's thinking, the implementation of all the stipulations of the Helsinki Final Act, including the observance of numerous individual rights, would influence the process of change in the socialist system. "Consequently, the Final Act contained from the West's stance an indisputable ideological aim." On the other hand, Müller had to admit that since the Helsinki summit the Soviet side had declared that the ideological struggle had not ceased. "By appealing to the principles of non-interference in internal affairs and the inviolability of borders, the Soviet Union seemed to be relying on a defence mechanism in the hope that, together with the status quo, regulated cooperation between states would work."

The declaration of martial law by Poland posed a totally new challenge for the CSCE process. Europe had not seen such a crisis since the occupation of Czechoslovakia in 1968 that, in its day, had developed into the dominant state of emergency. The behaviour of the Soviet Union was under close scrutiny. During the extended break in the meeting, in September 1982, the neutral countries held a ministerial meeting in Stockholm. President Koivisto, commenting on the declaration from the conference, said that other parties had finally assented to the amendments proposed by Finland, so that the accusations in the declaration could be erased in favour of a more reconciliatory formulation. In Müller's view, Switzerland was the most troublesome partner in the joint work of the neutrals. At times it wanted to appear as even more hawkish than the US and Britain. By stressing the righteousness of its own viewpoint, the Swiss had at the same time been critical of the Finns. "We were nevertheless able to gain the respect of the West, particularly the US, France and the FRG."

The joint communiqué of the foreign ministers of the neutral countries was significant in this situation. What it contained was not unimportant. The initial Swedish draft and the text that was finally adopted were, according to Müller, from completely different worlds. The joint manifesto of the neutrals was a revised and considered message on the current situation.

Müller observed in another context that the CSCE process would not be able to continue unless the N + N group were able to exercise realism and moderation. The Finnish delegation felt that it was between a rock and a hard place amidst the conflicting pressures. There were no options. And it was unthinkable to break away from the N + N's joint work.

Ambassador Brunner's article in the 23/1983 issue of *Europa-Archiv* on Switzerland's role in Madrid confirmed Müller's observations. He wrote that Switzerland's neutrality did not prevent its delegation from "saying loud and clear what they thought about problems such as Afghanistan or Poland. Neutrality did not mean being silent or indifferent." Neutrality did not mean being 'neutralised'.

In Brunner's view, the cooperation among the neutral and non-aligned countries was "confidential and harmonious" throughout the Madrid meeting.

But the work in Madrid also revealed the limits to this cooperation. Brunner gave Malta's behaviour as one example of this. Another was Switzerland's abstention from the joint appeal of the heads of the N + N participating states in April 1983. Brunner nevertheless came close to Finland's basic position in his final assessment. Madrid faced slow progress in agreeing decisions and making steps forward. These steps brought better results than an "all or nothing" posture. This work required maintaining both bilateral and multilateral pressure. The agreed texts and terms were legitimate instruments of multilateral policy, wrote Brunner.

The USA's European allies presented an appeal to Washington prior to the start of the 1982 autumn session in Madrid for the US to take a new, serious attitude to the work of the Madrid meeting. The FRG's Foreign Minister, Hans-Dietrich Genscher, defended the more active continuation of the Madrid negotiations despite the events in Poland. He called on the socialist countries to demonstrate a greater readiness for compromise. The long break in the negotiations had given them the opportunity to withdraw from the discussion concerning implementation. In Genscher's view, the mandate of the Stockholm conference to be negotiated in Madrid would significantly supplement the aims of the superpowers negotiations in Geneva and the alliance negotiations in Vienna.

In mid-November 1982, Chancellor Helmut Kohl visited Washington. The joint communiqué that was issued mentioned for the first time since Poland's declaration of martial law the readiness of the US to work towards achieving a substantive and balanced concluding document in Madrid. The US was ready for the more precise mandate required for a European disarmament conference provided that present sections in the draft text concerning human rights and civil liberties could be supplemented. At the same time, the US administration announced that it was lifting sanctions against the Soviet Union.

Ambassador Müller estimated that the work would restart in November 1982. A dramatic turnabout would have been if the Western alliance had decided not to take part at all. Such a decision would have endangered the entire CSCE process.

The countries of Western Europe did not want to take such a risk. Foreign Minister Genscher recalls in his memoirs that aborting the Madrid work would not have "punished the Soviet Union". The Western alliance would have simply harmed its own interests. Agreement on the continuation of the work was reached with difficulty. The West was prepared to continue working on the N + N proposal. This work required a host of significant alterations. There was no desire to shelve the N + N countries' proposal. It simply needed to better reflect the Soviet Union's current behaviour on human rights. Also needed were references to the legitimacy of the activities of the Helsinki groups, the right to criticize the shortcomings of government decisions on the implementation of the Final Act. Müller stressed in his report that the West did not propose changes to the content of the mandate on the disarmament conference. The attitude reflected caution so as not to upset the delicate balance or imperil further work on the matter.

A Soviet delegate commented calmly on the working situation to Markku Reimaa in November 1982. In Soviet thinking, the best way to demonstrate support for the draft of the concluding document of the N + N countries was to criticise the West's proposals for amendments to it. If they were to comment directly on the N + N's draft, it did not necessarily mean that they wanted to abandon the formulation of the draft. This Soviet colleague said with surprising directness that the N + N draft preamble to the section on Basket III was good to the extent that it would allow the Soviet Union "to probably survive more challenging operative texts in the future."

The military security of Finland and Europe

In November 1981, Finland's third Parliamentary committee on defence considered that the domestic politico-military situation was stable and that Finland had no strategically tempting targets. In the event of crisis and war, Finland's military importance concerned possible targets outside its territory. Lapland's airspace and the good network of roads could provide routes for advancing into an adversary's territory. "It is in everyone's interest that Finnish Lapland remains inviolable."

Also, there was keen interest in Finland in how the Nordic NWFZ could be advanced. In a letter on the subject to President Koivisto of 29 May 1982, Jaakko Kalela summarised the reasons according to which the Soviet Union assessed the Nordic NWFZ project. They were revealing. The Soviet Union considered that with the Nordic NWFZ project it would be possible to strengthen leverage on future security policy decisions of the Norwegian government, and via the Nordic countries, with their three NATO members, influence Western European public opinion and government policy. Kalela's conclusions included no reference to whether the Soviet Union's evident support for the Nordic NWFZ project, in the form proposed by Finland, had brought it closer to being realized.

Undersecretary of State Keijo Korhonen summed up his views on the same issue in a memo of 26 May 1982: "The Nordic NWFZ project is an essential part of Finland's foreign policy profile."

When President Carter's former National Security Advisor Zbigniew Brzezinski visited Finland in October 1982, he stressed that the Soviet Union's interests in Eastern Europe were mainly military. As to the role of the CSCE, Brzezinski admitted that the CSCE was thus far a victory for the West and Eastern Europe, at least in principle. Brzezinski was prepared in the future to support the CSCE process "on condition that it was used to the maximum to pressurise the Soviet Union."

In October 1982 the government in Bonn changed hands from the Social Democrats under Helmut Schmidt to the Christian Democrats under Helmut Kohl. The partner in the governing coalition continued to be the Free Democrats, with Hans-Dietrich Genscher as Foreign Minister and Vice-Chancellor. The programme of the new government stated that the unification of Germany was an objective which the new government would adhere to, "even though at this point there does not appear to be any possibility to alter the current situation. This state of affairs could last for generations."

In this situation President Koivisto felt that problems were piling up on the horizon. There were signs of this in discussions at the Madrid follow-up meeting. When Koivisto spoke with General Secretary Yuri Andropov on the 60th anniversary of the foundation of the Soviet Union, on 22 December 1982, the former mentioned that he was "anxious about 1983".

A few weeks previously, during discussions held on 9–10 December, Soviet Prime Minister Tihonov had told Koivisto that he expected much from the Madrid follow-up. The Soviet Union wanted a decision on a conference dealing with disarmament and security in Europe. But, according to Tihonov, "the United States wants a confrontation, and to undo the European security process." Fortunately, the roots of the process ran deep. "We highly appreciate

Finland's role in the CSCE and our cooperation in Madrid. We hope for success" Koivisto acknowledged that the Madrid meeting was important and that all the participants could influence its outcome. He admitted that the Finnish delegation in Madrid "faced difficult issues".

The Nordic NWFZ's minimalists considered that the coastal waters of Denmark, Sweden and Finland should be included in the arrangement. The maximalists, on the other hand, considered that the whole of the Baltic Sea had to be included. The Cabinet Secretary at the Swedish Foreign Ministry, Leif Leifland, had endorsed this latter position in presenting Sweden's position, on 2 March 1982. On 22 November 1982, Sweden's national day, Foreign Minister Bodström reiterated that submarines equipped with nuclear weapons should withdraw from the Baltic Sea. The Baltic Sea would not be included in the NWFZ per se. Instead, its status would be settled separately under international law. There had clearly been a debate in Sweden concerning the main point in Chervov's statement. One aim was to have an influence on public opinion in western Europe and on various peace initiatives.

In autumn 1979, General Secretary Brezhnev had made a wide-ranging proposal for a peace programme in which the key elements appeared to be a ban on the use of force in international relations, an agreement prohibiting a first strike and a proposal on freezing the number of members of the military alliances. The proposal also included the provision of security guarantees for nuclear weapons-free states. NATO's decision of December 1979 on the deployment of Pershing II missiles in Western Europe had an immediate impact on the Warsaw Pact's deliberations.

Soviet military specialists calculated that the Pershing missile deployments meant a reduction in the warning time on tactical nuclear weapons from half an hour to as little as five minutes. The programme was considered as a complete change in the global balance.

A broad formula of balance and reciprocity

At the end of the 1982 sessions of the Madrid follow-up the two superpowers submitted their comments on the mandate of the Stockholm conference in the military section of the N + N proposal. The main point of contention concerned the area of application for the notification of military manoeuvres, and its extent compared with the stipulations of the Helsinki Final Act. From the Soviet side this was expected to mean from the Atlantic to the Urals. In its comments submitted that December the Soviet Union adhered closely to its repeated principle that a correspondingly extensive area should be forthcoming from the West.

Initially, this was thought to mean primarily the inclusion of US naval manoeuvres within the sphere of the obligation on prior notification in the Atlantic. The Soviet Union was rescinding the strict geographical measure of reciprocity and the concept of "corresponding width". Moscow appeared to be prepared to reach its objectives by requiring that naval activities in the Atlantic should fall within the sphere of notification, if they were linked to "activities affecting the interests of security in Europe".

At the same time as nullifying its original stance, the Soviet Union expanded the agenda for negotiations to include the nature and purpose of manoeuvres. Western experts could not accept this European security linkage. It would have meant infringing on another forum, the negotiations on Intermediate-range Nuclear Forces. It was surprising that nearly 40 years after the Second World War, regional questions were so hotly debated in peacetime negotiations. Principles and achieved advantages were debated. Past achievements were treated as part of the present. The concepts of "respective obligations" and the demands of "balance and reciprocity" acquired completely new dimensions.

Before the Madrid meeting was brought to a successful conclusion, Finland had to admit that the Nordic NWFZ plan was for the time being on hold.

During talks between Prime Ministers Kalevi Sorsa and Olof Palme, on 7 February 1983, the two leaders affirmed their support for the Nordic NWFZ. Their positions on the issue were close. Only Denmark and Norway did not consider the scheme to be relevant at that point. NATO's joint priority was the deployment project for the Pershing missiles, "Euromissiles". A lively debate surrounded the project, which is why Nordic governments, too, had to focus on it. Sorsa acknowledged that the Nordic NWFZ plan was temporarily at a standstill. Prime Minister Palme said that he partly sympathized with the Western alliance's fears; they could not fail to be intensely aware of the Soviet Union's weapons' superiority in Europe. In Sweden's view disarmament should discuss a wide-ranging comprehensive solution that, in addition to nuclear weapons, would include conventional and chemical weapons.

In February 1983 Foreign Minister Pär Stenbäck entered a spirited debate on Nordic stability. The matter concerned discussion on the possible deployment of nuclear weapons in the Nordic countries, including Finland. A cable from the minister, dated 24 February, pointed out that the principal statements on Finnish disarmament policy of 1962, including the 28 May 1962 speech by Kekkonen on the Nordic NWFZ initiative, had been aimed at dispelling all suspicions that Finnish territory would be used for the deployment of nuclear weapons under any circumstances or with respect to any state. Unless such speculation was immediately rejected on the official level, it might feed further speculation and wreck efforts for the Nordic NWFZ.

If the policy based on supplementing the alliance agreements on maintaining the prevailing stability and balance in the North were rescinded, the situation would have become worrying, including from Finland's standpoint. It had been claimed that there were no treaty obligations that by themselves prohibited deployment of nuclear weapons in Finland under the authority of some State. If the Finnish-Soviet treaty could be interpreted in this way, then the effort and right to remain detached from disputes between the superpowers would become meaningless. This debate arose during the preparations for President Koivisto's visit to Norway.

Prime Minister Sorsa's discussions with Vice President George Bush on 2 July 1983, during the latter's visit to Finland, included the situation at the Madrid follow-up meeting. Bush said that relations between the superpowers had worsened since the heyday of détente. The reasons were the occupation of Afghanistan and the situation in Poland.

Sorsa reiterated the Finnish government's commitment to the CSCE process, including under difficult conditions. The CSCE corresponded to the basic objectives of Finland's foreign policy, in that it sought to improve the security situation on the European continent. Positive decisions made in Madrid would give cause for optimism.

At the same time as Bush's visit to Finland, the US Department of State confirmed to a Finnish Embassy representative that American reservations over the Nordic NWFZ remained. Because Norway and Denmark were US allies the theories and practices of their security policies were hard to consider in isolation. According to the Americans, a Soviet system of intimidation prevailed in Europe. "Messing with it would be crazy." In this way the Americans said clearly that the Nordic NWFZ idea would undermine NATO's defence efforts. "It even endangered general support for defence policy." Deputy Secretary of State Haass said finally that if the Finns were interested in other arms control breakthroughs, it would be better for them to give up setting obstacles to them such as the Nordic NWFZ.

A review of the international situation given at a meeting of Finnish ambassadors in Helsinki in August 1983 stated that the situation between the superpowers was bad. Talk of a new Cold War was nevertheless exaggerated. The deployment of "Euro-strategic" missiles in Western Europe had become the target of a propaganda campaign. If the implementation of the deployment decision was a low point in superpower relations, it could be followed by an improvement in relations and a gradual broadening of dialogue.

At the same meeting of ambassadors,when problems were reviewed from a Soviet point of view, they were seen as being elsewhere particularly in the form of US arms build-up. The US had not ratified the SALT II treaty. Economic sanctions were, according to the Soviet Union, an example of how Washington implemented its CSCE commitments.

An outside observer would have said that what was at stake was a struggle for authority, balance and equality in power politics. Different levels of contact were, as far as was known, going on in the area of arms control, concerning both the START and INF negotiations. There would also be, according to the review, another dimension to superpower relations opened up if the Madrid follow-up meeting decided on a substantive outcome.

Draft concluding document by the N + N countries, spring 1983

Finland continued to work actively following the change in its head of delegation. Richard Müller was appointed as head of the Foreign Ministry's Political Department. The Ambassador to Belgrade, Matti Kahiluoto, succeeded him in Madrid.

In spring 1983 Richard Müller started Finland's work from Helsinki on the latest initiative to bring the work in Madrid to a conclusion with a substantive document. The N + N countries presented a new comprehensive draft for a concluding document on 15 March. At the same time, there were signs of hope in the general international situation. After a long break, the leaders of the US and Soviet Union had met in Geneva on 7 January 1983. They agreed that talks at expert level on strategic and medium-range nuclear weapons would start in Geneva on 12 March that year.

At President Koivisto's initiative, on 18 April six N + N countries presented an appeal to the other CSCE participants for a speedy conclusion to the work of the Madrid meeting. The appeal referred to the N + N's draft for the concluding document, written in March. This was the latest demonstration of the commitment of these countries to the CSCE process and to a substantive outcome in Madrid.

Switzerland and Liechtenstein did not join the appeal. The absence of Switzerland was mainly due to the comments from the Americans concerning the N + N countries' draft for the concluding document. Switzerland did not want to commit itself to possible changes to the text. On the other hand, under the Swiss political system the role of the President was unsuited for presenting appeals on foreign policy. Malta, too, did not think that it could be involved, because it was not one of the original proponents of the N + N concluding draft. The significance attached to N + N cooperation on this matter was such that Austria eventually joined the appeal, although at the preparatory stage it had regarded Switzerland's presence important.

President Koivisto's appeal to the leaders of the CSCE was distributed in the capitals of 26 participating States. In Washington it was delivered by Ambassador Iloniemi to Assistant Secretary of State Richard Burt, on 18 April.

Burt was in a position to reply immediately to the N + N appeal. He was convinced that President Reagan's administration was prepared to support the CSCE and the objectives of the N + N countries for achieving a balanced and "sufficiently substantial" document. "Unfortunately, the most recent proposal of the N + N countries, RM/39, did not fulfil these requirements." The main source of concern was the concept of zone in the context of military activity. The word "ocean" was a problem. Moreover, the NATO group had voiced comments on other issues, including the position of free trade unions, an end to radio jamming, the rights of journalists and the situation of the Helsinki watch groups. Burt had good words to say about the N + N countries who, he said, had performed an extremely important and fair-minded role as mediator. He hoped that they would continue to do so.

In Iloniemi's opinion the reception was definitely appropriate but at the same time devoid of all enthusiasm. Iloniemi had noticed that in commenting on the N + N appeal Burt had referred to written notes, and so the response had been prepared in advance. In light of other factors, Iloniemi thought that the strict attitude on human rights, such as the release of dissidents or the granting of emigration rights, were due to the attitudes of the Congressional CSCE Commission. According to Iloniemi, a sense of mistrust prevailed in the State Department concerning the real purpose of the N + N appeal. There was suspicion that the appeal was due to Soviet pressure in Helsinki and Stockholm. Iloniemi and his Swedish counterpart Ambassador Wachtmeister had heard nothing along those lines.

The Soviet Union's first deputy Foreign Minister Kornienko said in Moscow that there was no need to comment at the time the appeal was submitted. The Soviet Union had appreciated and continued to appreciate the efforts of the N + N countries. The appeal that had now been made was regarded in the same way. On 19 April, *Pravda* published a TASS report on President Koivisto's appeal, which he had also presented in a Finnish TV and radio broadcast. This stressed that the purpose of the six N + N countries was to bring about "a substantial and balanced outcome in Madrid soon". Ensuring the continuity of the CSCE process was, according to Koivisto, the basic task of the Madrid meeting.

The N + N draft document received support from an unexpected source. The Soviet delegation announced in Madrid on 9 May that it was prepared to accept the document as it was, without further negotiations. President Koivisto expressed his appreciation on behalf of Finland for the way in which the Soviet Union had tried to further the attainment of a substantial concluding document in Madrid. The Soviet statement was decisively influenced by the fact that the mandate of the Stockholm conference on confidence and security-building measures was in a draft that was in an acceptable form. This had been one of the Soviet Union's priorities in Madrid. The Finnish delegation interpreted the Soviet comments as indicating that the Soviet Union was prepared to continue negotiations on the basis of the N + N document. In fact the Soviet Union announced that it would officially accept the text only after it knew the requirements for changes demanded by the West. In his report on the CSCE situation to the Finnish Parliamentary foreign affairs committee on 24 May

1983, Foreign Minister Paavo Väyrynen stated that now in Madrid, for the first time since December 1981 and the N + N countries' first draft for a concluding document, negotiations proper were under way. The 18 April appeal on the CSCE, initiated by Finland, had changed attitudes, including those of the superpowers. They were now directly negotiating among themselves. Iloniemi commented that the appeal made at head of state level departed from the usual negotiating situation in Madrid. This is why the Americans had been more cautious about it than Ambassador Max Kampelman normally was in Madrid

A key issue that arose was the convening of a separate meeting of experts concerning human contacts, before the Vienna follow-up conference.

During President Koivisto's visit to Denmark in April 1983, Prime Minister Schluter acknowledged Finland's active involvement at the Madrid follow-up meeting. The activities of the N + N countries had been a great asset. In Koivisto's view the Finnish representatives had played a major role in the meeting. Schlüter said that at his recent talks in Bonn with Chancellor Helmut Kohl and Foreign Minister Genscher, both had been optimistic about the Madrid meeting.

While Koivisto was discussing matters in Copenhagen, the political committee of the EEC held a meeting in Bonn, and the following day NATO was due to consider the N + N's latest proposal in more detail. In the view of the Danes the proposal was "mainly satisfactory" and the EEC/NATO countries would only propose minor amendments concerning:

- territorial definitions pertaining to the Stockholm conference
- stronger reference to the follow-up on the implementation of the Final Act, so that international organizations and citizens would be able to take part in monitoring.
- a decision to hold an expert meeting on human contacts, and
- an addition to the section on information exchange of something essential concerning the position of journalists or ending the jamming of radio broadcasts.

The Americans would refer to the requirement for improved performance in Soviet actions on human rights. It was not, however, realistic to expect that the Soviet Union would take any action in advance or by public announcement in Madrid.

On 8 June, Foreign Minister Väyrynen met Foreign Minister Gromyko in Moscow. The negotiating situation in Madrid was expected to be extremely difficult. The N + N countries had made their proposal with the aim of meeting the wishes of as many participating countries as possible. The Soviet Union had already announced that it approved the proposal. Some other countries still wanted changes to the text. Thus consensus had yet to be reached. Väyrynen assured Gromyko that Finland and the other N + N countries would not themselves propose any amendments.

Gromyko commented on the situation, saying that in the Soviet view the US wanted to unravel the progress made on the N + N text. The Americans tried to include leverage by which they would attempt to influence internal affairs in the Soviet Union and other socialist countries. "This is unscrupulous, and we cannot accept it." Gromyko wanted to assure Väyrynen that the Soviet Union had no room for manoeuvre beyond the N + N text. "If no agreement is reached in Madrid, it will be the fault of the Americans alone."

On 9 June, *Pravda* published a report saying that foreign ministers Gromyko and Väyrynen had declared their support for an end to the Madrid CSCE meeting as soon as possible on the basis of the concluding document proposed by the N + N group.

In communiqué negotiations the Soviet side had initially wanted to revert to the matter of earlier mass media practice. The proposal was that it would be stated that "the mass media was to promote, showing due responsibility, the important issue of further strengthening friendship and trust between the Soviet and Finnish people and not damage the development of the countries' friendly relations." Klaus Törnudd said that the role of the mass media in Finland was different from that of the mass media in the Soviet Union, and so Törnudd proposed deleting the paragraph. Farafanov put the matter to his superiors, who then accepted the Finnish position.

During a discussion between Ambassador Kahiluoto and Kondrachov on 13 June 1983, the latter estimated that the US had pushed through its stricter approach to human rights in Madrid with the support of the Western group. "If the Americans continue to impose on others, the prevention of a positive outcome in Madrid would be guaranteed." The Soviet Union had already made major concessions on the mandate for the Stockholm conference and on extending territorial stipulations for security and confidence-building measures across Europe as far as the Urals. Kondrachov said that the Soviet Union had not received anything reciprocal in response. The Madrid meeting was approaching a crisis. "It we now start to talk about having a summer break, it would mean that the N + N proposal would be sidelined." One alternative would be to go back to the Belgrade follow-up meeting, and only agree on the next follow-up. Kondrachov gave the impression that the Soviet Union was at that stage still prepared for all outcomes or none at all. There was also a repetition in Madrid of a few months of Mediterranean delay. Malta again wanted a decision on the holding of a new expert meeting on cooperation in the Mediterranean region.

General Secretary Andropov gave a spoken affirmation at the summit meeting of the Warsaw Treaty, on 28 June 1983, that the Soviet Union and the Warsaw Pact were ready to accept the N + N proposal as it stood. Deputy Foreign Minister Kovalev also announced in Madrid on 1 July that the Soviet Union was prepared to consider positively Spain's intercession to "take action".

Ambassador Max Kampelman considered this to be a constructive change in the Soviet position and that now an important advance had been made towards a decision at the Madrid meeting.

During the concluding negotiations the Soviet Union was in the end prepared to make major concessions on human rights issues on the assurance that the Stockholm conference would start in time. The concessions concerned for the first time the setting of more definite timeframes, of six months, on meetings between family members and the unification of families. Citizens were now guaranteed that they could conduct business at official foreign missions unimpeded. There were also new stipulations agreed on freedom of religion. The struggle against terrorism was included in a CSCE document now for the first time. On improving the working conditions of journalists, their personal links to their sources was written into CSCE practice, and they could carry with them information material needed in their work. When it was agreed that in spring 1986 in Bern there would be an expert meeting on human contacts, the Madrid decisions acquired, in a way, a boosted follow-up mechanism even before the Vienna follow-up meeting. It was decided to arrange follow-up meetings at regular intervals.

In his report on the proceedings, Ambassador Kahiluoto noted that in Madrid the US was able to retain its maximal objectives on human rights.

The CSCE remained a valuable forum in Europe for its allies, particularly for the FRG. But the socialist countries too played a role in developing the CSCE process in a pluralistic direction. The cultural forum arranged in Budapest was a good example. It was the first CSCE meeting held in a socialist country.

The final decision of the Madrid meeting took place under the direction of Ambassador Kahiluoto at the plenary session held on 15 July. The session lasted for 11 hours, with breaks. The positive and substantive outcome was due to the draft concluding document of the N + N countries and to the supplementary proposal made by the Prime Minister of Spain Felipe González on 17 June. The expert meeting on human contacts, to be held in Bern, was approved by consensus and in such a way that it was appended to the concluding document. The plenary chaired by Ambassador Kahiluoto decided at the start that the foreign ministers of the participating states would come to Madrid to close the follow-up meeting, on 7-9 September 1983. At that stage only the Maltese delegation did not join the consensus.

Prime Minister González told Finland's Prime Minister Kalevi Sorsa, in Helsinki in May 1984, that many of the key decisions at the Madrid follow-up were achieved with the help of the N + N countries. The mandate of the Stockholm Conference played a special role in this. The outcome of the Madrid meeting was an exceptional moment of détente in an otherwise tense international political situation. González affirmed the stance of the Spanish government, according to which Spain wanted to retain the level of cooperation with the N + N group during the Stockholm conference. Before joining NATO, Spain was the only CSCE participating state, along with the Vatican, that was not a member of any smaller reference group. This position required of the delegation much capability and resources.

Malta applies the brakes

Sergei Kondrachov of the Soviet delegation made an oral proposal on 25 July with which Malta's stonewalling could be moderated. Kondrachov suggested that all other participating states announce their acceptance of the draft text of the concluding document at the plenary session of 15 July. The meeting could then make the decision that there was no need to continue with business and the final outcome would thus be acceptable to all others.

Malta's obstruction was an annoying burden for the neutral and non-aligned countries. Everyone was now looking at the N + N group so that the Malta problem could be solved.

The consensus principle had, since the start of the CSCE, been an important emblem of its decision-making. It highlighted the equality of all the participants, big and small. In order for the usefulness and acceptability of the consensus principle to be preserved, it had, in Finland's view, to be used responsibly. It now seemed as if Malta had started to misuse it in a situation in which it already had most of its original demands included in the Madrid final document.

Foreign Minister Väyrynen was in contact by phone on 9 August with his Maltese counterpart, Foreign Minister Alex Skebarras Trigona. In addition, head of department Seppo Pietinen appealed to his counterpart Ambassador Camillieri on 23 August for Malta to join the consensus decision in Madrid. Apart from such bilateral appeals the other N + N countries decided to draw up a joint appeal for Malta to bend with the consensus.

Ilmar Bekeris, the Swedish Ambassador, coordinated the operation. A message was sent from Stockholm to all N + N countries, including Malta, containing the draft of a statement by the chairman and a separate appeal from the neutral countries to Prime Minister Mintoff. A sentence intended as a compromise had been inserted into Malta's section on security and cooperation in Mediterranean countries. Accordingly, "The participating states were prepared to carefully consider supporting initiatives that participants might possibly present during the follow-up process after the Madrid meeting, initiatives which sought to maintain and supplement contact and dialogue between the participating and non-participating Mediterranean states."

The appeal sent to Prime Minister Mintoff was signed by Chancellor Sinowatz of Austria, President Kyprianou of Cyprus, Finland's Prime Minister Kalevi Sorsa, Prime Minister Brunhart of Liechtenstein, the Captains Regent of San Marino Adriano Reffi and Massimo Roberto Rossini, the Prime Minister of Sweden Olof Palme, the Swiss Foreign Minister Aubert and the Prime Minister of Yugoslavia Planic.

The shooting down of a South Korean passenger aircraft during the last week of the Madrid meeting, on 31 August, caused an outburst of feeling but did not lead to the destruction of the meeting. US Secretary of State George

Shultz was considered to have played a constructive role over the issue, and towards President Reagan.

Finnish assessments estimated that Soviet-US relations were more conspicuous during the Madrid meeting than at any time earlier in relation to the CSCE. A second major finding was the need for unity within the Western alliance. The US eventually got its wishes on human rights included and the other member states of the Western alliance achieved a comprehensive and balanced outcome. The Soviet Union was prepared to be flexible on human rights issues in order to bring about the Stockholm conference. A good deal of the rest of the document was a counterbalance to the Stockholm conference and its preparatory meeting.

Foreign Minister Väyrynen stressed Finland's traditional CSCE policy in his final speech at the Madrid meeting, on 8 September. The achievement of a positive final result indicated that the participating states had a common will to develop multilateral relations. The hope was that the outcome would improve superpower relations and promote broader dialogue. Europe's richness lay in its variety. The neutral and non-aligned countries tried sincerely to act for and to promote consensus. "This of course requires realism, a businesslike approach and sometimes imagination."

The mandate for the Stockholm conference was an important step forward. It had a particular importance for countries that did not belong to military alliances. The accelerating arms race was a growing source of concern both to governments and citizens. "International stability and security can be increased only by limiting and reducing the levels of weaponry."

In the area of humanitarian activity, decisions were achieved that were based on the Helsinki Final Act and which supplemented it. Advances were made into many new areas.

The neutral countries had played a crucial role in Madrid. Due to their active mediating and negotiating work they contributed to the achievement of a balanced outcome. The role of the neutral countries had also been important in decisions concerning the follow-up: the Stockholm conference, its preparatory meeting in Helsinki and the next follow-up meeting in Vienna. In addition, there would be the expert meeting in Bern on human contacts.

CSCE paradoxes persist

In reviewing the work in Madrid, Finland's Parliamentary foreign affairs committee was able to state that the result was wide ranging and rich in content and that it safeguarded the continuity of the CSCE through a full follow-up programme. The concluding document was extensive, about 40 pages, and dealt with recommendations and stipulations in all CSCE areas. It had been possible to register decisions on all sub-themes that went further than the decisions of the Helsinki Final Act. The introductory part repeated the fact that the opportunities offered by the Helsinki Final Act to develop cooperation had not been utilised sufficiently.

Concerning the principles, there was agreement in Madrid on such matters as adding action against terrorism to the decisions, emphasising respect for human rights and fundamental freedoms and promoting freedom of religion, the protection of the rights of national minorities, promoting gender equality and the recognition and promotion of free trade unions.

The decisions on economic, scientific and technological cooperation had already been ready in summer 1981. The participants announced that they were endeavouring to eliminate all types of trade barriers. The ECE played an important role in this area. One of the most contentious subjects of Basket II was the discussion concerning the position of migrant workers. Their situation and rights, including the preservation of their language and culture and their rights of return to their countries of origin, were the subjects of animated debate.

For the first time, clear administrative time limits were set for dealing with applications for the reunification of families and applications for international marriages. There would be an effort too to keep the associated costs reasonable.

Efforts would be made to improve the availability of printed products imported from abroad and to keep their prices reasonable. Improvements to the working conditions of journalists would also be carried out, including privacy protection, possibilities for travel and the use of visas. Journalists would have the right to carry with them technical equipment and supplementary material needed for professional purposes.

In the area of cultural cooperation, one of Finland's priorities remained the protection of less widely spoken languages. Finland, together with Iceland

(NATO) and Hungary (Warsaw Pact), made the first joint proposal that covered representatives of all of the CSCE's political groupings. On the basis of the proposal a recommendation was entered in the concluding document.

The follow-up was comprehensive and diverse. It comprised altogether eight events, beginning with the preparatory meeting in Helsinki in October 1983 for the Stockholm conference, and a reference to the organization of a CSCE 10th anniversary event in Helsinki. It also comprised meetings on the peaceful settlement of disputes (Athens 1984), cooperation in the Mediterranean region, (Venice 1984), human rights (Ottawa 1985), a cultural forum (Budapest 1986), and a meeting on human contacts (Bern 1986). The next follow-up meeting would start on 4 November 1986 in Vienna.

The achievement of a substantial outcome was aided significantly by the problem-free interaction between the German delegations and especially by the close and smooth cooperation between the FRG delegation and the neutral and non-aligned countries. The FRG delegation was the first to request that the conference did not take long breaks and that despite martial law in Poland the meeting should continue its work.

The Finnish delegation estimated that the outcome of the Madrid meeting had been welcomed also by the small socialist countries. The CSCE offered them a framework, accepted by consensus, for cooperation and contact with the outside world at various levels and in various areas. While the superpower dialogue concentrated on the negotiations on medium-range missiles, the CSCE agenda provided a broader and more pragmatic basis for interaction. For Poland the outcome was of course of special value. It now finally became free from the burden of martial law.

CSCE enters sphere of military security

The mandate for the Stockholm conference on confidence and security-building measures and disarmament in Europe was one of the most difficult parts of the work in Madrid. The matter involved testing the waters of the principles and the specific task of starting negotiations among 35 countries. The first new opening was made with the expansion of the zone of application of confidence-building measures. Now it would cover the whole of Europe, from the Atlantic to the Urals and the adjoining sea area and air space. In addition to the mainland, the whole of Europe, it now also covered all European islands, the Azores, Spitsbergen, Iceland, Novaya Zemlya and Franz Josef Land.

In addition to enlarging the area concerning voluntary activities, agreed in the Helsinki Final Act, there were now clear criteria attached. These would be politically binding and militarily significant.

When advancing from the development of security and confidence-building measures to the next stage of the conference, a procedure was found in the form of a transition clause drawn up by Finland. According to the clause, known as the 'Laajava formula', some future follow-up meeting would have to make a new decision on the transition. In this context the results attained so far would be assessed along with other factors influencing European security. The content of the negotiations of the next stage of the CSCE remained completely open after Madrid.

A meeting of the neutral and non-aligned countries in Geneva, on 14-15 December 1983, prepared for the start of the Stockholm conference the following January. According to the Zurich newspaper *Tages Anzeiger*, on 16 December, the aims of the N + N countries had been clarified as increasing the transparency of military activity, limiting the deployment of military detachments in border areas and prohibiting the use of force.

Despite the tense nature of superpower relations, the incoming head of the US delegation, Ambassador James Goodby, made an encouraging comment to the *Washington Post* in January 1984. "The Stockholm conference could be the turning point in East-West relations. The biggest threat to the conference would be if it were to change into a propaganda forum for discussing nuclear weapons."

The Stockholm Conference, 1984–86

The Helsinki preparatory conference – small steps rewarded

The outcome of the Madrid meeting set an immediate challenge to the Stockholm Conference. It was complex. Now, for the first time in the CSCE framework, militarily important confidence and security-building measures would be outlined, measures that, at the same time, would seek a response to the growing pressure, in public opinion, for reducing military build-up and the nuclear threat in Europe.

It was agreed in Madrid that practical arrangements for the work of the Stockholm conference would be made in Helsinki, starting 25 October 1983 with a three-week preparatory conference. Under the direction of Ambassador Matti Kahiluoto preparatory visits for bilateral consultations were paid to all the participating countries. An exception was made, however, concerning the N + N countries. They agreed to hold a joint meeting in Geneva, on 10-11 October. The schedule was tight.

Taking part in the discussions in Washington DC, on 3 October, were Richard Burt, Deputy Secretary of State, Kenneth Adelman, Director of the Arms Control and Disarmament Agency, and Ambassador James Goodby, head of the delegation to Stockholm.

During the discussions the Americans had an opportunity to emphasise the importance of the ongoing bilateral negotiations with the Soviet Union, namely START, INF, the MBFR talks in Vienna and, soon, Stockholm. At that stage it was not considered necessary in Washington for Secretary of State George Shultz to take part in the opening stage in Stockholm.

Finland's Foreign Minister Paavo Väyrynen and the head of the US delegation Ambassador James Goodby at the opening of the preparatory meeting for the Stockholm conference, 25 October 1983. (Photograph: Lehtikuva / Marja Seppänen)

In Moscow, Ambassador Oleg Grinevski welcomed the Finns to the Soviet Foreign Ministry and asked them to "teach him what the issue was at the Stockholm conference". His appointment as head of the Soviet disarmament delegation to Stockholm had only been confirmed the previous evening. This was the start of useful cooperation between the Finnish and Soviet Stockholm delegations. It was of great importance in furthering dialogue and in producing the final document of the Stockholm conference.

There was broad consensus among the participants that the Helsinki preparatory conference was by nature a technical matter. Its duration was intentionally limited to three weeks maximum and its role was to reach agreement on the agenda for the Stockholm conference.

The smooth progress of the work of the preparatory meeting was significantly influenced by the success of the EEC's CSCE political cooperation group in agreeing, at a meeting in Athens on 17 October 1983, on a joint position for the EEC on the outcome of the preparatory meeting.

The deliberations of the EEC's ten member countries were comprehensive and calm. Their statements reiterated the mandate of the Madrid meeting for the Stockholm conference, and drafted points of a general nature for the conference's agenda – from the start of the conference and its various working stages, through to the adoption of a final document. According to EEC expectations, the conference would have to proceed in four sessions a year. The first four weeks would be used in plenary sessions for work on the subject index; general discussion would be in open sessions and with the presentation of proposals and drafting of texts taking place in closed sessions.

In Moscow, the attitude to the course of the Stockholm conference and the Helsinki preparatory meeting had not been finalised. This was the time of stagnation and the breakthrough of glasnost. The Soviet CSCE veteran, deputy minister Kovalev gave an instruction to Grinevski before the Helsinki preparatory meeting, "Show that the Stockholm conference is our baby!" The Helsinki preparatory meeting concluded its work ahead of deadline. The meeting only went into detail concerning practical arrangements and a smooth start to the opening phase. The general attitude was that the Stockholm conference would decide on its own arrangements only when the formal proposals concerning the work had been presented.

Foreign Minister Paavo Väyrynen said in his opening speech to the preparatory meeting that the decision made in Madrid concerning the Stockholm conference was an important political achievement. The CSCE was a positive exception amidst a difficult international situation. Finland saw the CSCE as a possible mechanism to revise outdated concepts of national security. "Security must aim for broader cooperation, and not rely solely on building up military strength."

The key decision of the Helsinki preparatory meeting was agreement on the agenda of the conference. This way the work would be sure to get off to a start without the customary disputes over procedure. The mandate was simple: the opening of the conference would take place without mentioning the level at which it would take place. This would be followed by opening addresses from all the participants. The conference would then proceed to its working phase: the presentation of proposals, the ensuing negotiations, and the adoption of an additional series of confidence and security-building measures, CSBMs. The fourth item would be the closing of the first part – the Stockholm part – of the conference.

Foreign Minister Väyrynen issued a press release on 11 November on the successful conclusion of the work of the preparatory conference. The work had been conducted in a constructive and businesslike spirit. All delegations had shown the necessary readiness to compromise. Given the international situation, the start of new negotiations in Stockholm was, in Väyrynen's view, encouraging.

It was agreed in Helsinki that the Stockholm conference would meet in four sessions during 1984, the first beginning on 17 January and the last ending on 14 December 1984.

No confidence, no security

Because the negotiations in Geneva on the Euro-missiles had just ended, the Stockholm conference attracted even greater attention. It was the only East-West discussion forum going on in 1984. Foreign Minister Väyrynen said that the neutral and non-aligned countries were among the first to decide to take part in the opening stage of the Stockholm conference at foreign minister level. By the end of December the NATO countries had decided to do the same.

The Warsaw Treaty countries began the New Year by saying that they too would take part at foreign minister level. The numbers of foreign ministers thenceforth snowballed. The result was that the opening of the conference took place at foreign minister level without any consensus decision. US Secretary of State George Shultz also took part.

The premise for defining security and confidence varied from country to country. Väyrynen expected that the forthcoming negotiations would be extremely difficult. Speaking to the Parliamentary foreign affairs committee on 2 January, he said that the Stockholm conference was a particular challenge for the neutral and non-aligned countries "For the first time they will be able to take part in a discussion on questions of continental European security policy." Because the negotiations and the diverse procedural matters were expected to be complicated, Väyrynen suggested that the work could adopt a path of gradual progress, up to the Vienna follow-up meeting.

The Stockholm conference was, in Väyrynen's view, the most important of the follow-up events agreed in Madrid. With this in mind Finland decided to set up in Stockholm a special representation for the conference comprising three officials from the Foreign Ministry and a military specialist.

The Finnish government, particularly the Foreign Ministry, made careful preparations for Stockholm. The defence administration was immediately requested to produce an expert analysis of the outcome of Madrid to support Finland's goals and interests in negotiations. In its response General Headquarters stated, in accordance with Finland's CSCE strategy, that the CSCE generally, and particularly the confidence and security-building measures, promoted security in Europe and served the overall objective of Finland's defence. On this basis the attitude of the defence administration to the forthcoming negotiation process was positive. Any compromises made would be unlikely to be contrary to Finland's national interests.

From the standpoint of the defence administration, Finland was prepared, to advance the cause of the joint N + N proposal presented in Madrid. A mandate required measures that were more binding. The only problems in work to come might concern limiting actions, as they were known. There could also be problems in defining the limits of peacetime exercises and in measures related to troop mobilisation during a heightened state of readiness. In a statement issued by Vice-Admiral Jan Klenberg he recommended that in the early stage of the negotiations there should not be commitments to excessively detailed proposals. There was reason to hold on to the Finnish delegation's freedom of movement in case there were situations in which there was need for a mediator and for a person to present compromises among the groupings.

In a preliminary assessment drawn up at the Foreign Minister it was generally believed that the possibility of a mediating role by the N + N group was more limited than earlier. The mandate clearly limited the chance of a comprehensive decision, although differences of interpretation and discussion would continue in Stockholm. It was therefore not expedient for Finland to table the sorts of proposals that could be immediately accepted or wholly rejected by either side. Originally, it was thought that the next opportunity to perform the task of mediator would only come about when the discussion entered the next stage, when it shifted to disarmament within the CSCE framework. The renewal of the Madrid mandate would then begin.

Form the outset, the inclusion of the Nordic NWFZ in the Stockholm proceedings had been under consideration. In January 1985 Undersecretary of State Klaus Törnudd drafted an alternative text on the Nordic NWFZ. He justified his draft by saying that it was fully in line with the text adopted by consensus at the 1978 UN Special Session on Disarmament. This unanimously called for the creation of nuclear weapons-free zones. A guarantee of this nature was, according to Törnudd, sufficient protection from the positions of the member states of the Western alliance. In a letter to Ambassador Kahiluoto, Törnudd mused that at least in theory it was possible to invent a zone that would not interfere with NATO's strategic calculations.

The opening address of the Finnish delegation to the Stockholm conference was given by Foreign Minister Paavo Väyrynen on 20 January. Väyrynen spoke of the results achieved by the prolonged negotiations in Madrid. Their precondition that new decisions must cover the whole of Europe, its sea areas and air space, was a challenge. The decisions reached must be militarily significant, politically binding and must contain corresponding forms of inspection. The timeframes must be set under the pressure of the gradual progress made. Only in Vienna, at the follow-up meeting, would it be possible to consider whether to move on to the next stage in the work, which was usually taken to mean dealing with definite disarmament measures.

Soviet Foreign Minister Andrei Gromyko contended that it was not possible in Stockholm to start discussions on the Euro-missiles. They were classified as prohibited weapons by Moscow. They could not be a subject for negotiation. Gromyko's attitude to the Stockholm conference was in other respects very traditional. If the Americans really intended to deploy medium-range Pershing missiles in Europe, the gathering in Stockholm could not be considered a normal CSCE meeting. "The Soviet Union might become angry and behave angrily during the actual conference." Because of this, it was not expected that the conference would see any significant results from the Soviet standpoint. For the sake of normal conference diplomacy, Gromyko stated that "the Soviet delegation would also look in the direction of the neutral countries; perhaps an idea or child of an idea might be found there and could take the work forward." Gromyko instructed Ambassador Grinevski in particular concerning Sweden. "Don't trust them. Sweden's neutrality is not genuine. During the Second World War they danced to the German's tune, and now they are fellow travellers of US imperialism. Ideologically, they are anti-communist."

Ministers of the superpowers met bilaterally in Stockholm. Information sent out from the meeting characterised it as "firm but constructive". The traditional positions of the superpowers were reflected in the opening speeches of their ministers. While the toughness of Foreign Minister Gromyko's speech provoked astonishment in Western comments, Foreign Minister Väyrynen told the Parliamentary foreign affairs committee in April 1984 that it came as no surprise to Finland. Gromyko simple related the Soviet Union's official stance in this first such multilateral event in the wake of the collapse of the Geneva negotiations.

The start to the work of the Stockholm conference was bogged down. Discussions were only held in the plenary sessions. Contention persisted about the mandate for the Stockholm conference given in Madrid. It was hard to interpret it unambiguously. An attempt was made to blend reflections of the international situation as firmly as possible into the outcome expected from Stockholm.

For the West this meant specific confidence-building measures according to the criteria agreed in Madrid. The West focused in its proposal on three subjects: information exchange, stability-building measures and means of verification.

The Soviet Union and the socialist camp continued to hold fast to a declaration on military-political measures, the drawing up of a non-aggression pact between the military alliances, and an agreement to prohibit the first use of nuclear weapons. The clear aim was to try to contain and resist the USA's aggressive military build-up. Ambassador Grinevski was to write in his memoirs that the Stockholm conference began according to CSCE tradition: at first someone presented publicly all their maximum objectives. Thereafter, the ensuing negotiations were clearly in a lifeless, motionless state. Finally, it was time to turn to the neutral countries, so that genuine negotiations could at last begin.

During a discussion in the Parliamentary committee on foreign affairs, on 10 April 1984, Foreign Minister Väyrynen said that it appeared that the US elections, to be held the following November, could create a situation in which actual negotiations would not have time to progress very far in Stockholm. His prognosis was right.

The Finnish delegation at the opening of the Stockholm conference, led by Foreign Minister Paavo Väyrynen. Also present, from the left, department head Seppo Pietinen, Ambassador Björn Ahlholm, Ambassador Matti Kahiluoto, Ministerial Councillor Markku Reimaa, Bureau Chief Jukka Valtasaari, Legation Councillor Tuomas Pekkarinen and Commander Jussi Lähteinen. (Photograph: Archive of the Finnish Foreign Ministry)

It was not until December that agreement could be reached on the start of the working groups. Finland led the decisive consultations on this. It was decided to set up two working groups. One would deal with the prior notification of military manoeuvres and activities concerning their inspection. The second would deal with all remaining possible proposals, including on matters such as restrictive measures and the exchange of information. At this stage there were five proposals on the table, among them the March 1984 comprehensive proposal of the N + N countries.

The head of the Soviet delegation, Ambassador Grinevski commented in the 4 December 1984 issue of *Pravda* on the decision concerning the working groups. The proposal was in harmony with General Secretary Chernenko's view that the combining of political-military issues with confidence and security-building measures was necessary for the success of the conference.

But the sluggish discussion went on about unofficial working methods and about the the neutral countries taking on responsibility for coordination of the five subjects. In November 1984 the neutral countries presented their first comprehensive proposal, which it was hoped would provide a basis for further negotiations.

Although the Stockholm conference was primarily a matter of military issues, it was clear that there was a desire to use the CSCE for more general and topical discussion. Foreign Minister Andrei Gromyko's opening speech to the conference on 17 January 1984 has gone down in history as the final delivery at a CSCE forum of a speech based on his Cold War experience.

The deployment of American medium-range missiles in Western Europe had just begun. The hallmark of President Reagan's first administration was its outspoken anti-Soviet and anti-communist rhetoric.

The US delegation at Stockholm was faced with a dilemma. Ambassador James Goodby, a disarmament specialist of long experience and known for his pragmatism, had a personal objective of bringing about a positive outcome as soon as possible. He entered into close discussions with his Soviet counterpart Oleg Grinevski, often with the contributory role of the neutrals and Finland.

But this attitude perhaps only reflected the stance of the US State Department. The Pentagon representative in the US delegation had quite different instructions. The Americans would not at that point concede to any results in Stockholm. What was more important was that the deployment of the medium-range missiles could proceed without outside disruption. There were problems in coordinating on various issues and positions within the Western group. According to the Americans it was particularly Norway, Canada and Turkey, the "peripheral nations" of the western alliance who were undergoing difficulties and were the weak points of a unified negotiating forum.

On military issues, the Americans now had to accept that the EEC countries would first hold their own meeting. Only after that would NATO convene in its own group meeting. The more that military matters were delved into in the CSCE framework, the more sensitive NATO's military specialists became to the danger of the alliance becoming a talking shop due to the CSCE. US Deputy Secretary of State Kenneth Dam remarked to Foreign Minister Väyrynen, in September 1983 in Washington, that the Stockholm conference must focus only on confidence and security-building measures. It must not interfere in strategic issues, in disarmament and not, for instance, nuclear weapons-free zones. Väyrynen, in principle, agreed. It was desirable to examine the enlargement of the task and mandate of the conference at the next follow-up meeting, in Vienna.

On 13 September, Ambassador Grinevski, evidently with the concurrence of Ambassador Goodby, requested, Ambassador Kahiluoto to begin consultations for the changeover to negotiations. On the basis of talks held in Moscow and Stockholm in autumn 1985, Goodby and Grinevski reached a joint understanding on the possible contents of the Stockholm document. It was therefore the right moment to hint to the other delegations at Stockholm that the time was ripe for moving on to the negotiation stage.

At first the Pentagon did not want to confirm that Goodby and Grinevski had arrived at an initial consensus. Goodby said that his job in Stockholm as head of the US delegation had come to an end. He left Stockholm a week later, in September 1985. His successor was Ambassador Bob Berry, who excelled more in general PR work. The final work on the agreement took time. And for once the CSCE process had time in abundance.

In an interview in Washington in February 2007, Martin Shletzinger, a long-time member of the Congressional CSCE commission, said that the role of the neutral countries at the Stockholm conference was highly positive and even of decisive importance at certain critical stages in the work. "The Americans trusted the Finns in this. In some respects they were the front line neutrals."

A new kind of détente

1985 – ten years on from Helsinki

Tenth anniversaries are generally unremarkable, but in many respects the tenth year since the 1975 CSCE summit conference was an exception. The difficult start to the Madrid follow-up hung in the background. Many CSCE veterans thought that the follow-up would face insurmountable difficulties in the quest to agree on any reasonable further schedule, not least concerning the next follow-up.

It was in this atmosphere that the Swiss Ambassador Brunner put forward the idea in spring 1981 that even if nothing else could be agreed, perhaps there could be a decision to arrange some sort of ceremonial function, a commemorative event in Helsinki, on the CSCE's tenth anniversary. In his memoirs, Foreign Minister Genscher later credited himself with the idea.

Despite its difficulties, the Madrid meeting continued working through many stages. No one proposed during the finalization of the concluding document that reference to a follow-up event should be deleted from the ensuing calendar. The feeling in Helsinki was that holding a CSCE meeting in the Finnish capital was always welcome.

In his closing speech to the Madrid follow-up meeting, on 8 September 1983, Foreign Minister Väyrynen said that the Finnish government intended later on to consult on the matter with the participating states. It was merely stated at the end of the Madrid meeting that the participating states would gather for the tenth anniversary of the CSCE "to commemorate the signing of the Final Act 1975". The purpose of the event, the level of participation, the duration, and so on, remained completely open. There was a desire in the

Foreign Ministry to make a full contribution to the event. The minimum aim would naturally be to have an appropriate political level in attendance, at least the foreign ministers of the participating states. The hosts would encounter many doubtful responses concerning this challenging aim. It could reasonably be asked what the foreign ministers would do in Helsinki. The natural response was that they would have an opportunity for various meetings. On the basis of ten years experience of the CSCE, they could give an assessment of where they had gone and where they should be going.

No preparatory mechanisms had been agreed for the 10th anniversary event. Everything depended on consultations by the host country and what they achieved.

During the first two weeks of September 1984, Finland sent a diplomatic note to all the governments of the CSCE participating states. The initial comments received suggested that all responded to it routinely, considering it a logical consequence of the Madrid decision and the announcement Finland made at the meeting. Only the British stated they would not have taken it amiss if such a decision had not been included in the Madrid concluding document.

The EEC countries decided to respond collectively. The Irish Ambassador, Richard Murphy, as representative of the EEC presidency, left the EEC reply with Ambassador Karhilo in Moscow on 23 November. Murphy stated that his reply was in the names of the Netherlands, Belgium, Denmark, the FRG, Greece, France, Ireland, Italy, Luxembourg and the UK.

The 10th anniversary event could honour the occasion appropriately as a two to three day gathering. The representatives of the participating states would each deliver a speech. "This would underline the significance of the CSCE process as a means to create greater security and cooperation among the participating states in all areas covered by the CSCE Final Act, and including the Belgrade and Madrid concluding documents." The EEC countries proposed that the speeches would form the true content of the event. They announced that they were prepared to take part in the conference "at a high level, assuming that the international atmosphere would make it appropriate".

NATO foreign ministers publicised their position in a communiqué of 14 December 1984. They too were prepared to take part in the Helsinki event at a political level, the international situation permitting. Clear guidelines and objectives had now been forthcoming for Finland's preparations. The responses

Helsinki 1985 and the 10th anniversary of the CSCE – the first simultaneous smiles from the
superpowers in a long time. US Secretary of State George Shultz and Soviet Foreign Minister

Eduard Shevardnadze met one another for the first time at the meeting hosted by Foreign Minister Paavo Väyrynen. (Photograph: Kalle Kultala)

of the US and the EEC countries suggested that the latter had been indirectly opposed to the creation of a concluding document. The Americans had made it plain that a dispute over the contents of a concluding document might only strain the conference atmosphere. In their view it would be better to be content with speeches only.

Preliminary consultations conducted in Helsinki by Ambassador Richard Töttermann appraised the situation in March 1985. Western remarks concerning a concluding document remained cautious. Moscow's attitude was also reticent. The view in Moscow was that the negotiation of a concluding document by the West's participants would be a predictable attempt to "to amend or re-interpret" the Final Act.

The summer of 1985 approached without any growing consensus on the content of the occasion or on a possible concluding document.

One final effort for a joint communiqué was made on 24 June. An informal draft communiqué was sent to all the participants. Compared with the draft sent out in May, it was devoid of all embellishments relating to the Final Act and its implementation. It was now stated that the speeches would only refer to "the political importance of the Final Document in promoting better relations between the participating states and in improving among them." The ministers would pledge to pay appropriate "due regard" to the implementation of the Final Act. Regardless of these changes, the US position remained negative concerning a general declaration.

The tenth anniversary event in Helsinki was nevertheless an impressive diplomatic get-together. Despite his initial promises, the UN Secretary General did not attend. In contrast, US Secretary of State George Shultz finally agreed to take part in the conference. News photographs of his meeting with the new Soviet Foreign Minister, Eduard Shevardnadze, who had been appointed just two weeks earlier, were flashed around the world and seemed to herald something new.

Foreign Minister Shevardnadze's speech contained criticism of the American and Western alliance's policy concerning assaults on the Yalta and Potsdam agreements, but also showed signs of possible new openings. No progress had been achieved at the Vienna negotiations. "Progress at the Stockholm conference was perhaps more dynamic."

Secretary of State Shultz spoke soon after Shevardnadze and stressed that "tensions remain for as long as some stubbornly violate all of the most cherished human rights." "The ten-year history of the CSCE had shown that the rights and interests of the individual were a fundamental part of European security and stability." The hopes inspired by the Final Document and the measures carried out on the basis of it were still far apart. As an example, Shultz mentioned the drop in emigration permits granted to Jews in the last five years from over 50,000 to less than 1,000 a year. Members of the Moscow-based group Helsinki Watch were under arrest. After listing many individual examples, Shultz ended with that of Andrei Saharov, who had been banished to Gorki.

When the two ministers met Shevardnadze asked his US counterpart why he had delivered such a stern speech. Shevardnadze had no opportunity to answer or even respond to it because of the order of speakers. Shultz replied that he was "just speaking the truth and was prepared to continue discussions privately with my colleague." Shultz later wrote that despite the tension and traditional posturing, Shevardnadze's approach to these issues was no longer polemical.

The Helsinki process could not be discussed without referring to individuals. They had to be the main beneficiaries of the Helsinki Final Act. There was a need for hard work, patience and effective cooperation among the participating states. The Final Act was a single entity that required progress in all its sub-areas. The preparations for the Vienna follow-up meeting gave an opportunity to reassess the progress made. Shultz noted with satisfaction Foreign Minister Shevardnadze's reference to possible progress at the Stockholm conference. A meeting between the US and Soviet leaders in November 1985 had been agreed. The United States was prepared to seize a new opportunity to reduce armaments, strengthen security and economic cooperation and enrich the lives of individuals.

In his speech, Foreign Minister Väyrynen affirmed the basic course and values of Finnish foreign policy in promoting the CSCE. He said that the CSCE provided Finland with "a unique forum for conducting a policy of neutrality." Finland sought to remain outside the disputes between the superpowers by maintaining good relations with all countries. The promotion of Finland's national interests was in clear harmony with the set objectives of the CSCE, namely the peaceful settlement of problems and the development of closer forms of cooperation. Decisions had to be put into practice if they were to remain credible. "Assessment of the defective implementation of commitments is both necessary and unavoidable," said Väyrynen. The continuity of the implementation process and the multilateral process were the way to reach out to seal the gap between visions and reality. At the end of his speech, Väyrynen outlined Finland's aims at the Stockholm conference and at the Vienna follow-up meeting.

It can be said in retrospect that the lack of a joint declaration from the 10th anniversary celebration did not diminish the significance of the occasion. The political preparations for the next follow-up meeting were started in Helsinki in a new manner. New hope was implanted in the CSCE and the European situation. In this development, the policies of General Secretary Gorbachev and Foreign Minister Shevardnadze were of crucial importance.

Soviet Marshal's negotiated breakthrough

Together with his American counterpart, Grinevski had produced a draft for the contents of an agreement at Stockholm. Foreign Minister Shevardnadze asked him to return to Moscow to present the draft to the Politburo of the Central Committee. After Grinevski had spoken to the gathering, Marshal Ahromeyev, one of those present, commented brusquely on the draft, describing the preliminary agreement as outright treason. It would mean that the Soviet area and its military activity would be opened up "to American and other Western spies". The Marshal made it abundantly clear that he for one would not give the agreement his blessing.

Following the meeting, Shevardnadze invited Grinevski to his office to discuss what should be done next. Although the CSCE meetings were usually the special preserve of foreign ministers, Shevardnadze asked Grinevski: because a decision would have a direct effect on the behaviour of the armed forces, wouldn't it therefore be more credible if Marshal Ahromeyev himself were to present the Soviet Union's latest position in Stockholm. Clearly, an order such as this could not come from the Foreign Ministry alone. It required a decision by General Secretary Gorbachev.

In this way Soviet Marshal Ahromeyev became the first marshal to speak at a CSCE session. He enjoyed considerable prestige among American disarmament experts. His position in the Soviet hierarchy was undisputed. He called himself "the last of the Mohicans", being the last of the Soviet officers to have fought against Nazi Germany who was still in active service.

On 19 August 1986 Ahromeyev delivered a speech to the Stockholm conference. Everyone understood that a historic breakthrough had taken place. He announced that concerning military manoeuvres the whole territory of the Soviet Union from its Western border to the Urals would be open to outside inspection. The opportunities for substantial results at Stockholm increased decisively. In the publicity surrounding the decade-old MBFR negotiations in Vienna the talk had been of 'hard core' issues. Now, due to the work of the 'soft core' CSCE conference, the Soviet Union's military secretiveness was being opened up for the first time to outside scrutiny. In line with the Madrid mandate, the movements and exercises of Soviet army units would come within the sphere of confidence and security-building measures from the Soviet Union's Western border to the Urals.

The Soviet Union announced a new readiness in principle to air the matter of how, and concerning what equipment, these inspections could be carried out. The question of inspections from the air became a decisive issue in the final negotiations. The neutral countries wanted to know immediately whether, as traditional mediators, they would be able to keep aircraft on 24-hour standby to carry out inspections. As regards the final outcome, the basic premise was that there would have to be a rapid response to inspection requests: inspectors would have to reach the area of manoeuvres within 24-36 hours. Kahiluoto's initial response to this was hesitant. He thought it an unrealistic option both politically and technically.

The marshal's important initiative from the Soviet side had to be re-interpreted. Ahromeyev's proposal was tied to the assumption that the country that was the subject of an inspection would itself offer its equipment for use by inspectors.

Military headquarters in Finland was asked about Finland's capability to participate in such an arrangement. The reply came by letter from Colonel Pertti Nykänen on 4 September. The attitude in Finland was in principle positive. The only problems concerned a shortage of aircraft and staff. Finland could only offer a limited number of small reconnaissance aircraft.

The Americans saw that the Soviet Union's political and military initiative required a response from them. It was to this end that they made an appeal on

9 September 1986 aimed at the neutral countries. The US was ready to make a significant compromise by consenting to the use of aircraft of the neutral countries for inspections of Soviet territory. The Americans appealed to Sweden and Finland to contribute a plane for the new inspection programme, in the manner of Austria and Switzerland.

The request received a single reply: Finland announced in an urgent message from Helsinki on 11 September that it was prepared to participate "in a generally acceptable solution by making aircraft and personnel available. The condition for Finland's undertaking was that a consensus decision on the issue be achieved in Stockholm". In Finland's view the offer by the neutrals included a principle between them on the rotating use of equipment and personnel." The finer details of the project would be agreed later.

Based on this development, Sweden drafted a joint announcement on the issue by the neutral countries. The aim was to present it to the plenary session of 15 September 1986. Its aim was to outline, on the basis of a report drawn up by experts from the neutral countries, the requirements and measures, in principle and in practice, on the basis of which the use of a third country's aircraft for air inspections could be carried out in accordance with agreed instructions concerning flight plans, the right of the host country to inspect aircraft, the possibility for a representative of the host country to be present during inspections and the obligation of the host country to provide all possible logistical support related to inspections.

At the last minute Moscow intervened. Deputy minister Vorontsov asked Ambassador Karhilo to meet with him on 16 September at 11.30. Vorontsov said that the Soviet Union placed great importance on the CSCE and therefore on the Stockholm conference. "There is an extremely fine text in the offing that the N + N countries have been of key importance in achieving. The Soviet Union appreciates this effort." But the Soviet Union could not accept the compulsory use of the neutral countries' aircraft for inspections. "This in particular would cause practical problems on Soviet territory." The Soviet Union's own aircraft would be able to act quickly and without impediment; there would be no difficulties over maintenance and the pilots knew the terrain. Vorontsov mentioned, by way of example, the longstanding practice according to which visiting heads of state were transported over Soviet territory by Soviet aircraft. Safety factors were paramount.

Vorontsov asked Finland to reconsider the matter and not to "demand" the implementation of the proposal to use aircraft of the neutral countries. It would, in his opinion, be "odd" if Stockholm were to now fail due to the proposal of the N + N countries. The Soviet Union had made a similar appeal to Austria, Switzerland and Sweden.

In the presence of assistant head of department Deryabin, Vorontsov said that the obligatory nature of the arrangement had been their main concern. A system based on voluntarism might be possible. This could be appealed to in a situation where the country to be inspected lacked the right equipment.

Helsinki wanted to give Moscow a quick reply. The same day, a message was sent via Karhilo to deputy minister Vorontsov. The message said that Finland also wanted a final result at Stockholm that was acceptable to all. Finland had not itself proposed the use of aircraft of a neutral third party. The proposal had come from the FRG delegation. When at one stage it appeared that an option of this sort could offer a solution, Finland too had been ready to consider it. If this did not bring about an agreement, Finland hoped that the forms of inspection could be clarified in another manner. The solution that finally came about was a system based on the equipment the country to be inspected.

The Stockholm conference ended on 17 September 1986 with a substantive outcome. It created for the Vienna follow-up meeting completely new starting positions.

Vienna 1986–89 – new surprises

The outcome at the Stockholm conference signified rapid change in the anticipated results of the Vienna meeting. In the follow-up to Madrid, the Stockholm conference was the only one that achieved a notable final result. It created a military security sector, an area in which, until that point, compromises had been the most difficult to attain.

The practical procedures for the Vienna follow-up were arranged at a short preparatory meeting held in the Austrian capital at the end of September and early October. The foreign ministers of the N + N countries met with their delegations at the end of October on the island of Brioni, at the invitation of Yugoslavia, shortly before the start of the follow-up meeting. The Vienna follow-up meeting thus raised new expectations. The outcome of the

Stockholm conference had been achieved at the last minute. It signified a new kind of breakthrough. It would now be feasible to expect that similar results would be forthcoming in other CSCE sectors. The Vienna meeting began in an extraordinary atmosphere. The 35 foreign ministers assembled on 3 November 1986 for the opening session in the historic Hofburg palace. One of the dignitaries was missing. Austria's President Kurt Waldheim did not attend the opening of the meeting. News of his Second World War activities during the German occupation of Yugoslavia had surfaced, marring his reputation. He was shunned and prohibited from travelling to the Western CSCE member states throughout his presidency. The Western representatives refused to meet with him.

The opening speech of the Finnish delegation was delivered by Foreign Minister Väyrynen on 5 November. He emphasised the dynamic nature of the CSCE. "Even though some participating state may not have fully implemented previously agreed commitments, its obligation to do so remains valid." The assessment of implementation must play a central role in the work of the Vienna follow-up, "because the implementation of all the stipulations has not, unfortunately, been satisfactory". Väyrynen thought that despite the numerous expert meetings held following the Madrid follow-up meeting and their valuable discussions, the follow-up meetings were the main decision-making forums for the CSCE's multilateral continuity. Finland hoped that follow-up meetings could be arranged at regular intervals.

Väyrynen stressed many examples of how the CSCE had not lost its relevance from the angle of the lives of ordinary citizens. The aspiration of peace, economic security and wellbeing, a safe and clean environment and an opportunity for people to live and enjoy individual freedoms and rights were all common objectives already set out in the Helsinki Final Act. It was now expected that the Vienna follow-up meeting would, as a continuation of the Stockholm conference, also enter into disarmament matters and naval activities as part of the military confidence-building measures. President Koivisto, too, had expectations of the Vienna follow-up, "because there is no other forum where a country like Finland has the same kind of opportunities to exert an influence on the design of international decisions concerning military security."

There were still many unused opportunities in the area of economic cooperation. Väyrynen promised that the Finnish delegation would make concrete proposals on environmental protection. In relation to the quality of life of the individual and the realization of human rights, the Helsinki Final Act and the concluding document of the Madrid follow-up meeting offered a ready long-term programme.

Väyrynen ended by referring to the recent meeting in Reykjavik between General Secretary Gorbachev and President Reagan. "It symbolised a great step forward in the nuclear arms negotiations between the superpowers. The negotiations must continue so that the arms race can be halted and be prevented from spreading to outer space".

The general discussion on the implementation of the CSCE process continued after the Christmas break until mid-February 1987. Proposals were made for measures by which the process could be improved and made more effective. By March there were 120 of them. They included over 30 proposals aimed at activities in the period after the Vienna follow-up. The Romanian delegation alone made more than 10 initiatives concerning the meeting. It later turned out that Romania's activity was disingenuous. The main aim of the Romanian government appeared to be to put an emphasis on events and not on the more effective implementation of actions or decisions already adopted.

It can be generally said of the neutral and non-aligned countries, in the preparations for the Vienna follow-up meeting, that environmental protection in Basket II and questions concerning information exchange in Basket III were issues that over the preceding decade had not been focused on in terms of follow-up. Thus at the beginning of the Vienna follow-up the N + N countries made a joint proposal, now seen as historic, for an expert information forum to take place after the meeting. Though the proposal was important from the stance of the N + N countries, and even momentous, it was not yet raised as part of the main negotiations on Basket III issues. Four neutral countries, Finland among them, made an additional proposal on the spread of information concerning human rights. The proposal was an upshot of the discussion at the Ottawa meeting of experts.

The real challenge at the Vienna talks remained the matter of a whole entity acceptable to all and striking a balance among the variety of subjects. When Soviet Foreign Minister Shevardnadze brought up humanitarian issues as the hub of Soviet policy, it was clear that the West faced an altogether new sort of challenge. The Western delegations took up the gauntlet. They proposed practical activities linked to human rights and human interaction and "on-site inspections concerning human rights", mechanisms that were to become routine for all the participating countries.

Another question, and a contributory factor to the central pillar of balance and completeness, was how the historic outcome of the Stockholm conference should be complemented in the future. Did the CSCE participants have the possibility to switch to the long sought process of disarmament? What would be the role of the Mutual Balanced Force Reduction talks that had been under way between the two alliances since 1973? Would disarmament matters be handled on an equal footing according to CSCE principles, or would the military alliances continue to discuss the 'hard core' issues of their own possibilities for arms reduction among themselves. France and the US in particular argued over these matters of principle.

A Finnish report produced at the end of the summer session of the meeting, at the end of July 1987, stated that the Soviet Union's openly proclaimed policy of *glasnost* and *perestroika* (openness and restructuring), and the general prospects for disarmament were breaking down the CSCE's customary boundaries and equilibrium.

During the Vienna meeting there were changes at the Finnish Foreign Ministry with the transition on 30 April from the government of Kalevi Sorsa to that of Harri Holkeri. Kalevi Sorsa succeeded Paavo Väyrynen as Foreign Minister. The CSCE continued to enjoy widespread support in Finland. The Finnish delegation in Vienna found that none of the original instructions had altered due to the change at the Foreign Ministry. Foreign Minister Sorsa attended the follow-up meeting in Vienna on two occasions: in May 1988, when the N + N countries' foreign ministers tabled the first comprehensive draft for a concluding document. The N + N foreign ministers also met among themselves. Sorsa also travelled to Vienna to deliver Finland's final address at the closing plenary session of the follow-up meeting, on 17 January 1989, and to welcome the participants to Helsinki in 1992.

The work of the Vienna follow-up meeting to a great extent followed the examples and experiences of the Madrid meeting. The neutral and non-aligned countries were again given the opportunity to contribute to the analysis and advancement of the work in the capacity of coordinators. The assumption was that on the basis of CSCE performance and experience there would no longer be anything to prevent the Finnish representative from leading any of the working groups.

The wish now was to test Finland's role as coordinator on questions of military security. When this happened, it was clearly an encroachment onto the turf of the host, the Austrian delegation. Its head of delegation had perhaps taken it as a matter of course that, in the capacity of the host country, Austria had first choice of what task it took. Following the successful conclusion of the Stockholm conference, matters of military security seemed to have become among the most important on the agenda. Military security was in fresh demand in the dialogue among the representatives of the alliances and the 35 CSCE participating states.

The follow-up meeting confirmed the demarcation of coordinating duties on 20 July 1987. For the first time in CSCE history, Finland was to lead the deliberations of the working group for military security. Austria was given the principles guiding relations between participating states, Switzerland took on economic cooperation, including environmental protection, and Sweden was given Basket III, comprising human contacts, information exchange, and questions of cooperation in the fields of culture and education. The representative of Yugoslavia was responsible for the coordination of the follow-up to the Vienna meeting.

State Secretary Matti Tuovinen considered the task allotted to Finland to be highly important. He wrote in his diary: "As a neutral country Finland has all along been able to provide useful services to all sides. This is in line with Finland's national interest."

The Vienna follow-up meeting gave an opportunity to demonstrate activity in many areas besides coordination work. There was almost daily collaboration among the neutral and non-aligned countries and they held two or three meetings a week. The Nordic countries held information meetings on a weekly basis.

In addition, at a fairly early stage Finland adopted the method of using the plenary sessions to speak on the current "work situation". The delegation discussed on a daily basis where the work was heading and what impressions each day's work had evoked concerning the issues in hand.

The Moscow human dimension conference

The Vienna follow-up meeting acquired its distinctive image, a wholesale departure from tradition, from Soviet Foreign Minister Eduard Shevardnadze's opening address. He invited the CSCE to a conference in Moscow on humanitarian issues. This was something different. The Soviet Union started the CSCE follow-up with a colossal bolt from the blue. This was the period of the *glasnost* and *perestroika* of General Secretary Gorbachev's Soviet Union.

Soviet politics had been under radical reform following the accession to power of General Secretary Mikhail Gorbachev. It became more open and shattered surface taboos. *Glasnost* and *perestroika* were buzzwords that signified something new. They were complete mysteries to many Soviet citizens and Western diplomats trained during the Cold War. Many considered them as mainly forms of propaganda, in the style of previous Soviet policy, a big bluff. Was transformation it just deception?

The activities of the Soviet delegation were closely followed. One often heard the allegation that Gorbachev's reform policy did not appear sufficiently concrete in the work of the Viennna follow-up. Our Soviet counterparts, on the other hand, would respond that the delegations found that West's hard line was an attempt to impose an all-or-nothing approach on the Vienna talks without serious negotiations. It appeared that Moscow had seized the PR initiative. Gorbachev was becoming a favourite of the Western media without his policies at home or abroad having acquired clear and irrefutable backing.

FRG Chancellor Helmut Schmidt considered the prospects for *glasnost* and *perestroika* in his memoirs, published in 1987. Schmidt did not think that Soviet policy concerning the other members of the Warsaw Treaty had changed. Their defection from the pact would not be allowed. The biggest question mark, in Schmidt's view, had to do with how Gorbachev would succeed in the reform of economic policy. If he failed on that front, the consequences could be disastrous. There would be no going back to the Brezhnev era's rigid but mainly covert police tyranny, centrally controlled command economics and dictatorial political relations with the Soviet Union's smaller allies.

US Ambassador Warren Zimmermann also had his doubts. He had earlier been the "number two" at the US embassy in Moscow. He and his wife he had been active observers of the course of Soviet social relations. They had also had the chance to get involved in the lives of representatives of the Soviet opposition, of dissidents. Zimmermann was Max Kampelman's closest advisor at the Madrid follow-up meeting. He continued along the path set by his previous superior and dealt in his official addresses with the persecution and fate of representatives of opposition movements in the Soviet Union. It was still a lengthy charge sheet.

Zimmermann had some tricky friends within his own Western grouping. The head of the Canadian delegation, William Bauer, was known for his colourful past. He had switched from being a Canadian communist to being a staunch defender of emigrants from Eastern Europe who had relocated to Canada and of people persecuted in Eastern Europe and the Soviet Union. In Washington those monitoring East-West relations, such as the Congressional CSCE commission, paid close attention to how Zimmermann and the US delegation fared.

Added zest was contributed to the internal cohesiveness of the Western alliance due to the fact that the FRG in particular wanted wholeheartedly to support Gorbachev's reform policy. This was so also in the work of the Vienna follow-up meeting. Foreign Minister Genscher voiced his immediate support for the Soviet Union's initiative for the organization of the Moscow human dimension conference. He did not understand why doubt should be cast over such support.

The meeting was approaching the summer break of its first year. This created timetable pressure for examination of the prospects for advancing the work.

There was more to report on the Moscow conference on humanitarian issues from talks involving Zimmermann on 16 June 1987. Zimmermann said that achieving a successful outcome of the Vienna follow-up depended crucially on whether Soviet human rights policy improved.

Particular attention was being paid in Washington to the increase in the numbers of emigrations and family reunifications, and to the way in which the Soviet Union was committed to pursuing its policy on these matters in the future. So far emigration permits had only been granted to people who had previously been refused them. The way of handling new applications was not encouraging, though the performance of the Soviet government was now better compared with the days of the Madrid meeting.

Zimmermann had held bilateral discussions with Ambassador Kashlev on the possibilities of solving problems. One way forward would be to change the clause in the Soviet penal code relating to the right to emigrate. Another option would be for a high level Soviet political representative to give a public assurance that the more liberal practice that had been started would continue after the Vienna meeting. Zimmermann said that Kashlev had responded to the suggestions "with gratitude", and had stressed that the latter option might be easier to carry out.

Zimmermann said that from the first days of the meeting he had only received vague and evasive responses about the Moscow conference. According to Kashlev, he had had no prior consultation about the initiative, and neither had he subsequently been able to work out what was behind the proposal. Because of this, it had not been much of a surprise to outsiders that Kashlev had spoken in bilateral discussions of his reticence about raising with Moscow all the questions and demands presented in Vienna. According to Zimmerman the Soviet representatives knew the American's preconditions for the conference. These concerned, inter alia, freer information, the right of former dissidents to be present in the work of the conference, and the possibility for NGOs to take part. Zimmerman said "the problem will be if these conditions are met". In his view the holding of a conference in Moscow linked to Basket III issues was hardly plausible. If the Moscow conference were to be part of the series of human dimension conferences, that too could be a matter of contention within the Western group. Zimmermann did not however rule out the possibility that agreement could be reached on all this.

The discussion ended with Zimmermann considering when the US and Soviet leaders might possibly meet. It would take at least four months to prepare a summit meeting. The respective foreign ministers had not yet confirmed the possibility of a July meeting. Zimmermann thought that the talk would now have to be of the end of November rather than October as the alternative date for the summit.

In this context it is worth remembering that in the preparations for the autumn 1985 summit meeting between President Reagan and General Secretary Gorbachev, Deputy Secretary of State Rozanne Ridgway and Aleksander Bessmertnyh reached an agreement that the agenda for bilateral discussions would regularly include human rights issues. The Americans considered this a "great victory".

In the light of all that had happened, the Soviet Union decided to clarify the concept of the Moscow conference before the summer break in July 1987. The subject of the conference was specified in a speech by Ambassador Kashlev to the 24 July plenary session as concerning "the broadening of humanitarian cooperation in the framework of the CSCE human dimension." The conference would deal with the effective implementation of human rights and cooperation on the exchange of information, the field of culture and education, contacts between people, organizations and institutions, including family-based contacts and questions concerning travel for personal or professional reasons. The conference would try to arrive at practical results. It would be open to the public and to the press. Ambassador Kashlev supplemented the address with the announcement that individuals and groups had access to the Soviet Union according to established CSCE custom.

Ambassador Zimmermann replied to the address a few days later, at the plenary held on 28 July. Kashlev's speech prompted fresh questions. Zimmermann said bluntly that the freedom for media access and public opinion, and for public and independent NGOs to operate in the Soviet Union did not, in the current situation, meet the conditions for holding the conference, and so it "fails to qualify". Moscow still had a long way to go when it came to implementation of human rights. There had to be an end to restrictions on emigration and immigration visas, including visas for former Soviet citizens. Soviet citizens had to be given the opportunity to take part in and register as participants in the Moscow conference. The work opportunities and security of those monitoring the Helsinki process had to be assured, as had the working conditions of foreign journalists.

Kashlev's speech and the ensuing discussion could be considered a concession to the basic conditions presented by the West. The Soviet Union was a novice in these matters. The Moscow human rights conference was to be the main topic of conversation during the summer break.

The test of glasnost and perestroika

The adoption of the concluding document as the result of the Vienna follow-up meeting, in January 1989, was considered the most important CSCE achievement since the Helsinki Final Act of 1975. The document, with its plethora of detail, had posed a particular challenge to the Socialist countries. For the first time in the CSCE's history the Soviet Union had not acted as a major obstacle to the document's stipulations. The flexibility and limits of Soviet reform policy were constantly being measured at the Vienna follow-up.

The importance of flexibility came as a surprise to many and generated problems. Some participating states considered that the Soviet reform policy should be given time to work. The Vienna follow-up meeting should therefore have reached a speedy agreement. The foreign ministers of the FRG and France, Messrs Genscher and Dumas, made an appeal to this effect in July 1988. The obstructionists were the socialist countries Romania, Bulgaria and the GDR.

At no stage in the Vienna meeting did the Soviet Union go into detail on the initiative for the Moscow conference. Shevardnadze refers in his memoirs to the heated discussion that took place in the Politburo. Had the speech been prepared without any discussion of details or how the issue would be pursued in Vienna?

In any case, the EEC countries had perhaps already been concerned that the varied opportunities offered by the Moscow conference might be lost. The EEC's presidency representative, Denmark's Ambassador William Friis-Möller, presented a reasonably positive assessment of the work of the Vienna meeting. Not all the EEC countries were prepared to accept the Moscow conference as an item in the concluding document. As a result, France had developed a novel idea. Due to the celebration of the 200th anniversary of the French Revolution in 1989, Paris could be the venue for the first human dimension event.

France was prepared to drop its opposition to the Moscow conference as long as Moscow focussed only on human contacts. More detailed examination of human rights issues could be taken up at some other venue. Friis-Möller thought that a conference of this nature could be held in Copenhagen. If the order were Paris-Copenhagen-Moscow, the pressure for performance in the human dimension, including the monitoring of human rights, would remain buoyant until Moscow. In this way the intervals between the CSCE's next follow-up meetings would be arranged more in line with the West's original goals.

The Soviet Union's skilful tactical and propagandistic initiative at the opening stage of the Vienna follow-up caused a fair amount of bother in Western capitals. Washington tried to deal with the situation by laying down strict criteria, which would have to be accepted before the US would be prepared to consider the Moscow conference. The head of the US delegation, Ambassador Zimmermann, presented the criteria to Kashlev on 6 October 1987. These supplemented the technical criteria he had presented in his plenary speech. Zimmermann said that the conditions with which the Americans would agree to the holding of the Moscow conference were:

- The release of all political prisoners and prisoners of conscience and their rehabilitation
- Reform of legislation in the Soviet Union in order to rescind the restrictive and narrow "concept of family and kinship".
- A significant increase by the Soviet Union in opportunities for Jewish emigration.
- The provision of possibilities in the Soviet Union for the Jewish community to receive instruction and schooling in Hebrew.
- Changes to the Soviet Union's existing penal code that would bring an end to the arbitrary arrest and imprisonment of people for their opinions.

Zimmermann informed America's allies immediately he had put the demands to Kashlev. This order of procedure indicated that the US was acting alone. It was not possible to start discussing demands presented at home, not even among one's own allies. It appeared that compromise among various agencies and congressional representatives in Washington was only possible by making such a list of maximum demands. In the view of the Soviets it was not appropriate – or reasonable – to compare the Vienna follow-up meeting with the Belgrade meeting or any other follow-up event. The behaviour of the Americans once again demonstrated that to them the importance and value of the CSCE lay in its being directed in particular at Soviet human rights policy and performance. It was a very similar situation to that of Belgrade, as far as the Americans were concerned. But now it was possible that Moscow would not act provocatively.

The timing of this measure may have been linked to the preparations for the superpower summit meeting. The list of demands would certainly not have made the follow-up meeting's work and negotiations concerning the Moscow conference any easier. Some EEC colleagues even thought that the conditions had "torpedoed" the development of France's idea of the human dimension as a common Western concept.

Weeks could have passed without any real work in Vienna before the Soviet Union was prepared to comment on the list of demands. The main question was of course whether the Soviet Union was ready to submit to a new round of negotiations on this basis. What would be its rejoinder? On the one hand, conjecture focused on scientific-technological cooperation, and, on the other hand, the binding of the MBFR talks and the 23-country negotiations more closely to CSCE frameworks.

The longer the negotiations in Vienna lasted, the more problematic the situation became. When even the balanced, comprehensive proposal of the N + N countries, which the other Western delegations had called for, began to lean towards acceptance of the Moscow conference, the Americans continued to hold back. They were unable to decide whether the de facto acceptance of the Moscow conference just before the start of the negotiations proper was in their interests. Ambassador Kashlev expressed a sort of flexibility from the Soviet side. He stated that he was prepared to discuss a series of up to three conferences in which Moscow would be a contributing factor.

In January 1988 Kashlev returned to the conditions that the Americans had set for the Moscow conference. They had caused only irritation in Moscow. Although the Americans had not declared their principle opposition to the conference, progress on the matter in the negotiations had remained stuck. In Kashlev's view now was the time to concentrate on delimiting, for example, the division of labour of the Paris and Moscow conferences. The Soviet Union was prepared to divide the human dimension conference into several parts. Decision on this should not, in Kashlev's view, be left to the last minute.

Balance of new dimensions

The momentous outcome of the Stockholm conference on CSCE military issues and the Soviet Union's astonishingly dynamic reform policy shook up the traditional negotiating positions in Vienna. Different schools of thought and attitude could be distinguished as yardsticks by which the attainment of progress and objectives were measured. The USA's bilateral contacts with Moscow were still the main measure of progress. For many other Western delegations the measure of the Soviet Union's new foreign policy were displayed in Vienna in Moscow's readiness to commit itself to new joint decisions.

The readiness to hurry, to hold back and to compromise at the right time was still discussed within the different groups. A report of the Finnish delegation on 31 July 1987 asked whether all the 35 participating countries were "ready to control their appetites before the hors d'oeuvres were served".

The head of the Soviet delegation, Ambassador Yuri Kashlev, was a long-serving versatile diplomat and experienced CSCE specialist already during the Geneva and Belgrade meetings. He once recounted that he got started in his career in multilateral diplomacy, as a young Soviet diplomat, after getting to know one of the s UN's official languages: Chinese. As an individual he was jovial and pleasant. He was also a credible exponent of General Secretary Gorbachev's and Foreign Minister Shevardnadze's reform policy. He socialised freely. He was the first head of a Soviet delegation at the CSCE to use more English than Russian in discussions, and he did not need an interpreter for German.

Kashlev was known to the Finnish delegation from earlier CSCE times – from Geneva, Belgrade and expressly in connection with Basket III. Finland proposed, immediately at the start of the Vienna follow-up meeting, a regular exchange of assessments bilaterally on the situation at the meeting. Kashlev readily agreed to this. He suggested that he could visit the Finnish delegation to exchange views on current issues. The reason he gave was that in this way he could come alone. The discussions were always rewarding. The longer the work of the conference went on, the easier it was to speak more and more openly of forthcoming challenges and even different options for decisions.

It was possible to assess the development of the CSCE and the openness of the work particularly from the manner in which the representatives of the socialist countries discussed future decisions. During the Geneva negotiations tight discipline and mutual solidarity had been almost total. Options for making decisions were hardly mentioned, nor was there any speculation about forthcoming decisions.

There were more pleasant experiences to record concerning the conclusion of the Vienna follow-up meeting and the new character of Finnish-Soviet bilateral relations. Finnish representatives were never once during the meeting summoned to the Soviet delegation for an admonition. Kashlev's superiors in

*The head of the Soviet
delegation in Vienna 1986–89,
Ambassador Yuri Kashlev.*

Moscow were CSCE veterans: the head of delegation at the Belgrade follow-up meeting Yuli Vorontsov, special Ambassador Lev Mendelevich and, for military affairs, Marshal Sergei Ahromeyev. They naturally tried to keep the Soviet Union's operational opportunities and options as broad as possible. Although the style of discussion and the level of information exchanged were qualitatively different from before, the Soviet delegation did not explain openly in advance everything to do with the limits of its flexibility.

The representatives of the socialist countries had first started to open bilateral discussions during the Madrid follow-up. This was not only to say what had been done and what had happened in the preceding days and weeks. They already dared to discuss their future intentions a little. The socialist countries no longer clung to the closest possible mutual solidarity in taking positions on matters being handled. In discussions concerning freedom of religion, the right to emigrate and national minorities, the spectrum of positions among the socialist countries was astonishingly broad.

In January 1988, Kashlev travelled to Moscow for a meeting of Warsaw Treaty CSCE heads. The Belgrade model was not yet excluded from the options for an outcome in Vienna, and a concluding document void of substance was still on the cards. According to Voronstov the situation was entirely different from Belgrade some 10 years earlier. "The international situation was in a powerful stage of development in many areas, not least in the main themes of the CSCE. What was now needed from Vienna was confrmation of the utilisation of those developmental possibilities through practical action."

Based on this, it was fairly clearly decided in Moscow that the Soviet Union wanted to perform as a true challenger with respect to the outcome of the Vienna follow-up. This role did not apply only to the Moscow conference.

Kashlev continued to refer to the possibility of a Belgrade type outcome in Vienna. The message was directed particularly at those Western delegations that were seriously interested in the CSCE. They would not support an advocate of a purely "all or nothing" course for long.

Kashlev concurred with with Vorontsov's line, according to which the most significantly substantial results were expected from Vienna. The discussions in Vienna up until February 1988 had indicated that some Western countries expected from the meeting, according to Kashlev, at least some sort of "conference on emigration". There were still people in high places in Moscow, such as deputy minister Kovalev and Ambassador Mendelevich, who had negotiated the Helsinki Final Act. "It was impossible for them to feed the impression that the possibilities for the continuation of the CSCE rested on registering rights of emigration and accepting the maximum conditions set by the West."

There were also constant discussions in Vienna of the effects of the November 1988 US Presidential election on the work of the follow-up meeting. Would the election campaign and the rise to power possibly of a new administration see a downswing in the USA's decision-making machinery that would affect CSCE affairs?

Shevardnadze wrote in his memoirs, published in 1991, that he was often asked in political discussions in Moscow in the mid-1980s how he viewed the interests of the class struggle in relation to general human rights. He said that he dismissed such questions. He saw no conflict whatsoever between them. At the same time the new foreign minister revealed the questionable practice whereby the Soviet government would certainly be prepared to sign all sorts of declarations, but remain non-compliant on their implementation. To his surprise the officials responsible for such implementation were often not even aware of the commitments made by the Soviet government.

The French and German foreign ministers, Messrs Genscher and Dumas, appealed on 20 July 1988 to their EEC and US counterparts to bring the work of the Vienna follow-up to a swift conclusion. When, at the same time, the French delegation in Vienna officially announced that it was ready to accept the N + N countries' comprehensive proposal as it stood, tension grew within the Western group. Astonishment and disunity prevailed.

France's emergence could be explained by frustration with the activity of the Western group. Even though a couple of months had passed since the proposal of the N + N countries was tabled, on 13 May, by mid-July the Western group were unable to agree on a single, detailed amendment in written form. There was plenty of discussion but no solid conclusions.

The Americans were now left with very few reliable friendly delegations – the British and Dutch. France had an advantage in the section of the N + N proposal on military security. The N + N countries were in principle in agreement with France that matters related to European military security should be negotiated as closely as possible within the framework of the CSCE, away from the discipline of the military alliances, whether this took place in the 23-country or 35-country format. The CSCE participating states were equal and European security was indivisible.

Paris versus Washington

While the two superpowers continued at high level to explore the possibilities for disarmament, including nuclear disarmament, the 35 countries of the CSCE had to discuss how the post-Stockholm work would be pursued. At the same time questioners asked what was the significance of the mandate agreed in Madrid to the work in Vienna when taking into account the results of the Stockholm conference. In Madrid, the Soviet and Warsaw Treaty representatives had set the condition that the mandate should open up the opportunity for progress in real disarmament.

As the 1987 summer recess drew closer the atmosphere in Vienna grew tense. The arrangement of work on military issues remained open. There was a major problem because of the internal discord in the Western group over the differences between Paris and Washington. The proceedings of the working group on military issues could not start until this friction was cleared up.

In mid-June NATO ministers gathered in Reykjavik for their summer conference. The Vienna negotiations were high on the agenda. Ambassador Zimmermann considered that the declaration of the conference was more a matter of the Americans' readiness to compromise than a result of France's flexibility. The CSCE connection of the negotiations now followed the concept proposed by Finland and the other neutral countries. The CSCE connection was versatile. There were now two mandates for the negotiations within the CSCE framework. The temporal and geographical connection was clear: both sets of negotiations would take place in Vienna. Countries outside the alliances also had the opportunity for dialogue and to present their own points of view. The concluding document of the Vienna follow-up meeting would also give attention to the mandate of the 23-country negotiations.

The Finns held discussions with British specialists in London in September 1987. These concluded that the 23-country and 35-country negotiations could "come closer together" at some point in the future. Because the CSBM and the 23-country negotiations anyway shared the same direction, the British would be represented at both by the same delegation. This practice became one of the most interesting symbols, indicating how the participants interpreted the proximity of the negotiations. The specialists had a reason to keep fully informed of the work of each of the negotiation processes. There was no need to resort to intermediary reports.

Now that the Western alliance's internal dispute was resolved, Zimmermann promised to take up the issue of the commencement of work by the working group on military matters. Though the Western group now had clear mutual standpoints on matters of principle, there was still no written proposal for a mandate. This would have meant having to deal with those proposals that had been tabled, namely the Warsaw Treaty's proposals.

In this situation the coordinator's opportunity to propose a new solution came to the rescue. The coordinator suggested that the work should not begin only with a written proposal for comment. There could first be joint deliberation "to assess the progress achieved at the Stockholm conference", the mandate that had been given for the Vienna follow-up already at the end of the Madrid meeting. At that time the results of the Stockholm conference were unknown.

The continuity of progress and the opportunity for assessing possible results had thereby in principle already been ensured over three years previously. The start of the proceedings of the coordinating group on military matters had constituted a harmful obstacle to the general work progress of the whole follow-up meeting. If the summer recess were to begin without this work having started, there would be a dampening effect on the overall mood of the meeting.

In autumn 1987 broad consensus was again brought about: the Madrid mandate could be interpreted widely and flexibly. In this new situation the mandate also became useable. It did not require further specification. If some of the proposals made in Stockholm had not been given more detailed treatment, they could be presented as they were in Vienna.

The first textual section dealing with security questions, composed under Finland's coordination, was written in the working group on 24 September. The text was based on a discussion held before the summer break that dealt with an assessment of the outcome of the Stockholm conference. It was stated that the Madrid mandate remained the practical precept of the work. The outcome brought about on 19 September 1986 – the series of confidence and security-building measures – was registered as a welcome achievement.

By comparison with the discussion at the time of the Madrid follow-up, the CSBM activity in Vienna took place in a new situation. The breakthrough on retaining on-site inspections as a CSCE routine behavioural norm had dramatically altered the atmosphere in which military matters were dealt with. What had only a few years before been taboo, had become a daily routine. Invitations to observe military exercises were sent out and were duly accepted. Truly remarkable was the fact that the most crucial and sought after area for inspections at the time of the Stockholm negotiations, the region of Central Europe and the Germanies, had by October 1987 been subject to inspection only t once.

According to the British, their request for an inspection in the GDR was not based on any particular suspicion. The aim was to perform the inspection as a matter of diplomatic relations. The GDR had handled the inspection programme in a businesslike and cooperative manner. The Western delegations, on the other hand, had become more cautious about making new initiatives. The practice of on-site inspections had lost a lot of its political symbolic value. The heated discussion in Stockholm on the maximum numbers of annual inspections to be carried out, the ceilings, now appeared rather unnecessary. The significance

The neutral and non-aligned, N + N, group was actively involved in bringing about the final outcome. From the right: Austria's Ambassador Rudolf Torovski, Sweden's Ambassador Curt Lidgaard, the Count of Liechtenstein Maria Ledebur-Wicheln, Malta's Ambassador Charles Vella, Switzerland's Ambassador Blaise Schenk, Yugoslavia's Ambassador Ignaz Golob, Cyprus' Ambassador Thalia Petrides and Finland's Ambassador Markku Reimaa. (Photograph: Archive of the Finnish Foreign Ministry)

of quotas was limited to the territory of the FRG, which could not be allowed to become a main theatre of inspection. Concerning disarmament, the main subject of the Vienna talks comprised the "link" between the 23-country negotiations and the 35-country CSCE negotiations. The issue was linking the two negotiating processes in a way that would secure the autonomy of the 23-country talks while taking into account the security interests of the 35 countries in new negotiations among the 23, integrity and generally accepted ground rules.

The Western alliance's cohesion and unity were now being frequently tested. Washington and Paris animatedly discussed the role of disarmament policy in general and its place in the CSCE in particular. A focus of attention was the idea of the N + N group concerning separate negotiating forums, particularly the possibilities for information exchange within the framework of the CSCE process. At the same time, the French wanted to emphasise strongly that the continuation of the Stockholm process did not merely mean developing confidence-building measures. The USA took the opposite view: the new 23-country talks were not part of the Stockholm process.

Certain suspicions prevailed in neutral and non-aligned circles that some of the Western delegations wanted a new mandate for starting negotiations among the 35 CSCE countries, where the objective of disarmament would be excluded and concentrated on instead by the 23 countries.

President Reagan and General Secretary Gorbachev's meeting in Reykjavik in October 1986 was a watershed in disarmament. NATO's member countries reached a mutual agreement at their meeting in June 1987 on the basis of which the West decided to propose a start to negotiations by the alliances involving their 23 member states "autonomously" and "in connection with the CSCE process".

On 14 December 1987, the 23-country negotiations registered consensus concerning the objectives of the mandate. The text followed largely the original proposals of the Western group. The text emphasised the importance of stability more clearly than the importance of reductions. The text also included a sentence, emphasised by the West, on eliminating the capacity for a surprise attack. Consensus opened up the possibility for arrangements concerning sectors. The East's goals reflected the mutual understanding that troops also meant armed forces.

As a supplement to the consensus attained, the Soviet Union delivered a letter to the parties specifying that conventional weapons included dual-purpose systems and that the elimination of the imbalance and the carrying out of reductions must be based on the principle of reciprocity. The letter was thought to reflect the dominant dichotomy in Moscow between civilian and military experts. Western officials thought it best to pay little attention to the letter in their comments.

After this, the more detailed mandate for the 23-country negotiations was decidedly open. Kashlev told Markku Reimaa in February 1988 that in connection with Foreign Minister Shevardnadze's visit to Bonn Soviet actions suggested considerable flexibility. The Soviet Union was prepared to leave short-range nuclear weapons out of the negotiations. It was nevertheless important that the mandate was balanced, and not only concerned a negotiating process dealing with Soviet tanks and troop numbers. "Dual-purpose weapons systems had to be included."

Kashlev said that the 23-country mandate and the follow-up work of the Stockholm conference had, from Moscow's standpoint, to be weighed up simultaneously with progress agreed on the humanitarian side.

The work of the Vienna follow-up meeting sketched out a code of conduct, in which support for the Soviet Union's aggressive reform policy came mainly from the Polish and Hungarian delegations. It was demanded of the GDR that, concerning border traffic, the obligatory daily fee paid by tourists be gradually revoked. This was a challenge both in principle and practice. During the final speeches at the follow-up meeting the GDR was put in the dock. There were calls for the Berlin wall to be torn down, as President Reagan had declared in his speech in West Berlin in June 1987.

N + N group in vogue

These developments already partly indicated that the N + N countries had an important role to play in advancing the Vienna follow-up meeting. The more there was a wish to discuss the target deadline for ending the new round of work, the more the N + N group was turned to so that it would present a draft for a comprehensive concluding document.

Ambassador Kashlev said in January 1988 that the Vienna meeting should reach a conclusion before summer, because with autumn other foreign policy matters would start to have a "retarding" effect on the work. He requested that a comprehensive proposal be made ready for use by the delegations before the Easter recess. It was stated by the Finnish side that the N + N had not yet progressed so far. "The position of the negotiations are far too vague and the main principle decisions are open. In this situation, a comprehensive proposal by the N + N countries would resemble guesswork rather than a seriously credible proposal for a final result."

When one considers the practical possibilities of the N + N countries for making a comprehensive proposal, it should be remembered that it was the first time in the CSCE process that the N + N countries were prepared to take on all the main subjects, including military security and the continuation of the Stockholm conference, and the principles of Baskets III and Basket I. Reference has already been made to Basket II's economic questions, in which environmental protection was becoming a new burning issue.

In connection with the Stockholm conference, the collaboration of the N + N countries had concluded fairly traditionally, with important differences of view, from Switzerland on the one hand and Yugoslavia and Sweden on the other, on whether or not disarmament negotiations were the business of the CSCE. A comparable major difference in interpretation concerned the role of the CSCE in general: was its 35-country consensus suitable for, or even capable of, having an influence over the arsenals of the main powers, including masses of nuclear weapons. Yugoslavia and Sweden, both of which were involved outside the CSCE in the disarmament activities of the non-aligned movement, took a different line to Switzerland, which tended to avoid the matter.

The idea of a joint proposal by the N + N countries was highly significant. And because the N + N countries presented a comprehensive proposal on military security on 24 March 1988, prior to the Easter recess, the comments of the other participants could wait until after the break. At the same time, the 23-country negotiations had taken a step forward on the issue of the mandate for the negotiations. The Soviet Union had also given an important signal of compromises on Basket III: the first 19 paragraphs could be preliminarily registered as adopted. EEC foreign ministers, meeting in Brussels on 23 March, had noted this as a positive sign. Things were now progressing towards substantial negotiations.

When the FRG's ambassador to Vienna, Ekkehardt Eickhoff, passed a message to this effect to one of the N + N coordinators, it was clear that the EEC group had prepared for a new phase of negotiations. From the EEC side this particularly concerned the post-Vienna follow-up, among other things, the Moscow conference. The EEC countries had a proposal of their own for a human dimension mechanism.

The original intention of the mechanism was that each of the 35 countries would have the right to convene a CSCE meeting to deal with individual cases concerning human contacts. Ambassador Eickhoff now said that the EEC countries no longer closely adhered to their original aim. It would be sufficient if, in the framework of the follow-up, there could be a more general return to unsolved matters, if they were not resolved beforehand bilaterally or otherwise.

The solution of problems was not in the EEC's hands alone. The US and Canada were also proponents of the initial idea. If they in any case required that the mechanism be included in the Vienna concluding document as a new dimension, it was clear that the same package would include acceptance of the convening of the Moscow conference.

The traditional competition surfaced in Vienna among the like-minded about who had been the most active. The State Secretary of the Swiss Foreign Ministry, Edouard Brunner, invited his N + N counterparts to an expert meeting in Geneva, on 6-8 April 1988, to prepare the countries' comprehensive proposal. A week later, on 15 April, the next session got under way in Vienna.

Geneva April 1988

The neutral and non-aligned circle of countries now convened amidst the general appraisal that the work of the Vienna follow-up meeting was approaching its decisive stage. Switzerland presented an invitation to an expert meeting in Geneva in April 1988. At that stage the Austrian side had already managed to confirm that the N + N foreign ministers would meet on 12-13 May in Vienna with the aim of proposing the group's draft comprehensive concluding document for the follow-up meeting. Because of this, the Austrians considered that the Swiss were "going solo".

The Geneva meeting went over all the remaining open questions. Alongside the traditional issue of the balance of the concluding document, there was a catalogue of Basket II and Basket III texts comprising a large body of detailed formulations. Based on discussions, a remaining open question was how complete and detailed the comprehensive proposal that the N + N foreign ministers would present in Vienna in May should be. Finland agreed with Switzerland and Yugoslavia that the proposal should be as complete as possible, including the part concerning the human dimension conferences.

The N + N attitude to the CSCE process was still up-to-date. Despite the period of *glasnost* and *perestroika* the N + N group worked from the assumption that the CSCE was emphatically a cooperative forum, that decisions were made by consensus, and that, from the standpoint of the process, it was important that all sectors of work could record significant progress. Gradual progress was typical of the process. The aggregate must be a politically acceptable balance.

The Geneva meeting was able to state that the joint N + N text on military security produced just before Easter corresponded to the group's common stance. There was no need for a more detailed discussion of the matter. The proposal was considered realistic and comprehensive. It could await comments from the other groups.

Principles

Austria, in the capacity of coordinator, presented a slightly reworked version of the draft text on 25 March 1988. The section on principles now contained the human dimension mechanism, as a "food for thought" draft and ideas paper, without having had the responses of the main parties. The human dimension was now defined as "Human rights, human contacts and other humanitarian issues". Switzerland considered the formulation to be acceptable from the East's standpoint, because there was nothing from Basket III except human contacts. Austria proposed that the human dimension conference should be in three stages.

The text concerning the peaceful settlement of disputes referred to an expert meeting and in principle the obligatory involvement of a third party in the settlement process. Finland wanted the mandate to more clearly delineate different types of dispute and their mandates. The coordinator entirely omitted from the text the recommendation concerning the abolition of the death penalty. Finland and Sweden considered this to be untimely. The section on principles now contained the first passage on measures against terrorism.

Half of the section on principles dealt with human rights, such as the right of individuals to promote the implementation of human rights, the means of remedy and freedom of religion, religious instruction and relations towards the media. The general assumption was that a text of this kind would now be acceptable to the Soviet Union. The passage on the death penalty was included particularly on the wishes of Finland and Sweden and for reasons of the balance of the comprehensive text. The group was aware that the US and UK would not be prepared to accept this part.

Kashlev said that the Soviet Union took a favourable view of Austria's draft proposals concerning the principles and Sweden's Basket III text. "Most of the

text is acceptable to the Soviet Union." He believed that a final outcome would
be reached on this basis with minor amendments.

Basket II

Questions of economic cooperation faced a contemporary international challenge in the Vienna meeting. The socialist systems sought to renew and make
cooperation more effective both among themselves and with the market econo-
mies. In Western Europe the process of integration continued, providing its
own dynamic to the discussion. The Soviet Union tried to make use of the
follow-up meeting's discussions to market perestroika: incentive, competition,
access to information and marketing were now concepts being used each day in
the speeches of the Soviet representatives. Likewise, the autonomy of industrial
plants and enterprises could be discussed. The possibility of the European Currency Unit being used as the means of exchange in East-West trade seemed to
be an interesting option for all except the Americans.

On the other hand, the Soviet Union held fast to its previous stand concerning trade barriers, offset trade, and restrictions on exports of technology.
It had not been prepared to give up its demands, even though the discussion
was free to cover subjects considered important by the Western delegations.
The Soviet Union only made one new proposal, concerning the establishment
of joint enterprises.

Throughout the whole discussion on the section concerning economic
cooperation the Soviet Union had tried to avoid giving emphasis to the old
dividing lines and disputes. The Western group and the EEC countries were
kept busy.

The biggest differences in view concerned economic cooperation. On this
too the Yugoslavian delegation, together with Austria and Sweden, aimed criticism particularly at the Swiss coordinator's text. He had drawn up the text to a
large extent independently. In Yugoslavia's view the proposal lacked dynamics
and specifics, particularly in the area of trade and scientific-technical cooperation.

There was an abundance of proposals on environmental protection. The
issue had been raised at the level of renewed discussion and calls for action at
the instigation of the neutrals plus Norway and Denmark. It was considered

as even having a healthy effect: the subject blended the old East-West arrangement in the discussions on Basket II. The first draft on the subject distributed by the coordinator on 1 June 1987 was below target in the opinion of Nordic experts. Later, in the autumn, Finland, Sweden and Austria made up a core group that aimed to make further amendments to the June text.

The Soviet Union agreed with the value of environmental initiatives and the urgency of measures related to them. It was not yet prepared, however, to commit itself in Vienna to targets; they would all too quickly lead to expensive investments. In the Soviet view, the work in Vienna should focus on emphasising programmes in principle and cooperation in research.

The Soviet Union kept up its developmental endeavours on overseas trade all the way down the line, with the EEC, the CMEA and bilaterally with the United States.

In Finland's view, the text paid unbalanced attention to differences between Eastern and Western aspirations. There were many detailed formulations from the West's proposals, while the areas favoured by the East – trade barriers and new forms of joint activity – had been left at a general level. The field of science and technology remained, in the opinion of Finnish experts, even below the target level of the Madrid concluding document.

The text concentrated on concepts of information exchange and scientific cooperation in general terms. The section on environment was formulated as a combination of the Nordic proposal and the EEC's vision. It was also detailed in terms of its follow-up. A better balance and acceptability of Basket II required, in Finland's view, a bolstering of the sections on economic and industrial cooperation and scientific-technical cooperation.

The question of the rights of return of migrants also divided the N + N group along traditional lines. Yugoslavia and Switzerland had completely divergent aims. The reference to the role of the ECE as a Basket II specialist agency was now alluded to in the preamble. The opinion of many was still that there had been an excess of references to the ECE in the Madrid document.

Basket III

During the drafting work Sweden proposed a summary of the text. This did not contain new proposals for decisions by the coordinator.

When it came to Basket III's section on human contacts, Switzerland worked from the conviction that objectives should be set markedly high, even at maximum level, in order that a balanced aggregate could be ensured. In contrast, the N + Ns' discussion re-examined what the primary aim of Basket III should be. The maximalists of the Western group aimed as clearly as possible to change the Soviet Union's human rights practices, and therefore to put pressure on Moscow through the Vienna decisions. For the FRG, however, it was important that regular contact with the GDR could be maintained more easily than before.

If the readability of the text depended on affirmative phrasings, the N + N group was prepared to highlight them. However, it sought to avoid repeating some of the socialist countries' contentious concepts and references. The facilitation of emigration was referred to as a "freedom" and not a "right". The processing time for applications concerning family reunification was given a compromise duration of four months, in place of the N + N proposal of two months and the East's suggestion of six,

One of the most difficult recommendations of the Vienna meeting concerned cases where previously people had left a socialist country "illegally" and their reunification with their families. According to the recommendation, the socialist countries would have to give retrospective pardons to verdicts of illegal emigration. The standpoint of the West was that innocent family members should not be punished in such cases.

Improved opportunities for faith communities to assemble and maintain contacts were now connected in a new way to neighbouring countries, as in the example of relations between churches in Austria and Czechoslovakia. The Eastern group thought that religious communities were now seeking special treatment at the expense of others. The section on information listed for the first time an expert conference on the exchange of information. The idea drew widespread support.

The head of the CSCE department at the Soviet Foreign Ministry visited Vienna shortly before the N + N countries' comprehensive proposal was officially presented to the meeting. Yuri Deryabin told Markku Reimaa on Saturday 5 May that the English-language comprehensive text must be translated into the languages of the socialist countries before experts could comment on it. In Moscow, deputy minister Kovalev had already decided that the Soviet Union should wait for the N + N countries' comprehensive text.

Different working habits emerged in the course of the CSCE process and in connection with the follow-up meetings. In Vienna this was seen in the excessive activity of the Romanian delegation in making various proposals. It was clear that written proposals were expected from the main countries that corroborated the viewpoints they presented in public and in their bilateral discussions. But there then came a crucial question with regard to the credibility of the negotiations and negotiators: how many times could an original proposal be amended without its author losing integrity, and how forceful was it worth making proposals, that in advance appeared fairly unrealistic, so that their impact would not be virtually the same?

The foreign ministers of the N + N countries presented the meeting with their draft document on Friday 13 May 1988. For the first time a comprehensive proposal contained the joint vision of a grouping, outside the military alliances, of what a possible outcome could be. The N + N countries' internal composition ensured that an effort was made to listen to the views of all the 35 participating states. The timing of the meeting and the presentation of the draft concluding document was such that the follow-up meeting could reach a conclusion by summer. The ministers clarified this timing at a joint press conference: they meant by the end of July.

Initial reactions: yes, but…

The more significant and important an initiative was, the more careful the reactions to it needed to be. And so in Vienna the week following the tabling of the proposal was taken up by internal discussions in the Western and Eastern groups. They each tried to craft their comments to be as comprehensive as possible. They had to try to choose what from their standpoint were the main questions and problems in the proposal. There was an informal competition over the popularity of the N + N proposal. In principle, everyone wanted to agree as much as possible with the N + N countries. In its content and timing, the proposal was considered "a decisive initiative" for bringing about an end to the work. It was timed to be before the Moscow summit meeting and the meeting of NATO foreign ministers in Madrid.

Thus, the initial responses to the proposal differed from one another only slightly. It was no surprise that the differences of opinion focused on human rights, freedom of religion, the possibilities for individuals and groups to monitor the performance of their governments, freedom of movement and emigration and currency exchange minimums. If the socialist countries felt embarrassed by such issues, the West was in difficulties over the section on military security, in particular the joint definition of the 23- and 35-country negotiating processes. The United States was not prepared to accept the proposal. The French declared frankly in private discussions that due to the formation of a joint position by the West, they were given to understand that there would still be some changes to the text. On the other hand, they were already prepared to accept the text as it was! The role of the US was decisive concerning issues to do with Basket II and military security. On the latter, France was the group's internal challenger, while on economic matters the aspirant host of the follow-up event was the FRG.

At the end of May 1988, the FRG's Ambassador Eickhoff turned to Markku Reimaa expressly on issues concerning the economic forum. US Secretary of State George Shultz had written a letter to his West German counterpart saying directly that the N + N countries' formulation of the "development and diversification" of trade was not acceptable to the US. The Americans suspected that behind the formulation lay a chance that the socialist countries would deal with the economic forum in connection with NATO's COCOM arrangement. When Eickhoff tried to get the relevant part of the text altered, with the assistance of the Swiss coordinator and other personal contacts, it turned into a question of prestige. Switzerland and Sweden in particular considered that unless there could be a discussion in a follow-up event – the economic forum – on "East-West trade", there was no need at all to convene a forum.

The formal comments by the groups were received in writing at the turn of June-July. The Soviet Union presented a response on the 27 June in the name of four socialist countries: the Soviet Union, Bulgaria, the GDR and Czechoslovakia. Amendments to the section on principles were proposed concerning the international obligations of national legislation, freedom of religion, the rights of national minorities and monitoring.

On 7 July, the Western delegations rejected the proposed amendments concerning national minorities and proposed amendments concerning monitoring that went beyond the suggestions of the N + N countries. This tactical

Foreign Minister Kalevi Sorsa took part on 13 May 1988 in the meeting of N + N foreign ministers for the presentation of the draft concluding document. Pictured here are ambassador Kaarlo Yrjö-Koskinen, Head of Department Matti Kahiluoto, Legation Councillor Päivi Blinnikka, Ministerial Councillor Tapio Saarela, Legation Councillor Harri Helenius, Legation Councillor Tuomas Pekkarinen, Major Yrjö Kukko and the author.

move only reinforced the position of the original N + N proposal. Concerning military security, the West's internal compromise was only possible in so far as the form and content of the further work of the Stockholm conference were increasingly vague. The West's internal compromise required magical flexibility by the conference diplomats in using "constructive ambiguity". The minimum demand of the N + N countries was that the follow-up work in Stockholm, the negotiations between the 35 and 23 countries, would take the form of a joint forum for information exchange on the customary terms of the CSCE process.

In his summarising report of 8 July, Markku Reimaa wrote that at the decisive stage of the N + N's internal negotiations different national emphases were clearly apparent. Austria's priority was that Vienna should be the venue for the continuation of the negotiations on military issues. Yugoslavia emphasised the central role of disarmament in the continuing work of the 35 countries. Switzerland repeatedly showed that its defence was based on the mobilization of a reserve army, which placed it in a special position. Finland stressed the importance of the continuation and credibility of the process started by the Stockholm conference.

The East's tactics in its comments on Basket II was that by being reticent it would bolster the position of the N + N's text and thus point out the abundance of the West's comments, which would slow progress towards completing the work. The Western delegations tried to put an emphasis on human dimension perspectives in this section. There had been much consensus on trade barriers, business contacts and information exchange. The follow-up to Basket II included a meeting of experts on environmental protection and an economic forum. Italy's initiative for a scientific forum was not affirmed at that stage. There was a positive and constructive atmosphere around the Basket II issues.

The Soviet Union and its allies made detailed proposals to amend and adjust the Basket III text. These stressed the traditional standpoints of the socialist countries: the primacy of legislation over international commitments, the attempt to limit the availability of religious literature to individual use, the effort in the section on the exchange and availability of information to stress "strengthening trust between peoples", radio broadcast reception was viewed as being free if broadcasts were national in origin and transmitted from the territory of a CSCE country. This way Radio Liberty and Radio Free Europe were excluded from international commitments.

The West's response to the East's proposed amendments was predominantly dismissive. The West's comments reiterated the view that the N + N text on Basket III "fell short of the West's aims". The West's "maximalists" still clung to the underlying view that a quick and comprehensive compromise was not to be expected on these questions.

Human dimension

The concept of the human dimension was new to the Vienna follow-up meeting. The initiative had come from the West. Because the expansion of military security demanded, in the West's view, a new development for the sake of balance, the humanitarian arena too had to progress onto new terrain. The West now proposed a new mechanism: an individual country could convene a meeting to deal with individual human rights cases. In addition, a separate conference on human rights would be organised. In the view of the Americans this mechanism, and on the other hand the autonomous negotiations by the 23 countries, constituted crucial new dimensions.

In the N + N countries' proposal the mechanism was slightly more embellished. According to the proposal, efforts would be made bilaterally and multilaterally to facilitate the resolution of humanitarian cases and situations. The N + N proposed a three-stage conference whereby there would be one held each year from 1989 onwards. The view of the West was that Paris and Copenhagen were already acceptable venues for 1989 and 1990, while the East's view was that Paris and Moscow were definite venues.

Washington's acceptance of the Moscow human rights conference was not confirmed until January 1989. Secretary of State Shultz was able to announce that the Soviet authorities had given binding and credible guarantees that the conference would be organized in an appropriate manner, following CSCE practice and openness. Only Canada at this stage withheld consent to the conference.

In addition to human rights questions, the three human dimension conferences and the follow-up mechanisms, the decision taken on 6 March 1989 for the start of negotiations on European conventional weapons was another new terrain for the CSCE. Though the negotiations were started between the 23 member countries of the alliances, the mandate for the negotiations and the decisions on the form of the work would be included in the document of the Vienna follow-up meeting. The results of the negotiations would be assessed for the first time at the Helsinki follow-up conference.

Who has the last word?

Apart from being always its own internal dynamo, the CSCE has also been a mirror of the outside world. In many countries eventual contentious solutions could become particular problems due to domestic policy issues. The successful conclusion of the Vienna follow-up was crucially tied up with the strict timetable. The USA's internal operational capacity was declining. The Vienna follow-up had to reach a swift conclusion before the change of power in Washington on 20 January 1989.

There were also problems in the Eastern camp. The Soviet Union, Poland and Hungary had on many occasions expressed a readiness to compromise so that the meeting could be quickly wrapped up. Ambassador Kashlev announced in a speech on 22 November 1988 that the N + N countries' latest proposals on Basket III issues were acceptable to the Soviet Union and other socialist countries without amendment. The information received by the Finnish delegation was somewhat different from this rosy view. The GDR had not yet agreed to the proposal for eliminating the minimum currency exchange rule, Bulgaria had a problem with the stipulation concerning national minorities, and Czechoslovakia and Romania had reservations about the establishment of monitoring groups.

The GDR's long-time CSCE ambassador in Madrid and Vienna, Peter Steglich, wrote in his 1996 book *KSZE-Fossil oder Hoffnung?* that the two Germanies acted in different ways as the CSCE's midwives. It was a different matter how each of them was able to use the CSCE for its own purposes. Steglich acknowledges that the GDR, particularly on the occasion of the 1988-89 Vienna follow-up meeting, clung to an obstructionist role. It felt that it was living a harassed and fearful existence.

On 7 December 1988, just before NATO ministerial meeting, the alliance's high level working group dealt with the issue of the relationship of the 23-country negotiations with the CSCE process. The US-French compromise followed the N + N working paper, presented in October, fairly closely though with some specifications. The arrangement concerned the end of the MBFR negotiations that had gone on since 1973, the mandate for the agreement of the new 23-country negotiations and their inclusion in the concluding document of the Vienna follow-up meeting.

One indication of the kind of detail necessary to reach a consensus was that the announcement of the start of the new 23-country negotiations had to take place simultaneously with the ending of the MBFR talks "that would last for a week at most, following the end of the Vienna follow-up meeting".

Apart from the end of the MBFR negotiations and the start of the new 23-country negotiations, from the Finnish and N + N position a decision was expected on the important new arrangements concerning information exchange. Consensus meant that these information exchange meetings were to be arranged on the basis of an agreement reached by the CSCE participating states.

The section on procedure referred to CSCE practice. The information exchange meetings were duly registered according to the aims of the N + N countries. They would be held every fourth week.

The third decision emphasizing the CSCE connection concerned the role of the follow-up meetings in following disarmament activity. A statement by the chairman, included as an appendix to the concluding document, explains "the Helsinki follow-up meeting would be the first in which an assessment of progress made would be possible". On the other hand, the continuation of proceedings by the 23 countries was left up to their own decision. The mandate would remain valid as agreed in Vienna, until the "activity of the 23 countries is changed".

In drawing up the working programme for the negotiations an effort was made to ensure that everyone had an equal opportunity to participate. The timetables of the meetings had to ensure there was no overlap, because many delegations used the same personnel for both sets of negotiations.

The Finnish delegation stated in a comment that the arrangements to do with the information exchange meetings largely corresponded with the ideas proposed by Finland and the other N + N countries. At the same time, it was considered noteworthy that there was now unanimity in the Western alliance concerning the role of the next follow-up meeting in relation to the new process being started.

Back to Helsinki

The decision on the subsequent work was confirmed at the final session of the Vienna follow-up. This generated a certain feeling of uncertainty that hung over all the proposed events. Nothing was engraved in stone until everything was prepared.

The post-Vienna follow-up events met with favour unique in CSCE history. There were from eight to 12 separate meetings and events to be arranged before the next follow-up meeting, in Helsinki in 1992.

The US delegation was the only one in practice to harbour fundamental reservations about the number of follow-up events. The Americans were particularly reluctant in their attitude to the meeting of experts on the peaceful settlement of disputes and to the FRG's proposal for organizing an economic forum.

The N + N countries endeavoured to dispel knee-jerk reservations with ideas such as proposing that the preparations for these follow-up events be trimmed or dropped altogether. The duration of the follow-up events would be four weeks instead of six as agreed in Madrid. From this one can calculate that the overall volume of follow-up work compared with the corresponding decisions made Madrid would not multiply in terms of working weeks, only in the number of events.

The number and duration of the follow-up events were to have an effect on the Helsinki follow-up meeting. Depending on the method of calculation and decisions taken, the next follow-up would be in 1991 or be moved to 1992. Ambassador Zimmermann said in a discussion at the beginning of December 1988 that the latter option depended on the organization of the Moscow meeting on human contacts.

The Vienna follow-up meeting decided that the representatives of the participating states would gather in Helsinki on 24 March 1992 for the next follow-up meeting. Instead of the meeting being organized against the grey backdrop of autumn and winter, the participants could meet during the light spring and white summer nights of the North.

The CSCE's 35 foreign ministers took part in the closing stage of the Vienna meeting, on 17-19 January 1989. The follow-up meeting had covered 92 working weeks. It was George Shultz's last conference as Secretary of State. In Washington, power changed hands from Ronald Reagan to George Bush on 20 January, immediately following the end of the Vienna follow-up. The closing stage of the meeting was also Kalevi Sorsa's last performance as Finland's Foreign Minister. When explaining the results of the follow-up meeting from Finland's viewpoint to journalists in Helsinki, on 24 January, Sorsa announced that he was leaving to see the President and to hand in his resignation. Pertti Paasio succeeded him at the beginning of February.

The return to Helsinki in the framework of the CSCE process was not an assumed fact. The formal decision on and confirmation of the Helsinki follow-up meeting were made in Vienna at the final session. However, with informal lobbying the idea had started to be accepted in good time. The delegation for the preparatory meeting had already estimated in Vienna in October 1986 that, based on experiences to date, Helsinki and Finland might have the possibility of hosting the follow-up meeting.

Following the Helsinki and Geneva rotation at the initial stages, from 1973 to 75, all main neutral and non-aligned countries had hosted follow-up meetings: Belgrade 1977-78, Madrid 1980-83, Stockholm 1984-86, and now Vienna. Though there were no CSCE written rules or decisions restricting a follow-up event solely to a neutral and non-aligned country, this had become the practice. From private discussions it was evident that this course was considered to be to Finland's advantage. Rotation had become one of the principles of CSCE practice. It did not prevent the possibility of returning to previous venues.

The Finnish delegation was given permission to continue with informal work on the matter. The Finnish head of mission had used the subject in a general speech in November 1986. The message was read loud and clear, which was the intention.

Back to Helsinki. State Secretary Åke Wihtol (left) held a closing reception in Vienna, 20. January 1989. Also pictured are Ambassador Matti Kahiluoto and hosts Varpu and Markku Reimaa.

Exploratory informal work on Helsinki's candidacy proceeded and intensified. The Finnish daily *Helsingin Sanomat* first published the news of Helsinki as a possible venue for the next follow-up meeting on 17 June 1987. The delegation duly conducted a review of the current situation at mid-summer. Finland's own interest in the discussion in Vienna concerned the discussion on the continuation of the Stockholm conference: where and when would the talks continue?

The matter of the venue for the military negotiations dealt with by NATO's ministerial meeting in Reykjavik was decided in favour of a single location. Naturally, the 16 NATO countries could not go further than this basic decision, for instance by naming the venue at that stage. The French let it be understood during the general discussion that their oblique attitude towards the MBFR negotiations supported the possibility for the negotiations to continue somewhere other than Vienna, in Geneva, for instance. The French estimated that half the NATO countries supported Geneva. The FRG was clearly in favour of Vienna. US Ambassador Zimmermann had the same preference for Vienna for both sets of negotiations.

Concerning the venue for the next follow-up, Ambassador Zimmermann had said in the *Helsingin Sanomat* article that the "United States was prepared to consider seriously the organizing of the next follow-up conference in Helsinki, if Finland were to offer itself as a candidate."

Zimmermann told Markku Reimaa a few days following the interview that the journalist who had written the piece had put "great stress" on the question. The ambassador mentioned having also said that if some other country that had been a host previously were available, the "option would include cities other than Helsinki, for instance Stockholm".

The delegation asked Helsinki how it should respond to the Zimmermann interview in favour of a quick solution. The fact that the issue was ripe for informal discussion did not ensure that the capitals of the participating states would go along with the process.

Foreign Minister Sorsa decided on behalf of the government to announce publicly in July 1987 that if the Vienna follow-up meeting so decided, Finland was ready to act as the host of the next follow-up meeting at a date to be arranged separately. Sorsa also announced that the government had decided to start the renovation of one of Helsinki's most prestigious edifices, the House of the Estates, with a view to the needs of the follow-up meeting.

The delegation formally presented Helsinki's candidacy in autumn 1987 at a plenary session of the follow-up meeting. There were not yet any other candidates in the race. Finland felt that it had gained an advantage that it would endeavour to safeguard and reinforce.

In December 1988, Zimmermann entered into the deliberations, for the first time on a more specific date for the Helsinki follow-up. He was positive about the idea of arranging the meeting in the spring, that the preparatory meeting would be as short as possible, lasting just a couple of weeks, and that the follow-up meeting could start immediately after the preparatory event. Zimmermann was pleased that the preparatory meeting, the opening of the follow-up meeting and the discussion on implementation could all take place before the 1992 Easter recess.

The final working week of the Vienna follow-up meeting was busy and its programme varied. Foreign Minister Sorsa arrived in Vienna on the Monday evening of 16 January and delivered his address on 18 January.

It had been agreed with State Secretary Åke Wihtol that he would be on standby to go to Vienna at short notice and host Finland's final reception on behalf of the Foreign Ministry. This was held at the residence of the CSCE ambassador on Friday 20 January at 18.00. The follow-up meeting made formal decisions on 19 January on the details and aggregate of the Vienna concluding document. Wihtol arrived in Vienna the same day. He hosted the reception, the purpose of which was to welcome the representatives of the CSCE participating states to the follow-up meeting in Helsinki in 1992.

Closing the circle

Three years were to pass from the end of the Vienna follow-up meeting, in January 1989, to the next follow-up meeting, in Helsinki in March 1992. The intervening period was filled with conferences and meetings that had been agreed in good time or were held at short notice. The functioning of the networks for cooperation and contact acquired by the CSCE were trimmed politically, and at the civil service level, in Europe and with the Americans and Canadians. It is hard to imagine that great upheavals and surprising twists and turns of the end of the 1980s and beginning of the 1990s could have happened in such good order, and without greater misunderstandings, without the CSCE. Despite all else, the main parties had the will to deal with the most painful issues by peaceful means – by negotiation. The mandatory principle of the peaceful settlement of disputes had become a European practice without the mandatory stipulation having ever been formally approved by consensus and recorded in a CSCE document.

The constantly turning "machinery" of the CSCE's interest groups and political level had also constituted a new type of crisis management mechanism. The CSCE was used to avoiding dramatic and sudden political decisions. Despite the continuation of the ideological war, the sabre rattling of the Cold War and, with the occupation of Prague, the arrival of the Brezhnev doctrine had become history with the rise to power of General Secretary Gorbachev. At his speech to the UN General Assembly in autumn 1988, Gorbachev said that the internal solidarity and internationalism of the socialist camp in the form of the use of force was over. The ideological dams had started to crumble.

The meeting of the Warsaw Treaty countries on 7-8 July 1989 took a momentous decision. The Treaty members "officially overturned the so-called

Brezhnev doctrine because it had endangered socialism and had given our communist brothers in neighbouring countries the right to interfere in the affairs of other by force". According to eye witnesses, the GDR party leader Erich Honecker was so irritated by this statement that he left the room early.

On the other hand, the 2 + 4-country process leading to German reunification later revealed that the issue was not only a major political and security challenge for Moscow. There were significantly more parties to the post-Second World War settlement in Western Europe. The UK's Prime Minister Margaret Thatcher was clearly dubious about the German reunification process. France's President Mitterrand was the last Western head of state, who on his visit to East Berlin in autumn 1990, attempted to restore faith in the future for his East German colleagues. Due to the CSCE, it was easier for the 35 participating states to confront a variety of unexpected events. It is hard to imagine that Poland's Solidarity movement would have been able to achieve its goals so quickly and clearly without the CSCE's Madrid meeting of 1980-83. Initially, Solidarity did not want to bind its trade union aims too clearly to the CSCE and foreign policy challenges.

The revolution in Portugal struck at the time of the CSCE summit conference and thus received special attention in the international media. The country's president came to Helsinki to the summit conference at a time of deep transition and without a legally functioning government. He signed the Final Act together with the representatives of the other participating states.

Cyprus's President, Archbishop Makarios, was also able to make a historic visit to Helsinki. The delegations of Greece and Turkey were usually present for the customary speeches of the final sessions of CSCE meetings. Their dispute concerned the division of Cyprus and governments' legitimacy as a party to the CSCE. The division of Cyprus has been an open wound for the CSCE, but not only for the CSCE, for the past 35 years. The Cypriot ambassador at the Vienna follow-up meeting, Ms Thalia Petrides, appealed to her counterparts that the division of Cyprus would not be reinforced as a permanent factor of European stability and security. The reunification process of the Germanies lent further authority to this statement.

The 20 years of the CSCE's alacrity constituted a new political challenge in nearly all the capitals. In the superpower capitals of Washington and Moscow this new challenge seemed surprisingly similar. The main organizations, the foreign ministries on the one hand, and the defence ministries on the other, were constantly the decisive factors in sketching out the future course of the CSCE process. Vast machines need plenty of time to ready themselves. Making changes was like turning a giant ship around – heavy steering.

The role of Congress in Washington altered fundamentally, when in autumn 1976 it established its own monitoring mechanism, the CSCE commission. The commission's representatives considered that through it the views of the Americans of the usefulness of the CSCE would become more positive. Thanks to human rights it acquired a definite policy. Along with the work of Congress it is said that the elevation of human rights policy as a conspicuous priority saved the CSCE in two ways: it did not cease despite the Americans' heavy rhetoric or the Soviet Union's polemics in Belgrade and Madrid. On the contrary, it revived the interest of the Americans in the CSCE process. It got enough done that was definite.

Moscow gradually had to face the challenge of a new kind of public opinion from its increasingly influential dissidents and the Helsinki group. Andrei Amalrik, who was killed in a car accident in Spain at the start of the Madrid follow-up meeting, asked in his book, published in 1969, whether the Soviet Union would last until 1984. Academician Saharov became the robust and logical critic of the traditional Soviet system.

Political decision-makers in both capitals were constantly cautious of being involved in détente, and therefore of being the guarantors of the CSCE's advancement. Both superpowers shared the mutual concern of how to preserve and ensure the internal solidarity of their own alliances.

The small and medium-sized states endeavoured to use the independent and equal roles of the CSCE participating states as effectively as possible. The role of the small states in discussions between the superpowers was easy to disparage. There was no desire to give the Micky Mouse states an undue right to speak under the umbrella of consensus, let alone the right of decision. The national goals of France and the FRG were considered by Washington to be fairly dangerous. For Moscow Romania's role in the early years of the CSCE was an open challenge to the unity of the Warsaw Treaty Organization. Ambassador Valentin Lipatti made this abundantly clear to everyone in Geneva when he spent the duration of the internal meeting of the Warsaw Treaty countries sitting in the conference centre café.

Finland's role — a myth?

From the viewpoint of Finland's original objectives the CSCE constituted a multifaceted process. Finnish diplomats and specialists from various ministries became accustomed over the years to increasingly smooth international cooperation, and to long-term negotiating processes with no automatic guarantees of successful outcomes. In addition, the readiness to organize international conferences in Finland was valuable training. The Spirit of Helsinki and Finlandia Hall are universal concepts, descriptive and palpable. The duties of host demanded up-to- date literacy in reading the international situation and the endeavours of the participating states. One learned to know within which type of framework one could operate.

From the standpoint of the foreign policy leadership, the original objectives of the initiative concerned were to try to nurture Finland's room for manoeuvre in foreign affairs. In this respect the CSCE's first years did not achieve clear results. In Moscow, the "channel" for handling bilateral relations with Finland ensured that internationalisation did not displace Moscow's priorities, despite all the speeches. The public liturgy was that the charter of Finnish-Soviet bilateral relations, the treaty of friendship, cooperation and mutual assistance, was the point of reference as before. The political axiom of the permanence of the Soviet Union and its system was a matter that one did not dare question in public, neither in speeches nor PhD theses.

It is warranted to ask what credible and critical research on the Soviet Union was performed in Finland during the 1970s. As has been mentioned, alongside the treaty of friendship, cooperation and mutual assistance bilateral relations faithfully sought to avoid breaking sensitive taboos. Soviet dissidents did not expect formal public support for them from Finland. Estonian emigrants were also quietly ignored in the speeches of Finnish politicians. The reception of Finnish YLE television broadcasts along the north coast of Estonia was a sensitive issue throughout the lifespan of the Soviet system in Estonia.

Despite the ideas aired by Foreign Minister Karjalainen in his speech delivered in Finlandia Hall in July 1973, the Finnish "model" and the manner in which relations were handled with the socialist countries did not become the main focus of discussion in the CSCE Basket III negotiations. Finland was more at ease expounding on its bilateral commercial relations with the Soviet Union and the CMEA.

Finnish involvement in the CSCE process had an increasingly clear twofold influence. Those in involved in the negotiating process held to the aim that the credibility of the involvement required coherent action in concrete negotiating situations, whether in Geneva, Belgrade, Madrid or Vienna. The neutral and non-aligned group of countries acted as a new operational reference group, even though the national starting points of these countries differed greatly.

After 1975, the vitality and continuity of the process constituted a clear, though general, priority of Finland's involvement. There was no alternative to détente and the CSCE. From a practical standpoint, the more general the instructions and frameworks sent from the capital, the better were the conditions for involvement.

The 1975 Helsinki summit conference brought together the long-standing aims of the domestic political leadership, President Kekkonen and the leadership of the Foreign Ministry, as well as of the delegation working in Geneva under the leadership of Ambassador Iloniemi. The personification of the Spirit of Helsinki in President Kekkonen had materialized. For its part, Ambassador Iloniemi's delegation had broadened the horizons of Finnish diplomatic expertise for the new forum. Despite the prevailing international trends, the summit conference took place in a spirit of conciliation. There were various critical factors. There was General Secretary Brezhnev's health. An apologetic President Ford found it hard to explain what the reason was for his participation in the conference. The President of Portugal arrived without the support of a functioning government in his capital.

Finland's domestic political routine displayed different features. The interpretation of this writer is that the domestic political competition for making

Moscow's road feasible, under the patronage of President Kekkonen, in the end became a self-installed brake on broadening Finland's foreign political room for manoeuvre. Thanks to détente and the CSCE the enlarging international cooperation did not eliminate intense ongoing debate about the role and meaning of the treaty with the Soviet Union. Moscow was offered an open, actively flexible and competitive alternative by Helsinki. It could hardly have been surprising that there was no need in Moscow to adapt to new ways in relations with Finland, regardless of the progress of détente and the CSCE. There was a definite instance of this when Ambassador Mendelevich asked his colleague and Finnish expert Juri Deryabin wasn't it time to shift the "brick" of Finnish bilateral relations into the present day. No, it wasn't.

On the disarmament front the tense situation in the North constituted a threat that even caused panic reactions in Helsinki. All sorts of initiatives were attempted, from a unilateral declaration of being nuclear weapon-free to the pan-European disarmament programme. As Professor Keijo Korhonen said, you have to run fast in order to stay where you are. To which one could add that you had to run with one eye covered.

The Soviet military-industrial complex supported neither détente nor the CSCE. The role of the SS-20 missiles in triggering an open disarmament race in 1976 indicated that political consensus did not extend beyond the Kremlin and Foreign Ministry elites in Moscow. The same applied with Finnish relations. The guidance of Finland's strict adherence to the 1948 treaty clearly united Finnish party-political and intelligence policy specialists for taking care of bilateral relations. At the same time the military clauses of the treaty involved the Soviet military-industrial complex as a guard in the event of possible change in the direction of Finland and the North.

Only General Secretary Gorbachev's unprejudiced initiatives unravelled the internal discipline of the socialist camp, and the Brezhnev doctrine, as well as the straitjacket of bilateral relations woven out of the treaty. When unrest and chaos threatened elsewhere on the Soviet Union's borders, the Finnish border in autumn 1989 visibly represented stability and continuity. For the first time in a long time Finns could feel satisfied. In October 1989 Finland was, in the words of President Mikhail Gorbachev, a clearly Nordic, neutral Finland.

Interviews

In Finland

AHO, Esko, Minister 18.5.2006, Helsinki,

BASSIN, Benjamin, Councillor of Foreign Affairs, 25.6.2007, Helsinki

BLOMQVIST, Leif, Ambassador, 18.10.2006, 27.5.2008 Helsinki

HELENIUS, Harry, Ambassador, 7.6.2007, Moskova

HOLKERI, Harri, Counsellor of State, 30.5.2006, Helsinki

HYVÄRINEN, Risto, Ambassador, 12.9.2006, Helsinki

ILONIEMI, Jaakko, Minister, 11.5.2006, 24.10.2006, 26.3.2008 Helsinki

IHAMUOTILA, Jaakko, senior industrialist, 12.4.2007, Helsinki

JAKOBSON, Max, Minister, 22.5.2006, Helsinki

KAHILUOTO, Matti, Ambassador, 9.6.2006, Helsinki

KANERVA, Ilkka, Member of Parliament, 9.11.2006, Helsinki

KARPPINEN, Antti, Ambassador, 16.6.2006, Helsinki

KEISALO, Paavo 23.5.2006, Helsinki

KOIVISTO, Erkki, Commodore, 19.1.2007, Helsinki

KOIVISTO, Mauno, President, 6.6.2006, Helsinki

KORVENHEIMO, Pekka, J., Ambassador, 2.5.2006, 20.3.2007, 7.5.2008, Helsinki

KORHONEN, Keijo, Professor, 25.7.2007 / by phone to Paltamo

KUJASALO, Pekka, Ambassador, 4.6.2007, Budapest

KUKKO, Yrjö, Colonel, 19.1.2007, Helsinki

LAAMANEN, Pentti, Colonel, 19.1.2007, Helsinki

LEHTOSUO, Kimmo, Colonel, 19.1.2007, Helsinki

LIIKANEN, Erkki, Director General, 29.11.2006, Helsinki

LIUKKONEN, Matti, Helsinki

LYRA, Markus, Undersecretary of State, 26.4.2006, Helsinki

LÄHTEINEN, Jussi, Commanding Officer, 19.1.2007, Helsinki

LÄNSIPURO, Yrjö, Foreign Affairs Counsellor, 8.5.2007, Helsinki

MANSALA, Arto, State Secretary, 22.11.2006, Helsinki

MICKWITZ, Margaretha, Cultural Affairs Counsellor, 1.2.2006,Helsinki

NEVAKIVI, Jukka, Professor, 13.12.2006, Helsinki

PALOSUO, Arhi, Ambassador, 27.11.2006, Helsinki

PASTINEN, Ilkka, Ambassador, 30.10.2006, Helsinki

POHJOLA, Raimo, Archival Counsellor, 3.4.2008, Helsinki

RANTANEN, Paavo, Minister, 9.5.2006, Helsinki

SORSA, Irene, 17.4.2008, Helsinki

STENBÄCK, Pär, Minister, 22.5.2006, Helsinki

SUOMI, Juhani, Professor, 20.2.2008, Helsinki

SUOMINEN, Ilkka, Minister, 28.11.2006, Helsinki

TORSTILA, Pertti, State Secretary, 14.2.2008, Helsinki
TUOVINEN, Matti, State Secretary, 14.6.2006, Helsinki
TÖRNUDD, Klaus, Ambassador, 3.10.2006, Helsinki
TÖTTERMAN, Richard, Ambassador, 9.3.2007, Helsinki
WARONEN, Eero, Director of Information, 5.6.2006, Helsinki
VALTASAARI, Jukka, Ambassador, 7.11.2006
VÄYRYNEN, Paavo, Minister, 7.5.2008 Helsinki
VÄYRYNEN, Raimo, Professor, 12.9.2007, Helsinki

Abroad

BERG, Göran, Ambassador, Vienna 23.2.2007
BILANDZIC, Vladimir, Vienna, 23.2.2007; Belgrade 8–10.3.2008
BOCK, Sigfrid, Professor, Berlin 13.6.2007
CESKA, Franz, Ambassador, Vienna 23.2.2007
CRITTENBERGER, Katharine, StD. Washington 7.2.2007
DEMUS, Helen, Legation Counsellor, Budapest 2.6.2007
DERYABIN, Juri, Ambassador, Moscow 27.10.2006, 6.6.2007
DOBROSIELSKI, Marian, Warsaw 12.12.2007
DUBININ, Juri, Deputy Minister, Moscow 7.6.2007
ERDÖS, Andrei, Ambassador, Budapest 2.6.2007
GOODBY, James, Ambassador, Washington 12.2.2007
KAMPELMAN, Max, Ambassador, Washington 6.2.2007
KASTL, Jörg, Ambassador, Berlin 12.10.2006
KONARSKI, Włodzimierz, Ambassador, Warsaw 11.12.2007
KONDRATSHEV, Sergei, Ambassador, General, Moscow 6.6.2007
KORNBLUM, John, Chairman, Berlin 12.6.2007
LÖFFLER, Sigfrid, journalist, Helsinki 16.3.2007
McNAMARA, Ronald, Washington 8.2.2007
MÜLLER, Richard, Ambassador, 10.2.2006 Richmond/USA
NILES, M.T. Thomas, Vice Chairman, Helsinki 17.4.2007
NOWAK, Jerzy, Ambassador, Warsaw 10.12.2007
OLIVER, Spencer, General Secretary, Vienna 23.2.2007
PETRAN, Janos, Ambassador, Moscow 7.6.2007
ROTFELDT, Adam, Professor, Warsaw 10.12.2007
SCHMIDBAUER, Werner, General, Kutvele 11– 15.7.2007
SHUSTOV, Vladimir, Ambassador, Moscow 26.10.2006
SLETZINGER, Martin, Woodrow Wilson Center, Washington 6.2.2007
STEGLICH, Peter, Ambassador, Berlin 13.6.2007
STRAUSS, Harlan, Dr, Washington 12.2.2007
TOWPIK, Andrzej, Ambassador, New York 16.2.2007
VEST, George, Ambassador, Washington 8.2.2007
ZAGORSKI, Andrei, Professor, Moscow 7.6.02007

Sources

ARCHIVES

Foreign Ministry of the Federal Republic of Germany, Berlin
Federal Archive: ZK, SED, Internationale Verbindungen, Konsultationen, Vorlage
Political Parties' Archive, Berlin

Foreign and Commonwealth Office, Kew Gardens, London
Cabinet papers 129
FCO 28, 66.

National Archives, Washington
Including documents on the cables and reports exchanged during the 1960s and1980s between the US Embassy in Helsinki and Washington in the possession of Hannu Rautakallio.

Archive Foundation of President Urho Kekkonen Orimattila
Annual reports of President Urho Kekkonen, 1968–1980.

Archive of the Finnish Ministry for Foreign Affairs
Documents concerning the CSCE meeting in Dipoli, 1972–73; the Helsinki first stage 1973; the Geneva second stage; the Helsinki Summit Conference of 1975; the Belgrade follow-up meeting of 1977–78; the Madrid follow-up meeting of 1980–83; the Stockholm Conference on Confidence and Security Building Measures of 1984–86, and the Vienna follow-up meeting of 1986–89.

Documents related to the visits to CSCE countries from 1970–1989 by the President of the Republic, the Prime Minister and the Minister for Foreign Affairs.

Documents concerning Finland's bilateral and multilateral consultations with the neutral and non-aligned countries and the Nordic countries.

Documents concerning Finland's policy on disarmament, including the Nordic Nuclear Weapon-free Zone, the Nordic Disarmament Organization and the EAO.

National Archive
The diaries of Matti Tuovinen, 1969–1989

The Finnish Labour Archives
The Kalevi Sorsa Archive for 1970–1989: foreign policy, visits, memos, correspondence, including the chairmanship of the 1978 Socialist International's working group on disarmament.

PUBLISHED PRIMARY SOURCES

Akten zur Auswärtigen Politik der Bundesrepublik Deutschland 1969–1976
Documents on British Policy Overseas, Series III, Volume II, CSCE 1972–1975, London 1997
Kekkonen, Urho, Päiväkirjat (diaries) I–IV, 1958–1981

Parliament Library:

Minutes of the meetings of the Parliamentary foreign affairs committee, 1970–1976 (in Finnish).
Europäische Sicherheit und Zuzammenarbeit; Voraussetzungen, Probleme, Perspektiven;
    Berlin, SDT, 1978
The Prague Spring 1968, A National Security Archive Documents Reader, Prague 1998
The Road to Helsinki: The Early Steps to the CSCE;
    Selected Documents from the National Archives, the Gerald Ford Library and the National
    Security Archive, Florence 2003
Sicherheit und friedliche Zusammenarbeit in Europa;
    Dokumentation zum KSZE-Prozess; Bonn 1990.
The Dipoli proposals of the CSCE Helsinki preparatory meeting, concluding document
Foreign policy statements and documents 1968–1989 (in Finnish)
Concluding documents of the Belgrade, Madrid and Vienna CSCE follow-up meetings.
Concluding document of the 1984–86 Stockholm Conference.

BIBLIOGRAPHY

Androsch, Hannes: Auf der Suche nach Indentität, Vienna 1988.
Akulov, Albert: Vuodet Tehtaankadulla, Keuruu 1996.
Apunen, Osmo: Paasikiven-Kekkosen-linja; Helsinki 1977.
Arbatow, Georgi: Das System, Frankfurt am Main, 1993.
Bahr, Egon: Was wird aus den Deustchen? Hamburg 1982.
Bartenjev-Komissarov: Yhteistyön taipaleelta, Keuruu 1979.
Brandt, Willy: Erinnerungen, Berlin 1989.
Cooper, James, Ford: Asemamaana Suomi, Helsinki 1998.
Derjabin, Juri: Omalla nimellä, Keuruu 1994.
Djilas, Milovan: Die Neue Klasse, Munich 1958.
Dobrynin, Anatoly: In Confidence, New York 1995.
Doubinine, Youri: Moscou-Paris dans un tourbillion diplomatique, Paris 2002/2003.
Dubcek, Alexander: Viimeisenä kuolee toivo, Juva 1993.
Falin, Valentin: Politische Erinnerungen, Munich 1993.
Ferraris, Luigi, Victoria: Report on a Negotiation, Geneva 1979.
Fischer, Thomas: Die Grenzen der Neutralität, Zurich 2004.
Ford, Gerald R.: A Time to Heal, London 1979.
Friedell, Egon: Euroopan kulttuurihistoria III, Porvoo 1933.
Genscher, Hans Dietrich: Erinnerungen, Berlin 1995.
    Wir wollen Ein europäisches Deutschland, Berlin 1992.
Goodby, James E: Europe Undivided, Washington 1998.
Gorbatschow, Michail: Perestroika, New Thinking for our Country and the World, New York 1988.
    Erinnerungen, Berlin 1995.

Grinevski, Oleg: Neuvostoliiton aseidenriisuntapolitiikkaa, Moscow 2004 (in Russian).

Gromyko, Andrei: Memoirs, London 1989.

Hemmo, Klaus: Helsinki mehr als drei Tage Sommer, Berlin 1978.

Hentilä, Seppo: Harppi-Saksan haarukassa, Helsinki 2004.

Hobsbawm, Eric: The Age of Extremes, 1914–1991, London 2004.

Holopainen, Kari: Orpo piru, Helsinki 2007.

Hyvärinen, Risto: Virkamiehiä, viekkautta ja vakoilua, Keuruu 2000.

Jakobson, Max: Kuumalla linjalla, Porvoo 1968.

    Pelon ja toivon aika, Keuruu 2001.

Jussila, Osmo: Suomen historian suuret myytit, Juva 2007.

Kallenautio, Jorma: Suomi kylmän rauhan maailmassa, Vammala 2005.

Kampelman, Max M.: Entering New Worlds, New York 1991.

Keisalo, Paavo: Hätäpotkusta voittomaali, Finnish Foreign Ministry Publications 2007.

Kekkonen: Nimellä ja nimimerkillä 2, Keuruu 1977.

Kissinger, Henry: Att återvinna världen, Vänersborg 1973,

    White House Years, London 1979,

    Years of Upheaval, London 1982.

    Years of Renewal, New York 1999.

    Diplomacy, New York 1994.

Koivisto, Mauno: Historian tekijät II, Juva 1995.

Kohl, Helmut: Ich wollte Deutschlands Einheit, Berlin 1996.

Korhonen, Keijo: Sattumakorpraali, Keuruu 1999.

Korhonen, Keijo, toim.: Urho Kekkonen – Rauhanpoliitikko, Keuruu 1975.

Kreisky, Bruno: Im Strom der Politik, Wien 1988.

Laqueur, Walter: A continent astray; Europe 1970–1978, Washington 1979.

Lehne, Stefan: The Vienna Meeting of the CSCE, 1986–89; Oxford 1991.

Lehtinen, Lasse: Aatos jaloa ja alhaista mieltä, Juva 2002.

Lourie, Richard: Sakharov, Brandeis University Press 2002.

Lukkari, Matti: Lauri Sutela, Keuruu 2003.

Maresca, John, J.: To Helsinki – the CSCE 1973–1975, Duke University Press 1985.

Matlock, Jack F. Jr: Reagan and Gorbachev – How the Cold War Ended, 2004.

Medvedev, Zhores A.: Andropov, New York 1983.

Rantanen, Paavo: Talviministeri, Jyväskylä 2000.

Renk, Hans-Jörg: Der Weg der Schweiz nach Helsinki, Bern 1996.

Rentola, Kimmo: Vallankumouksen aave, Keuruu 2005.

Rusi, Alpo: Vasemmalta ohi, Jyväskylä 2007.

Saarinen, Aarne: Kivimes, Otava 1995.

Schevardnadse, Eduard: Die Zukunft gehört die Freiheit, Hamburg 1991.

Shevchenko, Arkady, N.: Breaking with Moscou, New York 1985.

Semjonow, Wladimir S.: Von Stalin bis Gorbatschow, Berlin 1995.

Seppänen, Esa: Itäsuhteiden kolmiodraama, Jyväskylä 2007.

Shulz, George, P.: Turmoil and Triumph, New York 1993.

Smith, Hedrick: The Russians, UK 1976.

Soikkanen, Timo: UM:n historia 1970–1981; Uudistumisen, konfliktien ja suurten saavutusten vuosikymmen. (A history of the Finnish Foreign Ministry 1970–1981, unpublished)

Sorsa, Kalevi: Kansankoti ja punamulta, Keuruu 2003.

Strauss, Franz Josef: Erinnerungen, Berlin 1989.

Steglich, Peter-Leuschner,Gunter: KSZE-Fossil oder Hoffnung? Berlin 1996.

Suomi, Juhani: Urho Kekkonen 1968–1981.

Taistelu puolueettomuudesta, Keuruu 1996.

Liennytyksen akanvirrassa, Keuruu 1998.

Umpeutuva latu, Keuruu 2000.

Mauno Koiviston aika.

Pysähtyneisyyden vuodet, Keuruu 2005.

Epävarmuuden vuodet, Keuruu 2006.

Kohti sinipunaa, Keuruu 2008.

Suomi, Juhani, Ed.: Näkökulmia Suomen turvallisuuspolitiikkaan 1980-luvulla, Keuruu 1980.

Tarkka, Jukka–Karjalainen, Ahti: Presidentin ministeri, Keuruu 1989.

Tarkka, Jukka: Suomen kylmä sota (Finland's Cold War), Keuruu 1992.

Thatcher, Margaret: The Downing Street Years, London 1995.

Tuomioja, Erkki: Vaihtoehdottoman demokratian kritiikki, Keuruu 1980

Pekka Kuusi – alkoholipoliitikko, sosiaalipoliitikko, ihmiskuntapoliitikko, Helsinki 1996.

Törnudd, Klaus: Turvallisuus on ovien avaamista, Helsinki 2005.

Vladimirov, Viktor: Näin se oli…, Keuruu 1993.

Väyrynen, Paavo: On totuuden aika 1–2, Juva 1993.

Väänänen, Yrjö: Finlandia Bonn, Juva 1991.

Wilson, Harold: Final Term 1974–76, London 1979.

Zachovalová, Lieko: Prahan ääni, Helsinki 1998.

Index